Architecture and Architects in Socialist Poland

The book presents the history of Polish architecture and architects in the years 1944–1989, focusing on selected issues, including both the development of architecture itself and the conditions of practicing architecture in the socialist country.

The history of architecture and architects in socialist Poland is described not only from the perspective of an architectural historian and researcher but also from the perspective of active participants in the events described. The text is based on historical sources and literature, as well as on numerous interviews with architects and urban planners who played an important role in post-war reconstruction, implementation of the socialist-realist doctrine, creation of the most significant buildings and monuments, and development of the local version of socialist modernism or postmodernism. It gives the floor back to those whose voice was hardly heard after the collapse of the socialist system in 1989.

The book should become an interesting source of information for those interested in the material culture of former socialist countries. Although it focuses on socialist Poland, it can be used as material for comparative studies of mutual relations between East and West in post-war Europe, as well as for analysis of the situation of architecture and architects in socialist countries.

Błażej Ciarkowski, MSc and PhD in architecture from the Łódź University of Technology and MA in the history of art from the University of Łódź, is an associate professor at the Institute of Art History, University of Łódź, and three-term winner of the scholarship of the Minister of Culture and National Heritage. He has authored numerous books and articles on modern architecture and the preservation of the modern movement's heritage. Błażej's research interests focus on modernist architecture, mutual relations between architecture and politics, and the preservation and conservation of modernist architecture. He is a member of Docomomo International, the Polish National Committee of International Council on Monuments and Sites (ICOMOS), the Association of Art Historians, and the Association of Polish Architects.

Routledge Research in Architecture

The *Routledge Research in Architecture* series provides the reader with the latest scholarship in the field of architecture. The series publishes research from across the globe and covers areas as diverse as architectural history and theory, technology, digital architecture, structures, materials, details, design, monographs of architects, interior design and much more. By making these studies available to the worldwide academic community, the series aims to promote quality architectural research.

London's 'Big Bang' Moment and its Architectural Conversations
The Built Environment as a Subject of Public Discourse
Stephen Rosser

The Conquest of Istanbul and the Manipulation of Architecture
The Islamist-nationalist Rhetoric of Conquest and Melancholy
Berin F. Gür

Corporate Ethics and the Architecture of Asylum
Offshore Processing at Manus Island, Papua New Guinea and Nauru
Jennifer Ferng

Virtual Reality
Architecture, Culture, and the Body
Tatjana Crossley

Sacred Modernity
Anglican Church Architecture in Mid-Twentieth Century Britain
Lorenzo Grieco

Architecture and Architects in Socialist Poland
Between Stalin and Le Corbusier
Błażej Ciarkowski

For more information about this series, please visit: www.routledge.com/Routledge-Research-in-Architecture/book-series/RRARCH

Architecture and Architects in Socialist Poland
Between Stalin and Le Corbusier

Błażej Ciarkowski

LONDON AND NEW YORK

Designed cover image: Supersam deparment store in Warsaw, designed by J. Hryniewiecki and M. Krasiński. Author: Zbyszko Siemaszko. Source: NAC

First published 2026
by Routledge
4 Park Square, Milton Park, Abingdon, Oxon OX14 4RN

and by Routledge
605 Third Avenue, New York, NY 10158

Routledge is an imprint of the Taylor & Francis Group, an informa business

© 2026 Błażej Ciarkowski

The right of Błażej Ciarkowski to be identified as author of this work has been asserted in accordance with sections 77 and 78 of the Copyright, Designs and Patents Act 1988.

All rights reserved. No part of this book may be reprinted or reproduced or utilised in any form or by any electronic, mechanical, or other means, now known or hereafter invented, including photocopying and recording, or in any information storage or retrieval system, without permission in writing from the publishers.

Trademark notice: Product or corporate names may be trademarks or registered trademarks, and are used only for identification and explanation without intent to infringe.

British Library Cataloguing-in-Publication Data
A catalogue record for this book is available from the British Library

Library of Congress Cataloging-in-Publication Data
Names: Ciarkowski, Błażej author
Title: Architecture and architects in socialist Poland : between Stalin and Le Corbusier / Błażej Ciarkowski.
Description: Abingdon, Oxon : Routledge, 2026. | Series: Routledge research in architecture | Includes bibliographical references and index.
Identifiers: LCCN 2025023319 (print) | LCCN 2025023320 (ebook) | ISBN 9781032992501 hardback | ISBN 9781032992532 paperback | ISBN 9781003603153 ebook
Subjects: LCSH: Architecture—Poland—History—20th century | Architecture—Political aspects—Poland—History—20th century | Architecture and society—Poland—History—20th century | Socialist modernism (Architecture)—Poland
Classification: LCC NA1455.P6 C53 2026 (print) | LCC NA1455.P6 (ebook)
LC record available at https://lccn.loc.gov/2025023319
LC ebook record available at https://lccn.loc.gov/2025023320

ISBN: 978-1-032-99250-1 (hbk)
ISBN: 978-1-032-99253-2 (pbk)
ISBN: 978-1-003-60315-3 (ebk)

DOI: 10.4324/9781003603153

Typeset in Times New Roman
by Apex CoVantage, LLC

In memory of Professor Andrzej Basista

Contents

List of Figures	*ix*
List of Abbreviations	*xii*
Acknowledgements	*xiv*

	Introduction	1
	Introduction 1	

1	**The architecture and architects in socialist Poland**	5
	1.1 Political, geographical, and historical context 5	
	1.2 Architecture of the interwar period 10	
	1.3 Six stages of development of architecture in socialist Poland 15	

2	**Artist or worker? Architect in the socialist country**	19
	2.1 Education 19	
	2.2 State-owned architectural offices 23	
	2.3 Academic career 30	
	2.4 Architects in public administration institutions 35	
	2.5 Architects-politicians 39	

3	**Iron curtain or nylon curtain?**	48
	3.1 Foreign literature and journals 48	
	3.2 Polish architects in the Western world 54	
	3.3 International architectural competitions 60	
	3.4 Polish architects in the Middle East and North Africa 66	

4	**National in form, socialist in content**	77
	4.1 Between "old" and "new" times – architecture before 1949 77	
	4.2 The architecture of "Stalinist empire style" 83	

viii   *Contents*

4.3 *New cities, new estates 89*
4.4 *Post-war reconstruction of Warsaw 96*
4.5 *Western and Northern Territories 101*

5   Back to the modernism   114
5.1 *Architecture and modernization policy 114*
5.2 *"Prestigious developments" 121*
5.3 *(Critical) regionalism 129*
5.4 *New city centres 133*
5.5 *Housing estates 139*

6   Post-soc-modernism   154
6.1 *Post-socmodernism or soc-postmodernism? 154*
6.2 *Churches in the socialist state – architecture of
      resistance 158*
6.3 *Against the Athens Charter – postmodern urban
      planning 163*

Epilogue   171
Epilogue 171

Appendix 1: Biographies of selected architects mentioned in the book   *174*
Index   *192*

Figures

1.1	The house of Witold Kiltynowicz and Elna Gistedt in Warsaw, architects Helena Syrkus and Szymon Syrkus, 1936	12
1.2	The building of the District Court in Gdynia, architects Tadeusz Sieczkowski, Zbigniew Karpiński, and Roman Sołtyński, 1934–1936	13
2.1	Professor Zygmunt Skibniewski and architecture students at the Faculty of Architecture, Warsaw University of Technology	22
2.2	Architect Halina Skibniewska and the first Secretary of the Central Committee of Polish United Workers' Party, Edward Gierek in the lobby of the House of Parliament in Warsaw	42
3.1	Architect Jerzy Kurmanowicz and his wife Helena (also architect) in Leo Kammel's atelier in Vienna	58
3.2	Project awarded in the competition for the Leopoldville centre (Belgian Congo) by the team led by Józef Zbigniew Polak	62
3.3	Project of the city of Espoo in Finland. Project by Jan Chmielewski, Janusz Kazubiński, and Krzysztof Kuraś awarded the first prize in the international architectural competition in 1966	65
3.4	Submission awarded in the competition for the city hall in Amsterdam designed by Jerzy Buszkiewicz and Ewa Pruska-Buszkiewicz	66
3.5	Trade Fair Center, Accra, Ghana, designed by Vic Adegbite, Jacek Chyrosz, and Stanisław Rymaszewski	69
3.6	Sports hall in Latakia, Syria, designed by Polish architect Wojciech Zabłocki	71
3.7	Bus station in Baloush, Kuwait. Architects Krzysztof Wiśniowski, Anna Wiśniowska, and Leopold Chyczewski	73
4.1	Concept of the new centre of Warsaw designed by architect Maciej Nowicki in 1945	78
4.2	"Okrąglak," a modernist department store in centre of Poznań designed by Marek Leykam	80
4.3	Koło Housing Estate in Warsaw – a continuation of pre-war modernist ideas. Architects Helena Syrkus and Szymon Syrkus	82

x *Figures*

4.4   Palace of Culture and Science in Warsaw designed by Soviet architect Lev Rudnev. A gift from the fraternal Soviet nation and a symbol of Stalin's power over Poland   85

4.5   Community centre in Rzeszów (architect Józef Zbigniew Polak, 1950–1953) represents architecture national in form and socialist in content   87

4.6   Administrative centre of the Lenin Steelworks in Nowa Huta designed by architects Janusz Ballenstedt, Janusz Ingarden, and Marta Ingarden   91

4.7   Konstytucji square in the heart of Marszałkowska Residential District in Warsaw designed by architects Józef Sigalin, Zygmunt Stępiński, Stanisław Jankowski, and Jan Knothe. The socialist-realistic architecture and urban planning were made to host rituals of the new, socialist society   92

4.8   Housing Estate B designed by Kazimierz Wejchert and Hanna Adamczewska-Wejchert, part of the new town Nowe Tychy   95

4.9   Post-war reconstruction of Old Town in Warsaw by the Warsaw Reconstruction Office (BOS)   99

4.10 After World War II, Main Town in Gdańsk was nothing more than ruins and piles of rubble   104

4.11 New old town in Szczecin. On the site of destroyed tenement houses, new housing blocks were built   106

4.12 New frontage of the market square in Jawor – a rare mixture of modernity and traditional elements of architectural design. Architects Stefan Müller and Maria Müller   108

5.1   Collegium Altum – a dominant modernist 15-storey-high skyscraper in the centre of Poznań designed by architects Witold Milewski, Zygmunt Skupniewicz, and Lech Sternal   119

5.2   Main auditorium with a colourful panneau on the façade is a "gate" to the campus of Nicolaus Copernicus University in Toruń (chief architect of the whole complex – Ryszard Karłowicz)   121

5.3   Grunwald Victory Monument designed by architect Witold Cęckiewicz and sculptor Jerzy Bandura   123

5.4   Warsaw Central Station, one of the prestigious developments of the "Gierek's decade." Architects Arseniusz Romanowicz and Piotr Szymaniak   126

5.5   Palace of Sports in Konin, a relatively small town connected to the huge industrial site. Architect Wojciech Zabłocki   128

5.6   Harnaś resort in Bukowina Tatrzańska in Tatra Mountain – local reception of modernism, designed in 1962 by Cracow-based architects Przemysław Gawor, Leszek Filar, and Jerzy Pilitowski   131

5.7   Pyramid-shaped spa resorts in Ustroń-Zawodzie district, the largest newly designed health and recreation complex in Poland. Architects: Henryk Buszko, Aleksander Franta, and Tadeusz Szewczyk   132

Figures xi

5.8 Pedestrian passage in the centre of Warsaw, behind the so-called
Eastern Wall. Architect Zbigniew Karpiński   135
5.9 "Prefabricated gems," as the local press named them – residential
towers and commercial pavilions on Grunwaldzki Square in
Wrocław designed by Jadwiga Grabowska-Hawrylak   138
5.10 Sady Żoliborskie housing estate in Warsaw designed by architect
Halina Skibniewska   142
5.11 One of the so-called "wave buildings" in the Przymorze housing
estate in Gdańsk – large-scale mass housing designed by architect
Danuta Olędzka   144
5.12 It must have taken decades for a North Ursynów to meet the
expectations of the designers and users. Fragment of the North
Ursynów housing estate in Warsaw designed by a team led by
architect Marek Budzyński   146
6.1 The form released out of order – drawing by architect Romuald
Loegler   156
6.2 Postmodernist church of the Ascension between large panel
housing blocks of North Ursynów in Warsaw. Architects Marek
Budzyński and Piotr Wicha   160
6.3 The Church of the Blessed Virgin Mary Queen of Peace in
Wrocław's Popowice housing estate. Designed by architects
Wojciech Jarząbek, Wacław Hryniewicz, and Jan Matkowski   161
6.4 Nad Jamną housing development in Mikołów designed by
architect Stanisław Niemczyk.   167
6.5 Results of the retroversion of Elbląg's old town by architects
Szczepan Baum and Stefan Phillip, and preservationist Maria
Lubocka-Hoffman   168

Abbreviations

AK	(Armia Krajowa) Home Army
BOS	(Biuro Odbudowy Stolicy) Warsaw Reconstruction Office
CDT	(Centralny Dom Towarowy) Central Department Store
CIAM	(Congrés Internationaux d'Architecture Moderne) International Congress of Modern Architecture
CIRPAC	International Committee for the Resolution of Problems in Contemporary Architecture
CZMP	(Centrum Zdrowia Matki Polki) Polish Mother's Health Centre
DiM	(Dom i Miasto) Home and City
DWU	(Dzielnica Wyższych Uczelni) Higher Education District
GDM	(Grunwaldzka Dzielnica Mieszkaniowa) Grunwaldzka Residential District
GDR	German Democratic Republic
IPN	(Instytut Pamięci Narodowej) Institute of National Remembrance
KBUA	(Komitet Budownictwa, Urbanistyki i Architektury) Committee for Construction, Urban Planning and Architecture
KC PZPR	(Komitet Centralny Polskiej Zjednoczonej Partii Robotniczej) Central Committee of the Polish United Workers' Party
KUA	(Komitet do spraw Urbanistyki i Architektury) Committee for Urban Planning and Architecture
LSC	(Linearny System Ciągły) Linear Continuous System
MDM	(Marszałkowska Dzielnica Mieszkaniowa) Marszałkowska Residential District
NAC	(Narodowe Archiwum Cyfrowe) National Digital Archive
NEP	(Novaya Ekonomicheskaya Politika) New Economic Policy
NOT	(Naczelna Organizacja Techniczna) Supreme Technical Organization
NSZZ "Solidarność"	(Niezależny Samorządny Związek Zawodowy "Solidarność") Independent Self-Governing Trade Union "Solidarity"

Abbreviations xiii

PAU	(Pracownia Architektoniczno-Urbanistyczna) Architectural and Urban Planning Studio
PKiN	(Pałac Kultury i Nauki) Palace of Culture and Science
PKWN	(Polski Komitet Wyzwolenia Narodowego) Polish Committee of National Liberation
PPBO	(Pracownia Projektów Budownictwa Ogólnego) General Building Project Department
PPR	(Polska Partia Robotnicza) Polish Workers' Party
PPS	(Polska Partia Socjalistyczna) Polish Socialist Party
PRL	(Polska Rzeczpospolita Ludowa) Polish People's Republic
PZPR	(Polska Zjednoczona Partia Robotnicza) Polish United Workers' Party
SARP	(Stowarzyszenie Architektów Polskich) Association of Polish Architects
SD	(Stronnictwo Demokratyczne) Democratic Party
SL	(Stronnictwo Ludowe) People's Party
SSR	Soviet Socialist Republic
TUP	(Towarzystwo Urbanistów Polskich) Society of Polish Urban Planners
UIA	(Union Internationale des Architectes) International Union of Architects
USSR	Union of Soviet Socialist Republics
WPU	(Wojewódzka Pracownia Urbanistyczna) Provincial Urban Planning Studio
WSM	(Warszawska Spółdzielnia Mieszkaniowa) Warsaw Housing Cooperative
ZAPA	(Zespół Autorskich Pracowni Architektonicznych) Team of Author's Architectural Studios
ZOR	(Zakład Osiedli Robotniczych) Company for Workers' Housing Estate
ZUS	(Zakład Ubezpieczeń Społecznych) Social Insurance Institution
ZWZ	(Związek Walki Zbrojnej) Union of Armed Struggle

Acknowledgements

The idea of compiling a political-architectural history of the Polish People's Republic was born as an expression of opposition. Opposition to those who, unyielding in their position, believe that "the authorities bought architects." That the uneasy choices of individuals in the post-war reality could be summed up in a single pejorative word "commie" or the somewhat milder term "regime architect." That there are only two alternatives in the world, as in the Manichean struggle between good and evil. Black or white.

Jerzy Nowosielski said that in those troubled times "nobody had clean hands." Are the words of the prominent painter, however controversial, far from a true picture of the era? Architect Aleksander Franta warned against succumbing to the easy charm of simple questions and answers. "Under what influence did the man in question work? Who taught him, who influenced his education? What did he come into contact with, what influenced his work?" These are very uncertain things. We see a building or a project that is, so to speak, the final result of an architect's work. We analyse the form and often forget the "contact with life," the history that accompanies the process of its creation. Therefore, an extremely important part of my research on Polish architecture of the socialist era was (and still is) interviews with living people involved in its creation. In addition to written materials, archival sources, and literature, it is oral history that opens up a number of new ways of interpretation.

This book could not have been written without the kind help of the people who made it possible to carry out years of research and to include its results and the reflections derived from them in this volume. Special thanks are due to the interviewees – more than 40 architects, town planners, restorers, and builders who worked actively in the socialist reality and whose stories and memories became the basis of "Architecture and Architects in Socialist Poland between Stalin and Le Corbusier" (including those who did not live to see the creation of the book, but whose memory constantly accompanied me during the work).

I would like to thank Professor Michał Pszczółkowski for his support and critical comments, which helped to improve the quality of my work. For words of encouragement and support in difficult moments, I thank the Director of the Institute of History of Art at the University of Łódź, Professor Aneta Pawłowska. I am grateful to Caroline Church and Meghna Rodborne at Routledge Publishing House,

Acknowledgements xv

who made this book possible. Paradoxically, I am also grateful to those (fortunately few) who have disparaged my work and its results so far. The pettiness of their comments has only strengthened my conviction that the path I have taken is the right one.

I dedicate this book to the memory of Professor Andrzej Basista. Without his book "Concrete heritage: Architecture in communist Poland," and then without his many inspiring conversations, my view of architectural history would have been completely different. I would also look at academic work itself differently because it was Professor Basista who opened my eyes to the fact that the point of our activities is to reach the widest possible audience. And even if today I look critically at some of the professor's theses, I firmly believe that he himself would have been satisfied with this fact. After all, as he wrote, a plurality of views can be very welcome and very enriching, if it comes from real convictions, from experience, and from knowledge.

Introduction

Introduction

The history of Polish architecture in the period 1944–1989 and the subsequent reception of its legacy are complex issues, the evaluation of which has changed and continues to change. As time passes, both the social reception of certain phenomena and the research perspective associated with them evolve. The works of previous generations, which barely a quarter of a century ago seemed to be mistakes of the past, gradually acquire the status of heritage worthy of protection.

The first studies of Polish architecture under socialism, which had the character of a synthesis and an attempt to systematize the achievements of domestic design thought after World War II, were published as early as the 1960s (Zachwatowicz, 1968). In the following decades, further attempts were made to summarize both the analysis of trends and tendencies present in the theory and practice of design and implementation, as well as to synthesize the described phenomena and systematize the achievements of domestic architecture after World War II. The characterization concerned the achievements of the entire period beginning in 1944 (Szafer, 1988; Gliński & Kusztra & Müller, 1984), as well as the following decades or five years (Szafer, 1972, 1979, 1981). Among the monographs published after the fall of the communist system in 1989, "Concrete heritage: architecture in communist Poland" by Andrzej Basista (Basista, 2001). It was a pioneering study, the first to treat the architecture of the communist era not as a phenomenon "in statu nascendi," but as a completed stage of history. At the same time, the author did not limit himself to the presentation of the formal evolution but placed particular emphasis on the mechanisms that shaped architecture, such as politics, economics, education, or international cooperation. Another work presenting a cross-section of the architecture of People's Poland was published 17 years later. "Architecture in Poland 1945–1989" by Anna Cymer was an attempt to systematize knowledge about the construction of the period, taking into account the chronology of events and the main tasks undertaken by designers in successive, consecutive periods (Cymer, 2018). We should also mention the books "Shades of Gray. Architects and Politics in the Polish People's Republic" (Ciarkowski, 2017) and "The Architect's Word. Tales of the architecture of People's Poland" (Ciarkowski, 2023) by

DOI: 10.4324/9781003603153-1

2 *Architecture and Architects in Socialist Poland*

the author of the present book, which complements and develops the research carried out years ago.

This book is not only an analysis of the most important realizations and projects but also an attempt to present the various phenomena that determined the changes in domestic architecture in the years 1944–1989.

> Architecture . . . must be evaluated from the point of view of its desirability – both in terms of functional and aesthetic values. Thus, in the age of rationalism, the sources (or reasons) that determined the direction of development of modern architecture are all the more important,"

wrote architect Piotr Biegański (1972, p. 9). According to his words, it should be assumed that architecture is a process, an effect of the clash of political, economic, or social forces. Its fruit may (but does not have to) be a real object, a building, or a group of buildings.

The text of the book is divided into six chapters, preceded by an introduction and concluded by an epilogue. In addition, the book contains an appendix with short bigoramas of the most important architects whose names appear on its pages. The arrangement of the chapters corresponds to the successive sequences of events in the history of post-war Polish architecture, as well as – transformations on the political scene, which strongly influenced the shape of the domestic construction industry.

The first chapter, "Architecture and Architects in Socialist Poland," is an investigation into the background of the development of architecture in post-war Poland. It takes into account both the socio-political context and the development of Polish architecture in the first half of the 20th century. It also attempts to systematize the chronology of the development of building and architecture in Poland, based on the earlier work of such scholars as T.P. Szafer, B. Lisowski, and A.M. Szymski. The second chapter, "Artist or Worker? Architects in the Socialist Country," outlines various aspects of the architectural profession in socialist Poland. The architects' testimonies describe their personal experiences, including university studies, work in the state architectural office or public administration, and political careers. The chapter presents architectural education at Polish universities after World War II; working conditions in state architectural offices, including the idea of a work permit, salary issues, and career development; the academic career of architects, which separated from professional design practice at the end of the 1960s; and work in public administration, where architects held the positions of city architects, provincial architects, or urban planners, which provided them with a wide range of opportunities to shape reality but, at the same time, required certain compromises with political authorities representing the Communist Party. The last subchapter is dedicated to those Polish architects who decided to play an active role in politics at the central and local levels. In the third chapter (Iron Curtain or Nylon Curtain?), the following subchapters describe various aspects of Polish architects' relations with foreign architectural communities and their influence on the architecture of the Polish People's Republic. The literature – books and magazines reporting on architectural events from behind the Iron Curtain, which was the most common form of contact with the West – is analysed. Another way of contact, described in the second subchapter, was related to participation in international competitions. In addition, a significant number of Polish architects left their homeland to work or study abroad – both in Western Europe, the United States, and in countries of the Global South. The fourth chapter – "National in form, socialist in content" – describes: the architecture of the early post-war years, which can be described as a continuation of the interwar trends; the implementation of the socialist-realist doctrine; the construction of new cities and new estates for a "new" (socialist) man; the post-war reconstruction of the capital city; and the post-war reconstruction of the historic cities destroyed during World War II, which was under strong political pressure, especially in the western and northern part of Poland (which belonged to Germany before 1939). After 1956, in a wave of post-Stalinist thaw, Polish architecture returned to the ideas of the modern movement. The chapter "Back to Modernism" deals with selected aspects of this turn. It discusses the modernization policies of the communist authorities and their impact on architecture, using schools and university campuses as examples. The second subchapter is devoted to what Basista calls "prestigious development" – a group of buildings or monuments that were of particular importance to central and local authorities. The Polish reception of the idea of critical regionalism is described in the third subchapter. The next subchapter describes the modernization of city centres, where new buildings for public use and commercial facilities were built. The fifth and final subchapter focuses on what seems to be a well-described topic – housing estates. The decline of communism in Poland was connected with the decline of modernist ideas in Polish architecture. In the 1980s, a generation of young architects began to openly criticize their older colleagues and their devotion to the modern movement, which they saw as a manifestation of totalitarian oppression. The first subchapter refers to the idea of Polish postmodernism and the discussion about its essence. The second subchapter describes the postmodern churches that arose in the late 1970s and 1980s. The last part is devoted to postmodernism in late socialist urban planning. The whole book is crowned by an epilogue, which is a collection of reflections on the fate of architecture after 1989.

The book is an analysis of the history of architecture and architects in socialist Poland not only from the perspective of an architectural historian and researcher but also from the perspective of active participants in the events described. Research into the narratives of architecture in the Polish People's Republic was based on a critical analysis of source material, literature, and individual interviews with architects, urban planners, and engineers. The contribution of oral history to this study was crucial in determining the final form of the book, the aim of which is to present the history of architecture in the second half of the 20th century in Poland as a Benjaminian "dialectical relationship" in which the past is marked by discontinuity and catastrophe, while history is an open process. The text is based on historical sources and literature, as well as on numerous interviews with architects and urban planners who played an important role in: post-war reconstruction, implementation of the socialist-realist doctrine, creation of the most significant buildings and

4 *Architecture and Architects in Socialist Poland*

monuments, and development of the local version of socialist modernism or post-modernism. It gives the floor back to those whose voices were hardly heard after the collapse of the socialist system in 1989.

The subjectivity of memory (both individual and collective) and the complex nature of historical narratives make a clear assessment of the material heritage of the past difficult, if not impossible. "Cultural heritage is a process of constantly interpreting the past and using it for contemporary purposes," says Professor Jacek Purchla (2005, p. 33), an expert in cultural heritage preservation, emphasizing that the key to the "heritage game" is its immaterial layer. Its part is undoubtedly the history of architecture and the circumstances of its creation.

References

Basista, A., *Betonowe dziedzictwo: architektura w Polsce czasów komunizmu* [Concrete heritage: architecture in communist Poland], Warsaw-Cracow: PWN Scientific Publishing House, 2001.

Biegański, P., *U źródeł architektury współczesnej* [At the origin of modern architecture], Warsaw: PWN, 1972.

Ciarkowski, B., *Odcienie szarości. Architekci i polityka w PRL* [Shades of Grey. Architects and politics in communist Poland], Łódź: University of Łódź Publishing House, 2017.

Ciarkowski, B., *Słowo architekta. Opowieści o architekturze Polski Ludowej* [An architect's word. Stories about the architecture of the Polish People's Republic], Łódź: University of Łódź Publishing House, 2023.

Cymer, A., *Architektura w Polsce 1945–1989* [Architecture in Poland 1945–1989], Warsaw: Centrum Architektury, 2018.

Gliński, A., Kusztra, Z. & Müller, S., *Architektura polska 1944–1984* [Polish architecture 1944–1984], "Architektura" 1984, no. 1–6.

Purchla, J., *Dziedzictwo a transformacja* [Heritage and transformation], Cracow: International Cultural Centre, 2005.

Szafer, T.P., *Nowa architektura polska: diariusz lat 1965–1970* [New Polish architecture: A diary of the years 1965–1970], Warsaw: Arkady, 1972.

Szafer, T.P., *Nowa architektura polska: diariusz lat 1971–1975* [New Polish architecture: A diary of the years 1971–1975], Warsaw: Arkady, 1979.

Szafer, T.P., *Nowa architektura polska: diariusz lat 1976–1980* [New Polish architecture: A diary of the years 1976–1980], Warsaw: Arkady, 1981.

Szafer, T.P., *Współczesna architektura polska* [Contemporary Polish architecture], Warsaw: Arkady, 1988.

Zachwatowicz, J., ed., *Budownictwo i architektura w Polsce 1945–1966* [Construction and architecture in Poland 1945–1966], Warsaw: Interpress, 1968.

1 The architecture and architects in socialist Poland

1.1 Political, geographical, and historical context

Poland's situation in 1945 should be considered on various intertwining levels. World War II and the resulting international arrangements (including the Yalta Conference) changed the country's borders, its ethnic composition, and the balance of social and political forces.

Poland lost about 176,000 square kilometres located east of the so-called Curzon Line to the Soviet Union (or more precisely: the Ukrainian SSR, Belarusian SSR, and Lithuanian SSR). In return, it received some 100,000 square kilometres in the north and west at the expense of Germany. The so-called Recovered Territories (a name suggesting that they belonged to Poland in the early Middle Ages) were definitely more economically developed, with the large urban centres of Wrocław, Gdańsk, and Szczecin. Even so, it is impossible to speak of them as historically Polish lands, since Polish history was linked to such centres as Lviv and Vilnius. The shift of borders forced the migration of the population on a huge scale. More than two million Germans left the Western Territories and the Northern Territories, some of whom fled from the advancing front as late as the beginning of 1945, while the rest mostly left by 1950. They were replaced by people from the East, forced to leave their homes and colonize areas that were culturally alien to them. The taming of the so-called Recovered Territories would continue for generations to come.

Pre-war Poland was an ethnically diverse country. According to the 1931 population census, Poles made up just under 70% of the population, 16% were Ukrainians, 10% were Jews, 6% were Ruthenians and Belarusians, and just over 2% were Germans. After the war, Polish society was much more homogeneous. In 1947, nearly 96% of citizens declared themselves to be of Polish nationality.

By the decision of the Yalta Treaty, Poland found itself in the sphere of influence of the Soviet Union. The new authorities initially tried to maintain a semblance of a democratic system. Back in 1944, on 22 July, the establishment of the Polish Committee of National Liberation (PKWN) was announced. Formally, this was done by the State National Council; in fact, it was a political decision by Joseph Stalin, who was thus creating an administration in the Polish lands being liberated from German occupation that was entirely dependent on the Soviet Union. In late 1944, the PKWN was transformed into the Provisional Government of the Republic of

DOI: 10.4324/9781003603153-2

6 *Architecture and Architects in Socialist Poland*

Poland. Shortly after the end of World War II, a referendum was held on 30 June 1946, in which Poles were to vote for the abolition of the Senate, land reform, and the maintenance of the new western and northern borders. The rigged results resulted in a crushing victory for the communist option, which agitated for a long time to vote "3 x YES." Just over six months later, in January 1947, elections to the Legislative Assembly were held. As with the referendum, the results were manipulated, while the victory went to a pro-Soviet coalition of the Polish Workers' Party (PPR), the Polish Socialist Party (PPS), the People's Party (SL), and the Democratic Party (SD). Józef Cyrankiewicz became prime minister. The election results were not questioned by the Western powers, nor was the forcing of Cyrankiewicz's government to withdraw its preliminary agreement to Poland's participation in the so-called Marshall Plan.

Following the Soviet model, the economic system was changed, which, although in the first years after the end of the war, it retained elements of a free market economy (this time can be compared to the NEP in the Soviet Union), already in January 1946, it was replaced by a system of centralized planned economy. The nationalization of the industry then took place. Smaller companies could still remain in private hands. Until. By the end of 1950, private enterprises of a few to a dozen employees were also nationalized. This also applied to architectural studios. Individual author's studios, popular before 1939, were replaced by state-owned offices bringing together not only architects but also representatives of other trades (constructors, engineers, cost estimators, etc.). This led to many conflicts, as architects, seeing themselves as artists rather than workers, found it difficult to accept the rigid work regime of the company. At the same time, there is no denying that the reform made it possible to increase efficiency, which was extremely important, especially during the first and second five-year plans, when Poland was being rebuilt from war damage. This issue will be discussed further in Chapter 2, Subsection 2.2.

Comparisons of the material situation of the Polish People's Republic and the Second Republic seem indispensable insofar as they shed a different light on the modernization policies of the communist authorities. It is widely believed that the greatest challenge facing the state administration and ordinary citizens was the reconstruction of a country destroyed by war (destroyed cities, infrastructure, industry). This is true, but one should not forget the civilizational backwardness of the Second Republic in relation to the countries not only of Western Europe but also of its Central European neighbours (Leszczyński, 2013). The economy of the Second Republic was an agricultural-industrial economy, with a clear dominance of the first sector, as evidenced by the fact that, in 1938, 70% of the population was rural, two-thirds of the population worked in agriculture, and the rural share of social income was well over 60% (Ciborowski & Konat, 2010, p. 18–19). The authorities of the new, socialist Poland, planning changes in this area, had to reckon not only with huge financial outlays but also with the necessity of forcing thousands of people to change their previous model of life, sanctioned by multi-generational tradition. Not only was the latter not a matter of particular concern to the Polish communists, but it was actually part of the doctrine of forming a new

The architecture and architects in socialist Poland 7

(socialist) society. This is confirmed by the assumptions of subsequent plans. 1949 was the last year of the three-year reconstruction plan. It was followed by the six-year plan (1950–55), whose main goals were to build the foundations of socialism and to rug out capitalist elements (Eisler, 2018, p. 130).

It is worth noting that the model of collectivization of agriculture modelled on Soviet solutions did not take hold in socialist Poland. The agrarian reform introduced in 1945 solved the problem of "land hunger" to some extent by parcelling out large land estates. The years 1944–1948 thus saw the development of individual farms (another similarity to the NEP). Only from 1948 to 1956 was there an intensification of efforts aimed at collectivization. Even so, at their peak (in 1956), only 10% of all agricultural land belonged to cooperative farms. This was a rather brief but significant episode in the entire history of the Polish People's Republic, as, by 1956, the authorities had already decided to return to supporting individual farming (Ciborowski & Konat, 2010, p. 27).

The first few years of People's Poland were a time of major modernization projects. New industrial plants were established (e.g., the Lenin Steelworks in Nowa Huta near Cracow), and existing plants were expanded. A program of universal electrification was outlined and then implemented. It required the construction of a network of new power plants and combined heat and power plants, which, in turn, generated population movement and associated rapid housing development. Despite the efforts of the authorities, until the collapse of the communist system in 1989, it was not possible to completely satisfy the so-called "housing famine," although it must be admitted that a great deal has been done in this field compared to the interwar period. Although criticism of the multifamily housing construction of 1945–1989 is largely justified, as will be discussed in more detail in Chapter 5, subsection 5.5, it is necessary to outline the starting point from which they started then. First – cities such as Warsaw, Gdańsk, Wrocław, and Szczecin (as well as dozens of smaller centres) suffered massive destruction during the war effort. According to various estimates, about 70–80% of the urban fabric in downtown areas was completely destroyed or permanently damaged. Second, low-cost housing was a problem that the authorities of interwar Poland were unable to solve. According to the 1931 census, nearly 80% of Poles lived in one- or two-room apartments. The average density was 2.3 persons per room in cities and as many as 4.8 persons per room in rural areas. Add to this the supply of utilities, which looked as follows: only 13% of residential buildings had sewerage, 16% were connected to the water supply network, and 38% were connected to the electricity network (Ciborowski & Konat, 2010, p. 23). These figures applied only to cities – in the countryside, the individual rates were much lower. The absolute majority (96%) of residential properties were owned by individuals and companies (Jarosz, 2010, p. 18). Barely 0.2% – in the hands of housing cooperatives. Therefore, we should not be surprised that the authorities of the new socialist Poland set themselves the goal of building the maximum number of housing units, and their quality often receded into the background

A socialist state was, as it were, by definition, a welfare state. However much we may not evaluate, in retrospect, the propaganda significance of such measures

8 *Architecture and Architects in Socialist Poland*

as universal electrification or the fight against illiteracy, which were presented, as it were, in opposition to pre-war Poland (which was often described as "bourgeois"), their effects were as real as possible and by all means positive. Illiteracy was perhaps the most shameful legacy of pre-war Poland. As late as 1931, only less than 77% of Poles could read and write. Compulsory primary schooling, introduced as early as 1918, was often not enforced due to existing loopholes. Post-war legislation left no doubt on this issue by creating universal public schooling. On top of this, new schools were built on a large scale, or existing facilities were adapted for their needs (e.g., former mansions or palaces taken from their former owners and transferred to the state) (Słabek, 2015, p. 91). The apogee came at the turn of the 1950s and 1960s, when, under the slogan "a thousand schools for the thousandth anniversary of the Polish state," more than 1,400 so-called "schools – thousand-year schools" were erected in the country. A number of new universities were established and existing ones were expanded. In addition, it is worth noting that it was only after World War II that a system of universal health care was established in Poland. Ensuring that all citizens had access to medical care involved extensive investment plans. During the 45 years of the socialist system, nearly 10,000 new health centres were erected (just before the outbreak of war there were 201, and in 1990 as many as 9912) (Ciborowski & Konat, 2010, p. 35).

As already mentioned, the economy of the Polish People's Republic was centralized and planned. This meant that decisions on investments nationwide were made at the ministerial level, while their implementation was ceded to subordinate bodies. Planning, whose first and most ardent advocate was the post-war Minister of Industry (and later Industry and Trade) Hilary Minc, in turn, excluded all free market mechanisms, making the production of goods dependent on political assumptions rather than real needs (sometimes one went hand in hand with the other, but much more often, it brought negative consequences in the form of shortages of consumer goods). Although for nearly half a century of the Polish People's Republic, the framework set by the concept of a centralized, planned economy remained almost unchanged, the dynamics of the processes changed over the following decades (as in the case of agriculture, already mentioned). The years 1946–1949 saw a three-year reconstruction plan when most efforts were focused on lifting the country from the rubble. The six-year plan that followed (1950–1955) focused on industrial development, with particular emphasis on heavy industry, fitting the model of accelerated Stalinist industrialization (Leszczyński, 2013, p. 337). It was then that such combines as ironworks Nowa Huta, Huta Częstochowa, Huta Warszawa, and the Wodzisław Śląski Coal Mine were established. Shipyards in Gdańsk and Szczecin were rebuilt and expanded.

The thaw (whose beginning throughout the Eastern Bloc was Nikita Khrushchev's paper at the 20th Congress of the Communist Party of the Soviet Union) resulted in a change of government and, with it, a partial change in economic priorities. Heavy industry still remained a priority, but expenditures on the production of consumer goods also increased. At least, this was the premise of the next five-year plan (1956–1960), which increased investment spending in mining, metallurgy, chemical, and machinery industries. Among other things, more

The architecture and architects in socialist Poland   9

combines were built: a sulphur plant in Tarnobrzeg, a refinery in Płock, and new coal and copper mines. In the next five-year period (1961–1965), the growth of investment in heavy industry was sustained, with production increasing significantly. However, this was redeemed by a halt in the growth of the living standards of Poles, which, according to earlier plans, was to be one of the priorities of the authorities. Production of consumer goods grew much more slowly than expected. In the second half of the 1960s, economic growth was only 2–3%, and real wages were stagnant (Leszczyński, 2013, p. 350) which, combined with price increases, led to a lower standard of living and, ultimately, a deepening crisis. It should also be added that the entire period of Władysław Gomułka's rule (1956–1970) was characterized by a relatively low rate of housing development (although, to be fair, one should also mention the development of a network of schools, dormitories or resorts).

The economic crisis of the late 1960s and the ensuing social unrest brought Edward Gierek to power, who took over as First Secretary of the Central Committee of the Polish United Workers' Party in 1970. Gomułka's austerity and asceticism were due as much to the capabilities of the economy as to the personality of the First Secretary. His successor was a very different man in this respect (and many others). The new strategy of accelerated economic and social development of Poland that was introduced assumed not only to maintain the growth rate of the economy (large investments such as the construction of the northern port in Gdańsk and the construction of the Katowice steel plant) (Eisler, p. 301) but also to improve the living conditions of the citizens – both material and cultural. The modernization program, which was described by the propaganda of the time as the construction of a "second Poland," was based on loans taken in the West to enable the purchase of modern technologies and were to be repaid through income from trade in manufactured goods. "The decade of Gierek" is also a time when multi-family housing construction is developing rapidly based on prefabrication technologies. During the entire decade (1970–1980), more than 2.5 million new housing units were built, and in the record-breaking year of 1978 – as many as 283,600. However, even during the most prosperous period (1972–1973), there were problems arising directly from the rules of central planning. Companies were paid to underestimate planned investment costs and conceal problems (Kotowicz-Jawor, 1983, p. 76). Statistics were falsified, costs were concealed, and production costs were artificially inflated (Bałtowski, 2009, p. 253). At the same time, new technologies made domestic industry heavily dependent on the supply of raw materials and semi-finished products from the West. Foreign debt was growing, and debt service was consuming an increasing share of export revenues. Problems were tried to be remedied by reducing the scope of investment in light and food industries. This, in turn, led to shortages of goods available on the market and rising prices. The second half of the 1970s was a time when the Polish People's Republic gradually slipped into crisis, culminating in 1980 and the strikes that swept across the country. The NSZZ "Solidarity" trade union (whose sanctioning by the authorities was enforced by widespread protests) was established and later registered. It is worth mentioning that the genesis of the strikes and the creation of "Solidarity" were

10 *Architecture and Architects in Socialist Poland*

social and economic, not political. Such were also among the demands issued by the trade unionists.

The result of the social unrest was another change at the highest levels of government. Edward Gierek and his acolytes, discredited by its brutal action to suppress workers' strikes on the Coast, were forced to leave. Its successors decided to solve the problems by force by introducing martial law in December 1981, which lasted until 1983. At the same time, the already dire economic situation worsened. Significant price increases led to the pauperization of society. Even after the end of martial law, the economy of the Polish People's Republic was unable to break out of stagnation, and most investment activities can be described as either sham or as a continuation of earlier intentions and carried out by "force of inertia." The so-called "Wilczek Act" (named after Industry Minister Mieczysław Wilczek), passed in late 1988, introducing freedom of economic activity and equalizing the public sector with the private sector, could not stave off the inevitable end of the system. The end of socialism in Poland came with the 4 June 1989 elections to the Parliament, which resulted in the victory of the Solidarity Civic Committee. On 29 December 1989, the name of the country was officially changed – the Polish People's Republic was replaced by the Republic of Poland.

1.2   Architecture of the interwar period

Although the subject of this book is Polish architecture from 1945 to 1989, it is impossible to ignore the period preceding it, namely, the interwar period. The experience of 1918–1939 was an important point of reference for post-war designers, some of whom were directly connected with that period. Among important figures shaping the face of the architecture of the Polish People's Republic, one can find the names of the authors of significant projects of the 1930s, lecturers at the faculties of architecture in Warsaw, Cracow, or Lviv (until 1939 within Polish borders). Outlining the general situation of that era, it seems necessary to create, in the later part of the book, as complete a picture as possible of the Polish architecture of the socialist era.

Following the systematics proposed by researcher and architectural historian Andrew K. Olszewski, the years 1918–1939 can be divided into three main sub-periods. The first six to seven years (1918–1925) marked a return to historical forms. This was a time when traditional forms, referring to the residential architecture of the late 18th century and academic neoclassicism, dominated. The return to a past more than a century away could only seem surprising. In 1918, the Polish State returned to the maps of Europe after 123 years of partition (1795–1918), when its land was part of three powers – Prussia, Austria (from 1867 Austria-Hungary), and Russia. The use of forms considered traditionally Polish, and derived from neoclassicism or the Polish Baroque, was intended as a clear visual message emphasizing the continuity of Polish statehood. In turn, the popularity of academic neoclassicism was due to the fact that many prominent architects, such as Marian Lalewicz and Adolf Szyszko-Bohusz, were graduates of the Architecture Department of the Imperial Academy of Fine Arts in St. Petersburg

(Импера́торская Акаде́мия худо́жеств). The end of the so-called "manor house style" (national) came in the mid-1920s. Neoclassicism, in turn, lost its dominant position around 1930. At the same time, the "decorative" trend developed, which was, in its formal layer, a combination of applied art and expressionism, and whose apogee took place at the International Exhibition of Modern Decorative and Industrial Arts (Exposition internationale des arts décoratifs et industriels modernes) in Paris in 1925.

The years 1925–1934 can be described as the dominance of avant-garde and functionalist architecture. The development of Polish modernism ran parallel to the development of the trend in Western Europe. A.O. Olszewski, who was referred to earlier, proposed the following periodization. Olszewski proposed the following periodization: 1900–1925, 1926–1934, and 1935–1949. Recognized architects Lech Niemojewski and Bohdan Pniewski also systematized the evolution of the modern movement in a similar way (Olszewski, 1967, p. 28–29). It is worth noting that the time caesuras they set do not follow major historical events. The first phase of modernism, whose representatives include H. P. Berlage or Peter Behrens, and on Polish soil Karol Jankowski and Franciszek Lilpop, did not end with World War I, but in 1925. It was then that Le Corbusier and Pierre Jeanneret presented a new face of architecture to the world – the Pavillon de l'Esprit Nouveau. In Poland, too, it did not go unnoticed, especially in the circle of architects and avant-garde artists gathered in the Blok group, whose leader was the visual artist Mieczyslaw Szczuka, and to which the architect Szymon Syrkus belonged. It was he, a graduate of the Faculty of Architecture at the Warsaw University of Technology, who drew attention to the need to implement modern ideas (Wisłocka, p. 108). Around him gathered a group of young architects, graduates of the Faculty of Architecture of the Warsaw University of Technology: Barbara Sokołowska (later Brukalska), Stanisław Brukalski, Bohdan Lachert, Józef Szanajca, and Helena Eliasberg (from 1927 – Helena Syrkus). After the war, it was they, with the exception of Szanajca who was killed in September 1939, who would largely shape the image of Polish architecture. For the time being, however, they were a group of rookies who did not want to design the way the older artists also expected (as was clearly evidenced by the first issue of the magazine "Architektura i Budownictwo," published in 1925, in which it was in vain to look for even the Pavillon de l'Esprit Nouveau; instead, conservative buildings built in Warsaw were presented). In 1926, the circle of avant-garde architects organized the First International Exhibition of Modern Architecture in Warsaw. In the same year, Szymon Syrkus founded the Praesens creative group, which included all the aforementioned avant-garde architects, and which, unlike Blok, focused its attention on matters of architecture and urban planning. In 1928, the group became the Polish section of the Congrés Internationaux d'Architecture Moderne (CIAM).

The activities of Praesens-affiliated architects were largely focused on improving the quality of people's living environment. Hence, single-family and multi-family buildings and housing estates predominated among the projects and realizations (Figure 1.1). Among the most important were the housing estate of the Warsaw Housing Cooperative in Rakowiec in Warsaw (architects H. Syrkus

Figure 1.1 The house of Witold Kiltynowicz and Elna Gistedt in Warsaw, architects Helena Syrkus and Szymon Syrkus, 1936.
Source: Museum of Architecture in Wrocław.

and S. Syrkus, 1931–1936), a residential house on Katowicka Street in Warsaw (architects B. Lachert and J. Szanajca, 1928–1929), Brukalski family's own house on Niegolewskiego Street in Warsaw (architects B. Brukalska and S. Brukalski, 1927–1928), and WSM housing estates (architects B. Brukalska and S. Brukalski, 1927–1930, 1932–1934). However, the new spirit (l'Esprit Nouveau) concerned all aspects of human activity, not just the residential environment. Szymon Syrkus (together with Andrzej Pronaszko) created the concept of avant-garde simultaneous theatre. The Brukalscy or Lachert designed interiors and furniture, and Szymon Syrkus, together with Jan Chmielewski, created a concept for the urbanization of the Warsaw region titled – "Functional Warsaw," a concept that aroused great interest at the CIRPAC (International Committee for the Resolution of Problems in Contemporary Architecture) congress in London in 1934.

At the end of the 20s, there appears within the modernist trend a clear fascination with monumentalism, close to the official architecture of fascist Italy and the works of such artists as Marcello Piacentini and Adalberto Libera. It is worth mentioning at this point that Polish architects did not only hide their fascination but openly proclaimed the necessity of adopting in the field of architecture similar solutions to those in the state ruled by Benito Mussolini. The combination of modernist simplicity of forms with references to classicism (e.g., fluted pillars and profiled cornices) and the composition emphasizing vertical directions resulted in an architecture that was both modern and traditional. It built the image of a strong state, belonging to the circle of Latin culture (ergo Western European, not Eastern European), and at the same time a modern state. In this context, it seems understandable that the current of "classicizing modernism" found application primarily in the design of public edifices, such as the headquarters of ministries (the building of the Ministry of Religious Denominations and Public Enlightenment in Warsaw, architect Zdzisław Mączeński, 1927–1930), courts (the building of the District Court in Gdynia, architects Tadeusz Sieczkowski, Zbigniew Karpiński and Roman Sołtyński,1934–1936) (Figure 1.2), banks (the Bank Gospodarstwa Krajowego Building in Warsaw, architect Rudolf Świerczyński, 1928–1931), Catholic churches (the unrealized project of the Temple of Divine Providence, architect B. Pniewski, 1931–1933), but also . . . private villas (the Zalewski Villa in Warsaw, architect B. Pniewski, 1931).

At the same time, from 1934 onwards, Polish architecture saw a turn towards a specifically conceived modernity, which is sometimes referred to today as "semi-modernism" or "luxury modernism." Under these terms was an architecture that superficially drew on functionalism while abandoning the social ideas that were an

Figure 1.2 The building of the District Court in Gdynia, architects Tadeusz Sieczkowski, Zbigniew Karpiński, and Roman Sołtyński, 1934–1936.

Source: Photograph by the author.

14   *Architecture and Architects in Socialist Poland*

immanent part of any avant-garde movement. In the second half of the 1930s, due to legislative changes, there was a rapid development of higher-standard housing. Luxury rental buildings were built in all major cities – Warsaw (e.g., Wedel House on Puławska Street or apartment building on Przyjaciół Avenue, architect Juliusz Żórawski, 1935–1938), Łódź (e.g., tenement house of Tomaszowska Artificial Silk Factory on Piotrkowska street, architect Ignacy Gutman, 1937–1938), Katowice (e.g., skyscraper on Żwirki i Wigury Street, architect Tadeusz Kozłowski, 1929–1934), or Gdynia, a dynamically developing new port city on the Baltic Sea (e.g., the residential house of the National Development Bank "Bankowiec," architect Stefan Ziołowski, 1935–1937). In all the aforementioned buildings, the architects drew on Le Corbusier's five principles of modern architecture, designing flat roofs with terraces and ground floors supported by pilotis or ribbon windows. At the same time, they avoided "machine-like" aesthetics, were willing to use expensive finishing materials, and, most importantly, did not violate the social status quo with their designs.

The influence of the avant-garde on Polish architecture of 1934–1939 was much less than in the earlier period. Suffice it to say that even Syrkus designed multifamily buildings in Warsaw in a spirit closer to Żórawski's luxurious houses than to his designs from the early 1930s. This did not mean, however, that the progressive architects affiliated with the Praesens group, fell silent. The group of "followers of modern architecture" (Wisłocka, 1968, p. 192) consistently pursued its program by designing primarily cooperative housing estates.

As if next to the division into those architects who gathered in the Praesens group worshipped Le Corbusier, and those who presented a more conservative attitude, and communicated with the world through the monthly magazine "Architektura i Budownictwo" (Architecture and Construction) there were artists who were thoroughly individual and independent. They included Romuald Gutt, Romuald Miller, and Adolf Szyszko-Bohusz, among others. The former began his career with manor house architecture, to design small modernist public buildings in the 1930s (e.g., the post office building in Ciechocinek, 1933) and villas that are excellent examples of the fusion of modern architecture with nature (e.g., the architect's own house in Warsaw, 1928). Miller underwent a similar evolution – from forms drawing on historical styles, towards functionalist architecture. Szyszko-Bohusz, on the other hand, began with academic classicism, only to move through the various facets of modernism over time and to become passionately and devotedly involved in the conservation of monuments that are particularly important to the national identity of Poles.

The experiences of all the aforementioned groups of architects proved to be extremely important after 1945 when both representatives of conservative currents and those progressive tried (with varying success) to implement their ideas. The post-war choices of individuals, both artistic and political, were judged through the prism of pre-war achievements. In short – had it not been for close ties with the CIAM in the 1930s, H. Syrkus' conversion to Socialist Realism, which took place in 1949, would (probably) not have been so critically assessed; the post-war career of B. Pniewski, on the other hand, would have aroused less surprise if viewed in

The architecture and architects in socialist Poland 15

isolation from the fact that, before 1939, he was a favourite of the authoritarian Polish authorities.

However, before the new communist state was born in July 1944, the tragedy of World War II and occupation took place on Polish soil. Its results were not only millions of casualties and destruction amounting to, it is assumed, 25% of buildings and 60% of industrial equipment. World War II also constituted what philosopher Andrzej Leder called a "transplanted revolution" (Leder, 2014). In just a few years, from September 1939 to May 1945, not only Polish statehood but also its social structure lay in ruins. The extermination of the Jewish minority, the resettlement of Belarusian, Ukrainian, and German minorities, as well as the liquidation of the landed gentry as a social class, meant that post-war Poland was in almost every respect a completely new and different creation. It should therefore come as no surprise that many representatives of the pre-war establishment, such as the aforementioned Bohdan Pniewski, looked at the new reality with some anxiety (Czapelski, 2008). Pniewski himself, during the occupation, carried out minor design work in Warsaw and later in Kielce. The situation was similar for many Polish architects, who in 1939–1945 were primarily engaged in theoretical studies and in drawing plans for the future. This was the way in which H. Syrkus, Sz. Syrkus (until he was arrested and deported to Auschwitz), and Stanisław Tołwiński, among others, worked, who, in the clandestine Architectural and Urban Planning Studio (Pracownia Architektoniczno-Urbanistyczna – PAU), developed the pre-war concepts of functional Warsaw and social housing estates. In turn, Jan Zachwatowicz or Adolf Szyszko-Bohusz were involved in conceptual work on the preservation of monuments – the former of Warsaw's Old Town and the latter of the Wawel Royal Castle in Cracow. With the end of the war, their thoughts and conclusions became the basis for real action.

1.3 Six stages of development of architecture in socialist Poland

The development of architecture in Poland after the end of World War II followed a similar course to that in other countries that, as a result of international arrangements, found themselves in the Soviet sphere of influence. Significantly – in the first post-war years, it did not differ significantly from what could be observed in the West. The parallel development of Eastern and Western European design thought was interrupted by the introduction of the doctrine of socialist realism in 1949, which was given the status of an official style. The top-down imposed return to architecture with a monumental, historicizing character lasted until 1956. Nevertheless, it should be emphasized that, with the thaw after Stalin's death in 1953, designers from the so-called Eastern Bloc countries resolutely and wholeheartedly sought to return to the orbit of Western architectural influence. However, a certain backwardness, the main reason for which was the decisive retreat from modernity in architecture in the first half of the 1950s, could not be made up (Basista, 2001, p. 178).

One of the first attempts to systematize the achievements of domestic architecture after World War II was made by architect Jerzy Hryniewiecki, who proposed a

16 *Architecture and Architects in Socialist Poland*

systematization that took into account the specifics of political transformations and the dependence of architecture and urban planning on successive five-year cycles of economic plans (Szafer, 1988, p. 6–7). He distinguished seven successive stages, which were intended to most fully characterize the transformation of domestic construction during the communist era. Of course, Hryniewiecki's systematization was incomplete, as it did not cover the last decade of the Polish People's Republic and thus needs to be supplemented. At the same time, it shows with great accuracy the relationship between architecture and the politics and economics that determined its development. The first stage mentioned by Hryniewiecki was characterized by the continuation of pre-war schools and directions (1945–1949), the second was the time of the reign of socialist-realist doctrine (1949–1956), and the third period was marked by a return to modernist ideas of function and construction (1956–1960). The fourth stage heralded certain dangers associated with the dominance of urban design, the reduction of individual buildings to the simplest masses, and implementation restrictions (1961–1965). This dichotomy and discrepancy between planning activities and architecture deepened in the next stage (1966–1970). The breakthrough came in the sixth period falling in the first half of the 1970s. It was characterized primarily by the development of housing built with industrialized technologies, which, unfortunately, did not proceed as expected, as the country faced an economic crisis in the seventh period (1976–1980). The aforementioned systematization should be supplemented by the eighth stage, which would be the 1980s, when, despite the difficult political, social, and economic situation, Polish postmodernism began to sprout, while modernist ideas gradually died. The latter would pass away for good only with the 1989 breakthrough, and the end of the Polish People's Republic can be regarded as somehow identical to the end of modernism in Polish architecture, although this is not a sharp and completely defined boundary.

The year 1989 was a time of political transformation in Poland, which resulted in the end of 45 years of communism. The socialist system, as it were, by definition, was a modernization project (Juszkiewicz, 2013, p. 13), built on glorifying progress and striving to form a new society. Both modernism seen as a trend in art and as a philosophical direction or way of perceiving reality assume linear, continuous development. According to this idea, the eras that follow strive towards an imaginary perfection on the path of continuous progress. This concept was discredited by the policies of 20th-century totalitarian systems, which, despite their different attitude to modernism in architecture or fine arts, were guided by modernist ideas in social practice. The end of totalitarianism thus marked the end of modernist philosophy based on Darwinian evolutionism, as Karl Popper stated (Popper, 1999). From this perspective, the democratic and pluralistic Third Republic was itself, so to speak, the antithesis of modernism.

The systematics defined by Hryniewiecki was cited in its original form covering the years 1945–1980 by Tadeusz Przemysław Szafer, who similarly defined the time range covered in "Diaries of Modern Architecture." Three consecutive volumes describe Polish architecture from 1966–1970 (Szafer, 1972), 1971–1975(Szafer, 1979), and 1976–1980 (Szafer, 1981), respectively. In parallel, Szafer distinguished three generations of architects of Independent Poland (Szafer, 1988, p. 7). Representatives of the first built the foundations of domestic avant-garde architecture in the 1920s. Their successors were representatives of the Columbus generation, who were created during the first post-war five-year period. The third generation began independent activity in the 1960s. As in the case of Hryniewiecki's systematics, the division proposed by Szafer also needs to be supplemented by a fourth generation. These consisted of artists who graduated and began work in the 1970s and early 1980s and were disciples of those who entered architectural adulthood after 1956.

The systematization of Polish post-war architecture and its general characterization as a distinct phenomenon also became the subject of research by Bohdan Lisowski (Lisowski, 1989), as well as by Stanisław Latour and Adam M. Szymski (Latour & Szymski, 1985), who included it in broader studies of the world architecture of the 20th century. Nowadays, the problem of periodization of the domestic construction of 1945–1989 was taken up by, among others, architect Maciej Czarnecki, who, in one of his articles, described it as "up to a certain point . . . clear and lucid" (Czarnecki, 2017). He distinguished the following stages: the continuation of post-war modernism (1945–1949), social realism excluding industrial architecture (1949–1956), and the return of modernist tendencies (1956–1975). The second half of the 1970s has been described as a time of stagnation. In the 1980s, forms inspired by postmodernism appeared, but the dominant trend was "featureless construction," so that, as Czarnecki concludes, "the end date of modernism in Polish architecture remains uncertain and difficult to determine precisely" (Czarnecki, 2017).

References

Bałtowski, M., *Gospodarka socjalistyczna w Polsce: geneza, rozwój, upadek* [Socialist economy in Poland: Origins, development, decline], Warsaw: PWN Scientific Publishing House, 2009.

Basista, A., *Betonowe dziedzictwo: architektura w Polsce czasów komunizmu* [Concrete heritage: Architecture in communist Poland], Warsaw-Cracow: PWN Scientific Publishing House, 2001.

Ciborowski, T. & Konat, G., *Między II i III RP. Gospodarka Polski Ludowej* [Between the second and the third republic. Economy of people's Poland], [in:] *PRL bez uprzedzeń*, eds. J. Majmurek, P. Szumlewicz, Warsaw: Instytut Wydawniczy Książka i Prasa, 2010.

Czapelski, M., *Bohdan Pniewski – warszawski architekt XX wieku* [Bohdan Pniewski – Warsaw architect of the 20th century], Warsaw: Institute of History of Art, 2008.

Czarnecki, M., *Expressive forms as an example of creative pursuits in the architecture of postwar modernism in Poland*, [in:] *Architecture of the 20th century and its valorization in Gdynia and Europe*, ed. M. Soltysik, R. Hirsch, Gdynia: Gdynia City Hall & Gdańsk University of Technology, 2017.

Eisler, J., *Czterdzieści pięć lat, które wstrząsnęły Polską. Historia polityczna 1944– 1989* [Forty-five years that shook Poland. A political history 1944–1989], Warsaw: Wydawnictwo Czerwone i Czarne, 2018.

Jarosz, D., *Mieszkanie się należy . . . Studium z peerelowskich praktyk społecznych* [The flat is due . . . A study from the communist social practices], Warsaw: ASPRA, 2010.

Juszkiewicz, P., *Cień modernizmu* [Shadow of Modernism], Poznań: UAM Scientific Publishing House, 2013.

Kotowicz-Jawor, J., *Presja inwestycyjna w latach siedemdziesiątych* [Investment pressure in the 1970s], Warsaw: PWN, 1983.

18   *Architecture and Architects in Socialist Poland*

Latour, S. & Szymski, A.M., *Rozwój współczesnej myśli architektonicznej* [Development of contemporary architectural thought], Warsaw: PWN, 1985.

Leder, A., *Prześniona rewolucja. Ćwiczenie z logiki historycznej* [Transplanted revolution. An exercise on historical logic], Warsaw: Krytyka Polityczna, 2014.

Leszczyński, A., *Skok w nowoczesność. Polityka wzrostu w krajach peryferyjnych 1943–1980* [A leap into modernity. Growth policy in peripheral countries 1943–1980], Warsaw: Krytyka Polityczna, 2013.

Lisowski, B., *Rozwój nowatorskiej myśli architektonicznej w Polsce w latach 1918–1978* [Development of innovative architectural thought in Poland in the years 1918–1978], [in:] *Architektura i urbanistyka w Polsce w latach 1918–1978*, ed. W. Puget, Warsaw: PAN, 1989.

Olszewski, A.K., *Nowa forma w architekturze Polskiej 1900–1925* [New form in Polish architecture 1900–1925], Wrocław: Ossolineum, 1967.

Popper, K., *Nędza historycyzmu* [The Poverty of Historicism], Warsaw: PWN, 1999.

Słabek, H., *O społecznej historii Polski 1945–1989* [On the social history of Poland 1945–1989], Warsaw: Książka i Wiedza, 2015.

Szafer, T.P., *Nowa architektura polska: diariusz lat 1965–1970* [New Polish architecture: A diary of the years 1965–1970], Warsaw: Arkady, 1972.

Szafer, T.P., *Nowa architektura polska: diariusz lat 1971–1975* [New Polish architecture: A diary of the years 1971–1975], Warsaw: Arkady, 1979.

Szafer, T.P., *Nowa architektura polska: diariusz lat 1976–1980* [New Polish architecture: A diary of the years 1976–1980], Warsaw: Arkady, 1981.

Szafer, T.P., *Współczesna architektura polska* [Contemporary Polish architecture], Warsaw: Arkady, 1988.

Wisłocka, I., *Awangardowa architektura polska 1918–1939* [Avant-garde Polish architecture 1918–1939], Warsaw: Arkady, 1968.

2 Artist or worker? Architect in the socialist country

2.1 Education

It is impossible to outline the profile of an architect without even a cursory analysis of the educational system that formed him. Both scholars and architects themselves have commented on institutional and non-institutional learning, whose recollections were often surprising in the circumstances in which the foundations of future creative attitudes were laid. Suffice it to mention the almost symbolic role of Froebel's blocks (and, more broadly, homeschooling) in Frank Lloyd Wright's childhood or the youthful visit to Chartres Cathedral that enchanted Philip Johnson. These and dozens of similar colourful, captivating anecdotes, however, should not obscure the larger picture of the education system as a product of ideology and market needs. Even under a centralized socialist system, the education program sought to adapt not only to ideological requirements but also to real needs.

The problem of architectural education was the subject of public debate in the community for almost the entire duration of the communist era. Already the first post-war years and the pressing need to rebuild the country forced a change in the organization of the educational system from that in place before World War II. Its main goal was henceforth to prepare properly trained engineering personnel as quickly as possible to work on numerous new investments.

The first post-war years were (understandably) marked by a certain amount of chaos and, at the same time, great enthusiasm. Architects born in 1920 and 1930 repeatedly mentioned an overwhelming desire to study, seen in terms of "returning to normal life." This sometimes led to surprising situations. Witold Cęckiewicz, a native of Cracow, recalled that he was directly looking forward to the moment when he would be given the opportunity to study. As the situation of the Cracow universities in 1945 seemed uncertain to him he went to Warsaw. However, he did not find a place for himself there, so he was forced to return to his hometown, where in the spring of 1945, the headquarters of the Mining Academy, which had housed the German Government Office during the war, began to be cleaned up. However, before classes began for his architecture degree, Cęckiewicz attended lectures on mining. Years later, he laughed that "it didn't interest him at all, but it put him in touch with science." Fortunately, after only a few months, he was able to transfer to the desired faculty, because thanks to the personal efforts of Adolf

DOI: 10.4324/9781003603153-3

20 *Architecture and Architects in Socialist Poland*

Szyszko-Bohusz, the Faculty of Architecture at the Mining Academy began operating on 1 December 1945. Szyszko-Bohusz, in turn, became its dean.

Initially, teaching took place in somewhat makeshift conditions. The various departments of the university were assigned undeveloped buildings by the authorities – abandoned mansions, tenements, or former public buildings. At the same time, the auditoriums were bursting at the seams. "The studies began, the halls were filled to the brim," recalled Cęckiewicz, "Everyone who got in at that time (and it was well over 300 people) really wanted to study." Similar stories were also recorded by other representatives of the so-called "Columbus generation" (a term used to refer to Polish writers born in the 1920s who entered adulthood during World War II). Maria Piechotka described the difficult material situation prevailing in ruined Warsaw, where getting a warm coat or a decent roof over one's head bordered on a miracle. At the same time, in such realities, young people were undertaking the great task of rebuilding the capital and the country.

Post-war Poland needed architects, and the resurgent technical universities were expected to meet this demand. This was possible with a number of systemic changes relative to what architectural education looked like before 1939. The architect was no longer to be an artist, but first and foremost, a "creator of design documentation," one of many cogs moving the powerful machine of nationalized mass construction. A productivist view of the essence of a profession hitherto regarded as semi-artistic was nothing new. As late as 1932, leftist avant-garde architect Roman Piotrowski predicted that the future would belong to building factories and that the profession of architecture would share the fate of the professions of coachman, carriage driver, or telephone operator (Wujek, 1986, p. 200). The same Piotrowski was appointed Minister of Construction after World War II and implemented the idea of centralization in the structures of nationalized design offices. In such a reality, architecture departments could not be either a "talent breeding ground" for above-average individuals on the pre-war model or a structure based on a master-apprentice relationship, as was the case at the Bauhaus school.

Already at the beginning of the 1946/1947 academic year, the duration of studies was standardized, which was henceforth to be based on a grid of hours per subject, and the teaching period was set at 5.5 years. Two years later, it was divided into a 3.5-year engineering course and a 2-year master's course, so that young people were ready for professional work in less than 4 years after entering college (*Warszawska szkoła . . .*, 1967, p. 65–66). In this way, the authorities tried to meet the needs of the labour market, which absorbed any number of skilled workers. Two-degree studies survived until the 1960s when they were replaced by unified master's degrees (however, the solution of the second half of the 1940s was returned to in 1999, with the introduction of the so-called "Bologna Process").

The curriculum itself underwent various modifications, depending on the university and . . . leading trends in architecture (and politics). Thus, after 1949, with the introduction of the doctrine of socialist realism, more emphasis was placed on subjects related to the history of architecture. Students were expected not only to know them but also to put certain solutions into design practice. Years later, even those artists, who were commonly associated with the use of modern forms in the architecture they created, admitted that, during their studies (if they fell in the years 1949–1956), they designed bakeries pretending to be Greek temples and community centres looking like neoclassical palaces. Their memories were most often of graduation projects, which were not only memorable for their importance but also because of the unusual formula in which they were created. Until 1956, the so-called "cloister system" was in effect at architecture faculties in Poland. Students had to develop a given design topic (unknown beforehand) in designated studios in the university building. They had ten days to do so, during which they could work on the concept with the proviso that the drawings could not leave the walls of the university (the problem of "swapping" works for those developed at home was solved in such a way that each sheet was stamped). Unfortunately, not everyone complied with the regulations. Architect Tadeusz Mycek, a graduate of the Faculty of Architecture at the Warsaw University of Technology, recalled:

> Clauses of 10 days, the diploma lasted 10 days. There was an agreement that you work during the prescribed hours, you are not allowed to bring anything from home. What turned out: there were colleagues who opened files for colleagues, looked into them. Auxiliary scientific forces were involved.
>
> (Mycek, 1998, p. 37)

The cloistered system was eventually abolished and replaced by a solution that, by design, was conducive to raising the level of work and consisted of independent development of an assigned or selected project topic on one's own during the final year of study (Figure 2.1).

The changes in the curriculum that occurred over the years were the result of the architectural community's desire to profile the graduates of architecture departments in such a way that, upon graduation (engineering and then master's), they would be prepared for the challenges posed by the reality of a socialist state. In 1956, during the National Meeting of Architects, Bolesław Szmidt, outlining the "profile of a graduate of an architectural university," said that the goal of the university should be "to educate a social activist who is aware of his duties, and who has **the qualities of a technician and a humanist in equal measure**" (original spelling) (Barucki, 1956, p. 145). Among those who spoke during the discussion was Romuald Gutt, who expressed his conviction that the education of a few outstanding individuals should be abandoned.

> For me, the ideal would be for the school to be oriented to the most perfect mediocrity, and not to a "Meisterschule." The idea is that we should have this "average," but as an educated human being, truly prepared for the simplest, most elementary, but nonetheless constant tasks, of which virtually all life consists.
>
> (Barucki, 1956, p. 397)

Fundamental issues related to architectural education were also addressed in subsequent decades. The debates accompanying the National Meeting of Architects

Figure 2.1 Professor Zygmunt Skibniewski and architecture students at the Faculty of Architecture, Warsaw University of Technology.
Source: SARP Archive.

were reflected in the framework programs of study being developed by the Ministry of Higher Education. Graduates should not only be "prepared for creative conceptual and design work" but also "should have a broad vision and understanding of the significance and role of the achievements and direction of other frontier disciplines for architecture" (*Framework programs . . .*, 1966). As early as 1969, however, Andrzej Basista wrote: "There are few people satisfied with the current architecture curricula" (Basista, 1969, p. 1–2). The discussion about the state of education continued in the 1970s in the pages of the monthly magazine "Architektura," the most important and opinion-forming professional medium. The specific nature of the architectural profession was compared to that of a director, in view of which it was proposed that only those "who have graduated from other specified faculties closely related to the accepted concept of study" should be admitted to architectural studies (Piniński, 1971, p. 37, 44). Attention was also drawn to the "complex nature of contemporary architectural activity," in view of which, it was concluded, teaching "should be based on a comprehensive method of study" (Tyszkowski, 1971, p. 405).

Artist or worker? Architect in the socialist country 23

The image of the architect as a "Renaissance man" with versatile interests and knowledge guided the Polish academic community and reformers of the teaching system from the very beginning. Juliusz Żórawski, who taught at the Faculty of Architecture of the Cracow University of Technology since 1945, went down in history not only as a talented designer of modernist residential buildings but also (or perhaps above all) as an outstanding theoretician and educator. Years later, his former students, such as Aleksander Franta and Przemysław Gawor, recalled the non-standard questions Żórawski asked students during exams regarding general knowledge (understood very broadly – from the definition of "a capella" to the theories of Sigmund Freud). Żórawski's influence was so great that one of his students, also teaching at the Faculty of Architecture at the Cracow University of Technology, Bohdan Lisowski, even wrote about a "new school of architectural thinking," created thanks to the ideas and activities of the master. He stressed that "Juliusz Żórawski's theory, radiating from the Cracow university, has successfully stood the test of twenty-five years of proving itself in architectural practice, in life" (Żórawski, 1973, p. 7–9). Lisowski himself postulated a constant verification of the assumptions made (both design and didactic) through their confrontation with "life."

> The future of architecture should be built on a better quality basis of knowledge and experience. This base should be expanded with the proper depiction of diverse human needs, with adequate knowledge of the sociology and psychology of architecture, ecology and humanistic economics.
>
> (Lisowski, 1990, p. 18) – he wrote

Not surprisingly, the topics of design assignments he prepared for students reflected real problems that young architecture graduates could later encounter. The extensive scripts contained both a discussion of the topic of the exercises, all the data necessary for its correct execution, and the theoretical foundation from the borderline of the history of architecture and its sociology (Kardaszewski, 1998, p. 19).

Bearing in mind that Lisowski wrote about introducing a "practical" dimension to architectural education, i.e., bringing academic knowledge closer to real life, it can be seen that, to some extent, he was repeating the postulates of the 1950s or 1970s. This leads to a rather sad observation that despite the awareness of the need for reforms in the education system, for more than half a century satisfactory results have not been achieved. The problem of combining the interdisciplinary nature of education with its practical dimension remained largely unresolved. As late as the 1990s, architect Bolesław Kardaszewski, who taught at the Łódź University of Technology, postulated a return to the concept of two-stage studies developed in the 1940s and the introduction of curricular changes to deepen the issues of technical education and further humanize it.

2.2 State-owned architectural offices

Architecture in pre-war Poland was based on private ateliers and studios assigned to specific enterprises (e.g., the architectural studio of the Social Insurance

24 *Architecture and Architects in Socialist Poland*

Institution). After 1945, there was a partial return to this state of affairs only for a short time, when the communist authorities tolerated elements of the free market. When the process of nationalizing production enterprises began, it was only a matter of time when it would also include architectural studios. Although it should be remembered that as early as February 1945 the state-owned Warsaw Reconstruction Office (BOS) was established, activities on a larger scale began in 1948, when the first nationwide institutions were established. In subsequent years, municipal and provincial project offices were created, replacing private professional practice (Basista, 2001, p. 16).

In 1948, Minister of Reconstruction Michał Kaczorowski pointed out that private design studios were not effective enough for the growing needs of the rapidly expanding construction industry (Basista, 2001, p. 16). The result was the creation of, among other things, the Central Office of Architectural and Construction Projects, from which regional branches (e.g., the Łódź Chamber in 1949), as well as design offices assigned to particular centres or areas of the economy, were subsequently separated. In this way, the aim was to streamline investment processes and, moreover, as Andrzej Basista emphasized, to increase the control of the authorities over the entire professional group. State design bureaus in the first years of their existence "monopolized design activity," significantly limiting the freedom of architects. In practice, this meant depriving designers employed by the state administration and universities, among others, of the opportunity to practice their profession. The situation was partially changed when design studios began to be established at the Faculties of Architecture on the basis of auxiliary institutes (the situation at the National Councils was similar) (Basista, 2001, p. 51). As already mentioned, the idea of large design firms by no means originated under socialism. In the early 1930s, Roman Piotrowski predicted the end of individual design practice and its replacement by large, multi-discipline teams. His rather naive belief was shared by a section of the community centred around the leftist avant-garde. Thus, when architects were forced into the rigid framework of state design offices in the late 1940s and early 1950s, the pre-war predictions became a reality. In 1948, at the First Congress of the International Union of Architects, Helena and Szymon Syrkus spoke of the wide range of opportunities that a network of state-run, specialized design offices would open up for architects:

> An individual will not be able to cope with the enormous tasks posed to the architect by society. State Design Offices . . . are being organized as team studios of architects and other specialists, among whom not only builders, but also technologists, mechanics, workers of all branches will play a serious role. Through close cooperation with these specialists . . . the architect will deepen his technical knowledge.
>
> (Syrkus & Syrkus, 1948, p. 35)

It seems significant that the authors titled the paragraph devoted to architects "Design Contractors."

Artist or worker? Architect in the socialist country 25

The activities of state-owned design enterprises were evaluated differently by architects themselves. In addition to enthusiasts of this architectural collectivization, such as Roman Piotrowski or Helena and Szymon Syrkus, there was a much more numerous group of critics. Reading their opinions, it is hard to get rid of the impression that both sides selected arguments intended to confirm the a priori thesis they adopted, rather than to show the most nuanced and true picture of the situation. Undoubtedly, the beginnings of the state design offices were difficult, as Eugeniusz Wierzbicki pointed out at the National Meeting of Architects in 1956:

> Projects for the entire massive investment plan of the six-year period were developed in state design offices, which were organized in 1948. The enormity of the task created great difficulties due to the lack of experience in solving such serious and new problems in our country. The cadre of architects with extensive implementation practice was small. A significant burden of work and responsibility fell on young designers with little design and implementation experience. 80% of designers working in design offices graduated after liberation.
>
> (Barucki, 1956, p. IX)

Other designers pointed out the faulty organization of work:

> Design offices outsource the work started by one architect to other architects . . . What's worse, we ourselves take up the work entrusted to us started by our colleagues without agreement with them and without establishing a mutual copyright sharing relationship, we remake other people's buildings and thus violate the law in force.
>
> (Barucki, 1956, p. 180–181) – complained Józef Łowiński

At the same time, one can find isolated voices in defence of state design offices, or rather – attempts to rationalize the decision made at high levels of the political authorities. Tadeusz Barucki recounted that Piotrowski, as Minister of Construction, was responsible for creating a new legal framework for architectural activity. With great consistency, he enforced reliability, punctuality, and discipline – qualities that in themselves seem highly desirable, but proved irritating to the artistic mentality of some architects. The very fact of starting work at an early hour of the morning and the introduction of attendance lists seemed to many artists to be somewhat inappropriate, and a popular anecdote cited by Barucki spoke of the particular indignation of Romuald Gutt, who stated that "The hour of 7 am is too late to milk cows, but too early to do architecture!" Barucki believed that "the very idea of creating multi-discipline offices seemed good."[1] The assumption was that architects would be relieved by administrative staff who would take over tedious office tasks, so they could spend more time on creative work. Unfortunately, the people hired were often incompetent, and the designers had to fulfil their duties without being paid for it. As early as 1956, Bolesław Szmidt stigmatized the "psychosis of money," which led to the creation of "elaborate administrative cadres and staffs

26   *Architecture and Architects in Socialist Poland*

of taxmen occupied solely with calculating salaries" in design companies, while architects "instead of being the stewards of their collective workshops, are now treated as **one of the trades**, as burdensome 'decorators' who have finally been given a thumbs-up" (original spelling) (Barucki, 1956, p. 155).

Despite the efforts of the architectural community to change the unfavourable state of affairs, Jerzy Wierzbicki could only sadly conclude years later that "all the new reorganizations do not bring improvements" (Wierzbicki, 1974, p. 37). In the meantime, the issue of separating from the state structures of design offices into smaller units centred around prominent artists was increasingly raised. Of course, already before that, figures of such stature as Bohdan Pniewski operated on slightly different principles than "ordinary architects," but, as Barucki stressed, "these were cases unique in Polish conditions."[2] Although the author of the Sejm building functioned within the framework of a state enterprise, he worked in his own villa on Skarpa in Warsaw (Piątek, 2021). The first fully independent author's studio was not established until 1958 (Żmudzińska-Nowak, 2017, p. 151) in Katowice. It was created by Henryk Buszko and Aleksander Franta. Barucki was the General Secretary of SARP at the time – "I convinced the then director of ZOR (Zakład Osiedli Robotniczych – The Company for Workers' Housing Estate) that there was nothing to prevent us from separating author units associated with specific individuals."[3] The Katowice studio was an experiment. Its success was to determine whether the concept of authorial studios would be developed. PPBO (Pracownia Projektów Budownictwa Ogólnego – General Building Project Department), which was the name of Buszko and Franta's office, was subject to the same rules and regulations as the large state-owned design companies. "The organization was legally defined. We had to take formal and legal matters on ourselves, because that's why we sought independence, not to have a director over us," Aleksander Franta recounted. "We worked and decided about the enterprise in two, but the appointment of the manager was held by Henryk Buszko. I, in turn, was the deputy for technical affairs," he explained.

> The enterprise must be arranged hierarchically, and authorial cooperation requires partnership. The two arrangements are mutually exclusive . . . one must have goodwill, be guided not only by what the law says, but also by what ethics says about camaraderie, about cooperation"[4]

Despite the undoubted professional successes that Henryk Buszko and Aleksander Franta have become, author design studios have not become a common phenomenon.

As the years passed, the list of accusations against state project offices did not diminish. "The atmosphere of the project offices is poisonous. They are not studios, but documentation factories," – wrote in the 1970s Jerzy Wierzbicki (Wierzbicki, 1974, p. 37). His voice was not an isolated one, and the negative attitude towards the system was rather widespread. It is only in retrospect that design companies have gained partial rehabilitation in the eyes of former employees, who appreciate, among other things, their multi-discipline nature and the good atmosphere in some studios. The activity of the offices themselves is, as it turned out after time,

Similarly, a longer time perspective allows a more nuanced assessment of another phenomenon that was unanimously criticized under socialism – the so-called labour order. Under this term was the administrative referral of high school and university graduates to the place of practicing their learned profession, it was supposed – according to the recommendations of the authorities – "to prevent the liquidity of workers in professions or specialties of particular importance to the socialized economy" (*Act of March 7, 1950*). In this way, it was centrally decided to evenly distribute representatives of particular professions preventing, for example, shortages of architects in certain cities or regions. It should be noted, at this point, that this did not mean "exile" and was often associated with specific benefits. Young designers right after graduation were directed by the selection committee to enterprises located in various cities – usually outside the centre where they received their education. Due to the relatively high demand for architects in the labour market, some design offices tried to attract graduates by offering favourable conditions and assistance in obtaining housing. This was especially true for those centres that appeared to be "less attractive" in the popular perception. Architects mentioned that where a job was assigned could depend on two factors: the grade on a graduate's diploma and connections.

Thus, architecture graduates could end up in a locality where they did not want to live and work at all (as a rule, there were a couple of possibilities, so they could choose the "lesser of two evils"). They could also be assigned to a company that did not match their career interests in any respect. Ewa Dziekońska, a graduate of the Wrocław University of Technology, was happy when she was assigned to the Provincial Office of Rural Construction Projects in 1955. Not only did she not have to leave Breslau, but she also had to deal with subjects that particularly interested her. It was only the reality of working "in the field" (i.e., in the provinces) that came as a surprise to the young architect. On the other hand, architect Władysław Hennig, who had been involved in the urban planning of Rzeszów and its surroundings for years, was initially assigned to the Coal Industry Design Office in Cracow. He was eventually assigned to the Provincial Urban Planning Office in Rzeszów, which was urgently looking for new employees. Another architect, Mieczysław Gliszczyński, as a result of an administrative mistake, ended up at the State Office of Projects for the Fermentation Industry in Warsaw. He worked there from 1951 to 1952. "Nobody had time for training and discussions," wrote Gliszczyński, whose first assignment was the design of an industrial boiler house for a sugar factory in China. "Having the technological design, I tackled the architecture without any problems . . . The installation designs and cost estimates, fortunately, were done by my neighbour from the studio." Fortunately, Gliszczyński the designer managed, not without problems, to change his place of employment.

After explaining to the personnel department that there was a mistakenly faulty information on the job assignment that I was a civil engineer, not an

28   *Architecture and Architects in Socialist Poland*

architect, I managed with great difficulty to change the assignment to an office with architectural studios.

In the face of such situations, the story of Bolesław Kardaszewski, who had to leave his native Warsaw, seemed quite ordinary. His wife, Irena, was ordered to work in Łódź, a large, rapidly growing industrial city located not far from the capital (about 120 kilometres to the west), and in addition, the city's design office guaranteed them a new apartment. With a permanent housing shortage, having their own place was quite an incentive.

The beginnings of young designers looked different, but it can be noted that the system of large design offices, consisting of many studios, was conducive to professional advancement. Cracow architect Stanisław Spyt began working in a local design office in the late 1940s. His supervisor was Tadeusz Ptaszycki, an architect and urban planner with an established reputation in the community as co-designer of the plan for the reconstruction of Wrocław, destroyed during the war, who was seconded to Cracow as general designer of the newly formed socialist city, Nowe Huta. Despite a number of architects with more experience than Spyt, it was he who was entrusted by Ptaszycki to head one of the studios in Miastoprojekt-Cracow. Thus, the subordinates of the 20-something Spyt were architects who had begun their careers even before the outbreak of World War II, such as Stanisław Juszczyk (at with whom Spyt began his professional practice) and Stanisław Murczyński. "This was Ptaszycki's approach: to bet on young people," Stanisław Spyt recalled years later.[5] Young architects not only had prospects for professional advancement but also, perhaps more importantly, professional fulfilment. They were relatively quickly entrusted with ambitious, large-scale subjects. They often saw with their own eyes how what had barely been a drawing plotted on paper a few weeks earlier turned into a building or architectural detail. This was largely the result of staff shortages. In the decades that followed, when these were met, many architects complained that everything they designed ended up in the archives instead of on the construction site.

The system of work orders was finally abolished in the 1960s. Regulation of the architectural profession did not begin to change until 20 years later. The 1980s not only brought changes in views on architecture and a definite turn to postmodernism but also initiated the search for a new formula for practicing the profession. A number of different, previously unpractised, forms of work appeared, such as companies, cooperatives or Architectural Services Laboratories of the Association of Polish Architects (SARP) formed at its various branches (Syska & Jaworski, 2017, p. 153–154). The most important change, however, was the beginning of independent design studios. Until then, any manifestation of independence from the structures of state design offices was limited to isolated exceptions on a national scale. Meanwhile, thanks to the loosening of restrictions, "in 1985 already about three hundred architects were working outside the state design offices, which accounted for 10–18% of the total workforce" (Basista, 2001, p. 52). "The 1980s are already the disintegration of the Polish People's Republic and the disintegration of the concept of state professional organizations. Cooperatives are beginning to

Artist or worker? Architect in the socialist country 29

emerge, there is a move towards private practice" – Tadeusz Barucki recounted. "In those years, however, no insurance company in Poland was geared towards insuring architects, which is an obligation, and without which the profession does not exist in the West . . . It was full improvisation."[6]

> In 1983 I was probably the first architect in Łódź to leave the state office. I always joked that I had no other choice at the time, because as the person who was in charge of new forms of work at SARP, I had to set an example that it was possible

– recalled Andrzej Owczarek, who moved his work from a city design office to his own home. It quickly became apparent that the room allotted for this purpose was too small, as he needed a team of draftsmen in the face of a rapidly growing volume of orders.

> This all started to happen quite rapidly. At that time, the first economic changes were taking place, people's investment opportunities were being freed up, and mini-cooperatives were being formed in an avalanche, communities that were able to buy land from the state or municipality, and then divide it into building lots for terraced housing," Owczarek recalled.[7]

Around the same time that Andrzej Owczarek was starting his private professional practice, ZAPA (Zespół Autorskich Pracowni Architektonicznych – Team of Author's Architectural Studios) was founded in 1982 in Gdańsk. It was the first company in socialist Poland to bring together architects acting individually. A loophole in the law was exploited and it was given the form of a cooperative of creative work, although, in practice, it was already a substitute for a private business. The atmosphere of the last years of the communist system (although, in the early 1980s, I do not think anyone yet sensed that these were the "last years") and the enormous social energy unleashed by Solidarity were conducive to non-standard activities. One of the co-founders of ZAPA, architect Szczepan Baum, organized a nationwide architectural congress, raising slogans of freedom of practice and fair remuneration (Piątek, 2007, p. 90). Together with his colleagues Daniel Olędzki, Józef Chmiel, or Stefan Philipp, they set an example for others by founding a cooperative. At first, they worked in the attic of a medieval shooting range – the headquarters of the Pomeranian branch of the Association of Polish Architects. They quickly moved to more comfortable premises – their names had a reputation in Gdańsk and the surrounding area for years of work in state design offices, so they could not complain about a lack of orders. The structure of ZAPA itself provided considerable freedom for individual architects running author's studios (such as Baum or Olędzki) while, at the same time, ensuring all the benefits of cooperation within a larger organism.

The transformation concerned not only the organization of the architects' work itself and its legal anchoring in the current system but also relations with investors. In view of the difficulty or even impossibility of receiving large orders (of which

30   *Architecture and Architects in Socialist Poland*

there were relatively fewer during the crisis of the 1980s than in earlier decades), private principals and the Catholic Church began to play an important role. The participation of individual investors in the process of renewing Polish architecture was not limited to breaking the state monopoly but directed designers towards new areas (single-family housing) and ways of doing things (participation). It was not without reason that, in the mid-1980s, SARP representatives spoke of a resurgence of construction visible in the realization of small houses. Their creation was connected with close cooperation with the investor –in terms of both design and execution. It required architects to be flexible in responding to the needs of the principal but also to adapt to the limited technical and material possibilities.

The design of single-family houses was a testing ground for architects before the later entry into the realities of the market economy and was, to some extent, a substitute for it. The widespread enthusiasm for the free market, which was supposed to be a panacea for all the ills of the domestic construction industry, was clearly felt. In 1984, architect Krzysztof Herbst proclaimed that "the only sensible solution . . . is to let the market in architecture and construction. The private investor, the owner of the money, can already see to it that the projects please the residents, that the houses please the tenants" (Herbst, 1984, p. 4). This and many other similar opinions of the Polish architectural community of the 1980s were close to the views of American postmodernists, who treated architecture as a product and part of the market game (Bielecki, 1996). "Architecture will become good when the architect offers his products to many subjects, to many private buyers, and when he realizes their desires and demands" – Herbst claimed. The spatial chaos that prevailed in Polish cities and towns after 1989, and which was extremely vividly described by reporter Filip Springer in his book "Bathtub with a Colonnade" (Springer, 2020), seemed to contradict his words.

2.3   Academic career

The academic career, like all other aspects of practicing the architectural profession, was subject to various regulations in successive periods lasting within the Polish People's Republic. Like education, work in state administrative bodies, or work in design offices, it was conditioned by changing external factors – personnel shortages, bureaucratic sprawl, economic problems, or ideological struggles. In the first post-war years, it was necessary to fill the significant staff shortages in the newly opened architecture departments. This resulted in relatively easy access to assistant positions (not even a college degree was required), as well as a wide openness to architects combining design and academic work. In subsequent years, however, the system underwent some regulation – a fairly rigid framework for the course of a career path was introduced, and the possibility of combining employment in and out of academia was restricted. Finally, staff fluctuations were fostered by turning points, in the field of both architecture and politics (examples include 1949, when the simultaneous imposition of the style of socialist realism and the increasingly repressive actions of the authorities took place, as well as the events of 1968 and the anti-Semitic events that also affected the academic community).

The first post-war years can, with some exaggeration, be described as a time of spontaneous action. It could not have been otherwise, since on the one hand there was a huge social need for education, and on the other – a lack of adequate structures and material resources. This resulted in situations such as the one related to the Faculty of Architecture of the Academy of Mining (since 1954 – Faculty of Architecture of the Cracow University of Technology), which not only began its activities on 1 December 1945, i.e., in defiance of any academic calendar, but its first headquarters were rooms in the Wawel Royal Castle complex. This was possible thanks to the personal efforts of Professor Adolf Szyszko-Bohusz, the first post-war dean of the architecture department and also the architect responsible for the conservation of the Castle since 1916 and taking care of it during the German occupation. One of the faculty's students was Witold Cęckiewicz, whose works presented at an internal exhibition of student works caught the dean's attention. Szyszko-Bohusz summoned Cęckiewicz to his office and communicated to him that he saw the second-year student (!) as his assistant in the Monumental Composition Department. He was entrusted to teach an exercise in perspective sketches, a subject lower in the hierarchy than design classes. Despite this, the start of teaching by a second-year student should be considered a special case. Cęckiewicz was not an isolated case of a student becoming an assistant even before obtaining his master's degree (although one should do justice to the Cracow architect and admit that the author of this book is not aware of any other case of such an early start in teaching). At the State Art School in Łódź (which was transformed into the Academy of Fine Arts in the 1960s), Edmund Roman Orlik studied and worked in the Department of Architecture at the Faculty of Spatial Arts. He, however, was hired at the time of his graduation, but long before he finally received his diploma.

Relations at the university soon began to mirror the reality in the socialist state, in terms of both structuring and political dependencies. When the doctrine of socialist realism was proclaimed in 1949, successively in literature, fine arts, and architecture, and repression affected people associated with the anti-communist underground, a number of changes – programmatic and personnel – took place in the architecture departments. The former have already been described in the subsection on education. In turn, the history of the Faculty of Architecture at the Warsaw University of Technology can serve as an image of personnel changes. The former supporters of the avant-garde had to remove themselves into the shadows or change their views. Marek Leykam and Jerzy Hryniewiecki were removed from teaching architectural design, leaving them with only a few hours a week of classes in architectural history. Juliusz Żórawski left the capital and returned to his native Cracow. The dean of the Faculty of Architecture at the Warsaw University of Technology from 1947 to 1948, Lech Niemojewski, opposition to the implementation of socialist realism in the curriculum paid with his dismissal (Kucza-Kuczyński, 2004, p. 8–9). Tadeusz Mycek recalled that students were unequivocal in their assessment of the politicization of the university. They admired Jerzy Hryniewiecki, who "preached unconventional views, opposed the theory of socialist realism that was being promoted at the time." Also widely respected and liked was Jan Bogusławski, whom young people "considered a true master-teacher,"

32 *Architecture and Architects in Socialist Poland*

while they loathed successive party "professors 'brought in briefcases'" (Mycek, 1998, p. 37). When in 1956, on the wave of the post-Stalin thaw, architects made settlements of the past era, Romuald Gutt recalled the situation of the late 1940s and early 1950s in academia:

> And what was the situation in the Faculty? It was necessary to bring in new-comers, and in the process remove others. Col. (colleague) Niemojewski left, Col. (colleague) Hryniewiecki was forbidden to lead the chair of design, it was apparently considered harmful.
>
> (Mycek, 1998, p. 260)

The end of the Stalinist era and the so-called Thaw of 1956 brought significant changes to academia. Former dissidents such as Hryniewiecki and Żórawski were restored to favour. Political control over curriculum and personnel matters diminished significantly. However, the de-politicization of the academy was apparent, and this was revealed in full force after 1968. Architect Zbigniew Karpiński, who took over as dean of the Faculty of Architecture at the Warsaw University of Technology in 1972, recalled that "This also reflected on my enthusiasm for my work and in teaching at the Faculty of Architecture, where the independence of professors was erased and directors of institutes were imposed" (Karpiński, 2018, p. 70). At the same time, in the late 1950s, new rules were introduced for promotions up the academic career ladder. The Higher Education Law of 1958 made academic careers dependent on earning degrees and, as Andrzej Basista recalled, "was modeled on Soviet solutions." According to the intentions of the creators, it was supposed to enforce constant upgrading of academic staff qualifications. However, according to many (most?) representatives of the academic community, these assumptions were not achieved – "at any rate, not with respect to architects" (Basista, 2001, p. 163). Jerzy Hryniewiecki in 1961 criticized the situation in which architecture "was drawn into some general scheme, without understanding and without any attempt to bring out architectural specifics" (*Sprawozdanie Zarządu Głównego . . .*, 1961, p. 11), and academic work was separated from professional practice. "Our best artists – colleagues who are great educators and wonderful creators – are excluded for months or even years in order to write a scientific paper, which is only needed by a personnel officer of the Ministry of Higher Education" – criticized the existing state of affairs. Indeed, universities imposed significant restrictions on faculty architects for non-academic work, thus giving rise to a phenomenon that remained unresolved throughout the socialist system.

Cracow architect Tomasz Mańkowski, a student and assistant to Juliusz Żórawski at the Faculty of Architecture of the Cracow University of Technology, wrote:

> Teaching architecture is particularly responsible. This is because it is the most enduring art, the most costly and the most ubiquitous. . . . For the transmission of design skills, one must develop one's own architectural workshop. A workshop that can only be improved by building, by confronting the

Artist or worker? Architect in the socialist country 33

vision formed in the imagination, the lines sometimes easily laid on paper, with the concrete reality of implementation.

(Szafer, 1988, p. 135)

Juliusz Żórawski himself, although he practically did not design after the war and occupation, considered it indispensable to combine extensive theoretical knowledge with professional practice. This became increasingly difficult as time went on, because, after 1960, the academic authorities strictly limited the so-called "multi-job" and did not accept parallel full-time employment in design offices. Thus, when Przemysław Gawor became an assistant to Juliusz Żórawski at the Faculty of Architecture at the Cracow University of Technology in the early 1960s (although the supervisor of his doctoral dissertation was Tomasz Mańkowski), he had to choose between a design job at the Cracow Miastoprojekt and an academic career. In the end, the faculty authorities agreed that he should keep his part-time job in both places. Perhaps this decision was influenced by the fact that Gawor was eager to get involved in the work on his dissertation. His supervisor, Mańkowski, suggested to his doctoral students that they tackle topics that made up the picture of one larger and more complex problem – the optimal minimum in housing. Gawor studied the issue of housing complexes. His colleagues dealt with programming (Zofia Nowakowska, dissertation topic – "Furnishing of apartments"), psychological perception of various housing solutions (Jan Meissner – "Human needs for housing"), or the practice of cooperative activity and quantitative analysis of its effects (Jerzy Chronowski – "Compilation of apartments"). In a different situation was the architect Danuta Olędzka, employed since 1952 at the Faculty of Architecture of the Technical University of Gdańsk in the Department of Utilitarian Construction as an assistant. She reconciled her teaching work with her ¾-time employment at Miastoprojekt – Gdańsk. In 1961, she herself terminated her employment contract. New conditions of employment at the university forced her to resign from her job at the design office, which she could not and did not want to do – hence the uneasy decision to leave the university. In the end, her relationship with the Department of Architecture continued for three more years. In a letter to the Dean (the same one in which she asked for the termination of her contract), she wrote: "I ask you to consider hiring me on other terms. I can undertake to teach on contract hours at any time." The part-time employment lasted until 1964 when the authorities of the Department of Architecture began to push Danuta Olędzka to write her dissertation. She, not feeling a calling to strictly scientific work, refused. Thus, the Gdańsk University of Technology lost a didactician valued by students and a recognized, experienced practitioner.

However, the case of Danuta Olędzka cannot be considered a rule, as subsequent stories convince us that the practical enforcement of the regulations depended to a large extent on the people who implemented them. For example, Bolesław Kardaszewski, a graduate of the Faculty of Architecture at the Warsaw University of Technology, was employed at the Miastoprojekt – Łódź design office in 1956. At the same time, from 1959, he was an employee of the

34 *Architecture and Architects in Socialist Poland*

Łódź University of Technology. Over the years, he held the positions of assistant (1959–1960), senior lecturer (1974–1976), and contract docent (since 1976). At the same time, it should be noted that he received his doctorate in technical sciences only in 1977, which, in practice, entailed automatic employment at the Institute of Architecture and Urban Planning of the Łódź University of Technology as an independent teaching and research employee with the rank of docent. At this point, it is worth looking at Kardaszewski's dissertation itself, entitled. "Higher Education Building System, District of Higher Education Institutions in Łódź. Optimization of solutions under given environmental conditions," which was not just a strictly theoretical work but also a de facto analysis of his own project and its (partial) implementation. Thus, not only did it occupy a special position among the dissertations created by architects, but it also did not have the basic flaws that became the main subject of criticism by Hryniewiecki or Basista (Basista, 2001, p. 163–170). The adoption of his own design achievements as the foundation of his doctoral dissertation reflected well the attitude of Kardaszewski, who remained primarily a practitioner throughout his career. A different fate befell the Cracow architect, a specialist in industrial architecture, Bohdan Lisowski. This student of Juliusz Żórawski wrote and defended his candidacy dissertation (this is how doctoral dissertation was still referred to in the early 1960s, following the Soviet terminology) much earlier than Kardaszewski, in 1960. From then on, Lisowski's design activities were limited by his teaching and research activities. In a nutshell, he spent the time he would otherwise have devoted to designing buildings and development complexes on developing numerous scripts, textbooks, design guidelines, and expert opinions. In this way, he tried to confront theoretical assumptions with "life."

From 1968 to 1992, Bohdan Lisowski headed the Department and then the Department of Industrial Architecture of the Institute of Architectural Design at the Cracow University of Technology. The memoirs of his students and subordinates revealed a particular, one might say "corporate," way of managing the unit. While Lisowski's mentor, i.e., Żórawski, manifested a kindly attitude towards young employees, Lisowski himself could be quite ruthless and "adhered to radically different methods – the so-called high bar and staff rotation, according to the principle: every year the weakest one leaves, and in his place we hire a new candidate for a scholar" (Złowodzki, 2010, p. 16).

As the aforementioned examples show, it is difficult to create a single coherent picture of the academic environment of architects under socialism. Much depended on political conditions, but even more – on the individual decisions of the authorities of individual universities and departments. However, it can certainly be said that, throughout the 45 years of the Polish People's Republic, architects made efforts to treat the discipline they practiced with their own distinctiveness and specificity in mind. Regardless of external circumstances, they postulated the necessity of combining theoretical knowledge with practice, because they believed that only in this way would Polish architecture be able to develop. Let us summarize, therefore, the words of the Poznań architect and lecturer Jerzy Gurawski, who

Artist or worker? Architect in the socialist country   35

throughout his life contested both the prevailing methods of training architects in Poland and the way architecture is perceived as a science:

> It is the duty of every architect who has anything to say in this country and really feels like an architect to protect young impressionable people. . . . If we don't protect them, we the next generation of forty-year-olds, Polish architecture will end once and for all. There will be no architecture in Poland at all! After all, the competitions we participated in were the last wave. After that, there is emptiness – only big-plate houses are standing.
>
> (Gurawski, 1982, p. 38)

2.4   Architects in public administration institutions

Architects in the Polish People's Republic were able to influence the quality of space not only by designing and teaching but also by creating the legal and administrative framework for new investments. Working in public administration is not a widely described and recognized issue. Moreover, it is virtually absent in most studies of architecture and architects in Poland under socialism. Meanwhile, among the architects who served as provincial architects/urban planners/conservators of monuments, one can find names so significant for the history of Polish architecture under socialism, such as Witold Cęckiewicz, Jerzy Buszkiewicz, Józef Sigalin, Władysław Hennig, and Wiesław Gruszkowski.

Shortly after the end of World War II, the new communist authorities began to build not only central power structures but also administration at the local level. This applied not only to areas as fundamental to the functioning of the state as the political authorities, the forces of law and order, or the ministries responsible for the various branches of the economy and infrastructure. At the same time, architects, urban planners, and conservationists were appointed at the provincial levels. The organizational units they headed were strictly subordinate to the presidiums of the provincial national councils. Only at a later stage, did they begin to organize appropriate units at the municipal level, such as the Municipal Planning Offices operating at the Municipal Boards of the time. In this way, a highly politicized and centralized model of architectural, urban planning, and conservation administration was created. The point of reference for its creators was, not surprisingly, the solutions used in the Soviet Union.

A model example was the changes that took place in the late 1940s among Warsaw architects. On 30 December 1949, following the Soviet model, the Committee for Urban Planning and Architecture (KUA) was established, reporting directly to the Prime Minister. A month earlier, the Urban Planning Office of Warsaw had been created, which was subordinate to the Presidium of the National Capital Council. A natural consequence of this decision was the creation of the office of the chief architect of Warsaw, also modelled on solutions used in the USSR, where the largest cities, led by Moscow, had their "chief architects" (Skalimowski, 2018, p. 208). In Warsaw, the architect Józef Sigalin became them. The centralization

36 *Architecture and Architects in Socialist Poland*

allowed greater control of the party leadership over the architecture and construction administration, a fact that Sigalin himself admitted years later, writing that the decisions of the party leadership were more important than the opinions of professionals, which in retrospect he considered "an undoubted mistake" (Skalimowski, 2018, p. 219).

The KUA was directly subordinate to the prime minister or, in the realities of a socialist state, the first secretary of the PZPR Central Committee. This position was held in 1953 by Bolesław Bierut, and it was he who appointed Zygmunt Skibniewski as chairman of the committee. At first, the architect resisted and tried to persuade Bierut to change his mind. However, the latter remained firm in his decision. At least this was Skibniewski's version of events years later (Barucki, 2000, p. 306–307). The purpose of the KUA was to develop the activities of architectural and urban planning services and studios, and, according to its first chairman, by 1960, it was satisfactorily fulfilling its activities. At that time, however, the committee was absorbed into the much more powerful Committee for Construction. Skibniewski managed to force a name change to the Committee for Construction, Urban Planning and Architecture (KBUA) but was unable to defend its eventual liquidation in late 1963 and early 1964. Most of the former tasks of the liquidated committee passed to the Minister of Construction and Building Materials Industry, while some matters (in the field of planning and urban planning) were transferred to the Planning Commission of the Council of Ministers, as well as to the Minister of Agriculture. The position of architects and urban planners as a professional group began to gradually weaken. Krzysztof Nawratek described this event as "one of the worst moments in the history of communist architecture." "This, in a formal sense, political decision, perhaps without any ideological goals, caused a radical collapse of Polish architecture in the near future" (Nawratek, 2005, p. 113). What, then, guided architects to begin their careers in public administration, largely losing the opportunity for design work and exposing themselves to pressure from political authorities? As usual, there is no single answer to such a question. However, the stories of individual cases and individuals reveal different backgrounds of the decision to accept a position as a municipal architect or provincial conservationist.

The architect of the province was, among others, Wieslaw Gruszkowski, a graduate of the Faculty of Architecture at the Gdańsk University of Technology. He was appointed chief architect of the Gdańsk Voivodeship in 1955, at a time when a certain relaxation after Stalin's death was already being felt, but no one dared to speak of a "thaw" yet. This was a rather unique case since it was customary for the Party Provincial Committee to decide on the staffing of leadership positions. Meanwhile, in Gdańsk, an employee of the Provincial Committee, responsible for selecting a candidate, asked the president of the local branch of the Association of Polish Architects to recommend a suitable person. Gruszkowski recalled years later that architects were not at all keen on the idea of taking office. "They preferred to design and were afraid of such positions, which it was known that you had to put your chest on the line," he said. At SARP, more candidates were feverishly analysed: "how about Kadłubowski, how about Gruszkowski?" – they debated. Architect Lech Kadłubowski briefly disposed of the proposal. "Give me a holy peace, I am an artist," he said. In this situation, one candidate remained – Gruszkowski. "Agree, please, because then they will give us some idiot" – pressed fellow architects, and the person concerned himself did not know that the appointment was agreed with the party, and he rightly regarded the appointment as an expression of confidence of the environment. Just as interesting as the circumstances of his employment was the story of Gruszkowski's dismissal (and subsequent reinstatement) from his post. In the first half of the 1960s, the central authorities said that provincial architects, along with provincial conservationists, were to blame for an overly liberal (in their view) policy towards new religious investments. They should have been exemplarily punished, i.e., fired from their jobs. As Wiesław Gruszkowski recalled, in most provinces, one person (either the architect or the conservator) was fired, but, in Gdańsk, they got rid of both officials. One of them was Gruszkowski, who 60 years later recounted the story with some amusement. "It was a funny story," he recalled, "they fired me from my position, but they didn't sack me. The deputy ruled, and I worked."[8] This state of affairs, however, did not last long. Events took an unexpected turn when colleagues stood up for the dismissed architects. Jerzy Hryniewiecki filed a parliamentary intervention in the Sejm, and in Gdańsk itself, the deputy provincial secretary Antoni Bigus, a pre-war communist who had taken Gruszkowski on barely three years earlier, returned from leave. He already knew about everything and took his first steps to his superior's office, to whom he explained the awkwardness of the situation. Gruszkowski recalled that the matter was eventually settled by the intervention of Zygmunt Skibniewski, thanks to whom he was appointed head of the provincial urban planning studio. Informal interpersonal relations and the peculiar chaos prevailing at many levels of government effectively mitigated the authoritarian nature of the state apparatus. However, even unofficial arrangements between designers and representatives of the power apparatus were not able to mitigate harmful decisions affecting the conditions of the architectural profession. However, it is necessary to maintain proportions in assessing the events of that time and the situation of architects and the architecture and construction administration in socialist Poland. "It's not worth overemphasizing the importance of these political inspirations, because they really weren't that deadly effective," Gruszkowski explained years later. "There were undoubtedly pressures, but our colleagues from the USSR and East Germany were in a much worse situation."[9]

In a similar vein, were Jerzy Buszkiewicz (Chief Architect of the City in Poznań 1973–1975, Chief Architect of the Province 1975–1981), Witold Cęckiewicz (Chief Architect of the City in Cracow 1955–1960), or Władysław Hennig (head of the Municipal Urban Planning Studio in Rzeszów 1963–1971, acting head of the Provincial Urban Planning Studio in Rzeszów 1972–1975). Hennig, whose adventures with the work order have been described in earlier subsections, began working at the Provincial Urban Planning Studio in Rzeszów in March 1956. He worked his way through all levels from designer to team leader, to deputy manager and acting WPU (Provincial Urban Planning Studio) manager. When he started, the studio was headed by Michał Mermon, a graduate of the pre-war Lviv Department of Architecture, who found his way to Rzeszów as one of three architects active in

38   *Architecture and Architects in Socialist Poland*

the city after the war. He first established a private design office, then moved to the Provincial Office, and, as head of the urban planning studio, began organizing its structures in 1955. Employees (seven in all) came from various cities in Poland – Gdańsk, Warsaw, or, like Hennig, Cracow. Hennig's duties as a WPU employee included the development of general plans for a number of cities in the Rzeszów province. He was the main designer of plans for Strzyżów (1957), Jarosław (1958 and 1979), Przemyśl (1961), Rzeszów (1966 and 1971), Krosno (1978), and Sandomierz (1988), among others. After the 1975 administrative reform, when new units were designated, he drew up development plans for the Krosno, Przemyśl, and Tarnobrzeg provinces (1977). This was a special moment in history, as the newly created provincial capitals were given rather large financial injections to prepare for their new functions. Performing such responsible tasks related to the long-term strategy of regional development, Władysław Hennig constantly witnessed political interventions. His personal ties with the PZPR will be outlined in the following chapter, but the relationship on the line: urban-architectural administration bodies and local authorities, was not limited to party affiliation. Sam recalled that he had to personally negotiate with newly appointed party dignitaries and together with them set the program of cities or centres. That this was not an easy task can be seen from stories that, years later, took on the character of anecdote but actually illustrate the corruption of the decision-making process. The chairman of the Presidium of the City Council in the small town of Krosno dreamed of an airport and expected urban planners to plan a runway in the place he indicated. In turn, in the Piastów housing estate in Rzeszów, the city authorities decided to develop the vacant space contrary to the plan (which envisioned a service and commercial centre in that place) and contrary to the expectations of the local community (which, in turn, wanted to build a church there). The party authorities of Rzeszów, with the approval of the city architect (sic!), without a second thought "inserted" in the vacant space two typical residential blocks – "located contrary to all urban planning principles"[10] – described the situation to Władysław Hennig. As can be seen, the authorities' pressure on architects working in leadership positions in the architecture and construction administration or urban planning bodies was related not only to the strictly political situation but also to the economic one. The 49 provinces, established in 1975, had relatively large budgets, which, combined with the burgeoning ambitions of local activists and politicians, resulted in projects of "hundreds of thousands of dead-end volumes without coverage." A number of investments were planned, which the editors of "Architektura" described as "the madness of local authorities who want to erect monuments to themselves" (*Marian Fikus* + . . ., 1982, p. 30).

The stories and cases described earlier involve established architects whose professional achievements went beyond strictly administrative work. However, one should not be fooled by appearances. The daily reality in the field administration looked bad, and sometimes even tragic, in terms of the saturation of administrative bodies with architects. Beginning in 1957, "Communications of the SARP" ("Komunikat SARP") a periodical published by the General Board of the Association of Polish Architects, published job offers for architects, including, especially numerous, job offers in field administration. By 1960, some needs had been met in this regard, but there was still a shortage of architects at the county level and of urban planners. When, in 1971, the SARP General Board appointed a committee to investigate the state of employment in the offices, the committee presented data that was quite shocking. Not a single architect was employed in the 126 architecture departments at the county level. It should be added that the entire country was divided into 400 counties at the time, which means that almost one-third of them lacked architectural professionals. Not surprisingly, with such staff shortages, self-construction and starting investments (both private and public) without proper paperwork and permits were commonplace (Basista, 2001, p. 44–45)

2.5 Architects-politicians

In 1980, the membership card of the Polish United Workers' Party (PZPR) could boast more than three million Poles. How many of them were architects? Contrary to a fairly common popular opinion, the careers of designers in socialist Poland were not strictly determined by party membership. The mere fact of having a "red booklet" (the ID card had a red cover) did not become any guarantee of success. As Tadeusz Barucki emphasized years later, the percentage of "party" architects was relatively low in Poland. Those who "belonged" mostly compensated in this way for the moderate creative potential, although, among the "party," there was also no shortage of artists who were outstanding in many respects.

Among them were Helena Syrkus, Bohdan Lachert, Ryszard Karłowicz, and Bolesław Kardaszewski. They can be considered artists of above-average creativity who decided to join the ranks of the PZPR. Why? There is no single right answer to this question. Behind each decision was a different motivation, a different story, and experiences. Karłowicz came from a Jewish family and before the war bore the surname Mandel. He was the son of a Warsaw lawyer, Karol Mandel and Stefania Warszawska. Both parents most likely perished in the Krzemieniec ghetto in 1942. Even before the outbreak of World War II, Ryszard graduated from the Evangelical high school named after Mikołaj Rej as one of only three boys of Jewish descent. During this time, he became close to leftist groups, being active in the Socialist Youth Organization "Life" and the youth section of the Democratic Club. In 1939, he was sent to Lviv and then to Uzbekistan. Probably because of his origin, he was not accepted into the Polish Armed Forces forming in the Soviet Union in 1941, i.e., the allied troops of the Western Allies, subordinate to the Polish government-in-exile. Instead, he served in the First Infantry Division named after Tadeusz Kościuszko, fighting against the Germans alongside the Red Army. He walked the combat trail from Lenino to Warsaw. After the war, he adopted the surname Karłowicz (after his father's name, Karol) and, as a member of the Warsaw Reconstruction Office, became involved in rebuilding the country. From 1944, he belonged to the Polish Workers' Party, and when the party was united with the Polish Socialist Party in December 1948 and the PZPR was constituted, he naturally became a member.

40　*Architecture and Architects in Socialist Poland*

Kardaszewski was more than a decade younger than Karłowicz. He came from a working-class family with socialist traditions. His father, a pre-war PPS (Polish Socialist Party) member, worked at the Polish Aircraft Engines Factory – Okęcie near Warsaw. In 1945, he joined the party, which may have influenced his son's later political decisions and choices. The latter, in turn, being too young to belong to an "adult" organization, was active in the Union of Polish Youth. He did not join the ranks of the Polish United Workers' Party until 1966, when he was 35 years old, and had made a name for himself in the Łódź architectural community.

Party affiliation or lack thereof was determined by a number of factors. In addition to individual inclinations and beliefs, there were a number of unwritten rules according to which managerial positions in the architecture and construction administration were filled by party members. However, this did not necessarily mean that they were incompetent or treated with hostility by their subordinates. Interpersonal relations do not always fit into the black-and-white division of the world into "ours" and "theirs," as Bogdan Wyporek's recollections from his time working at the Warsaw Urban Planning Bureau attest well. "We were somehow unbelievably lucky that there were no political activists in our midst," he recounted.

> (Adolf) Ciborowski was a party member, but without that he could not have held the position (of Chief Architect of Warsaw). Later there was Czesław Kotela, who was also a party member. But these were all very decent people, excellent urban planners. They were not politicians, but professionals.[11]

Wyporek's words coincide with Marian Fikus' account of Jerzy Buszkiewicz. "If he had not been a party member, he would have been neither Chief Architect of the City nor Chief Architect of the Province,"[12] said Fikus, a colleague and for many years a subordinate of Buszkiewicz. However, there were exceptions to every rule. The case of Wiesław Gruszkowski, described in an earlier section, who was appointed Chief Architect of the Gdańsk Voivodeship in 1955, proved that membership in the Polish United Workers' Party was not a sine qua non for an administrative or even political career. For Gruszkowski, non-partisanship proved to be an asset on more than one occasion. "I was not given any party instructions," he recalled with undisguised satisfaction. And he added: "They could not give them, because I was not a party member."[13]

Wiesław Gruszkowski admitted that by the time he took over as chief architect of the Gdańsk province, he already had an established professional position. In the face of a designer respected in the environment with considerable achievements, the authorities had to show some forbearance and even subtlety. It was not possible to simply, unceremoniously suggest to Gruszkowski or Cęckiewicz that they join the ranks of the Polish United Workers' Party. Such behaviour would be frowned upon, yet the Communist authorities were careful to keep up appearances. When 31-year-old Witold Cęckiewicz took up the post of Architect of the City of Cracow in 1955, he was non-partisan. His situation was aptly and wittily described by Rzeszów architect and urban planner Władysław Hennig: "Cęckiewicz did not have to be a party member, because he was already a professor and a prominent architect."[14]

Artist or worker? Architect in the socialist country 41

Hennig himself, however, held a party card and made no secret of the circumstances of his joining the PZPR. Listening to his account, one could get the impression that this was simply another of many episodes in the long and fruitful work of a designer in People's Poland. During one of the meetings of the Provincial Urban Planning and Architectural Commission, Hennig, who held the position of head of the Provincial Urban Planning Studio, presented the plan for Rzeszów in the presence of the First Secretary of the Provincial Committee of the Polish United Workers' Party, the Chairman of the Presidium of the Municipal National Council, and all higher-level comrades. The presentation was followed by an intimate meeting.

> Listen Hennig, you guys would like this to be implemented, yes? And do you know what influence you have as a party member and what influence you have as a non-party member? If you are a party member, you will participate in all these procedures that will lead to the realization of this, and if not, you won't.[15]

And so Władysław Hennig became a member of the PZPR.

Jerzy Sołtan, an architect-dissident, once stated that a designer "works by building" (Sołtan, 1996, p. 49). He was willing to forgive his fellow architects for political conformism if it was not accompanied by artistic servility. In the case of Hennig (and many of his ilk), "politics" became a complement to the work of architects and urban planners providing an opportunity to increase the effectiveness of their own efforts to improve the quality of the surrounding space.

Party membership was not a requirement for an architect to receive prestigious state commissions or . . . sit in the Parliament. What is more – these honours could be obtained with "stains" in the resume as serious as membership in the Home Army. Halina Skibniewska belonged to the Home Army during World War II, which did not prevent her from being an MP during the communist era for five consecutive terms, as well as holding the position of deputy speaker of the Parliament (Figure 2.2). Her husband, Zygmunt Skibniewski, was involved in the underground activities of the Union of Armed Struggle (ZWZ). He sat on parliamentary benches from 1952 to 1956. The Party, guided by the usual pragmatism in life, was willing to turn a blind eye to various manifestations of "iniquity." Maria Piechotka remained non-partisan throughout her life. She was a participant in the Warsaw Uprising and a prisoner of the Zeithain camp. From her words and actions, it is impossible to infer any sympathy for the communist authorities. Nonetheless, she became a member of the Polish People's Republic's Parliament of the third term.

The beginning of her activity in politics was surprising for the designer herself. As she recalled, one day in March 1961, she was summoned to the headquarters of the Warsaw Committee of the Polish United Workers' Party, where she was met by communist secretary Walenty Titkow. He proposed that Maria Piechotka's name be included in the list of candidates for the Parliament during the upcoming elections (which, of course, had nothing to do with freedom of choice or democracy). He rolled out visions of how this experienced architect with ties to housing could help the parliamentary Construction Committee. He stressed that her past active work

Figure 2.2 Architect Halina Skibniewska and the first Secretary of the Central Committee of Polish United Workers' Party, Edward Gierek in the lobby of the House of Parliament in Warsaw.

Source: SARP Archive.

in the Warsaw Metropolitan Council had not escaped the benevolent attention of the authorities. Recalling the whole situation years later, Piechotka suspected that she had been singled out because of the policy adopted by the authorities, according to which all social groups should be represented in the parliament of a socialist state. "It was clear from the Electoral Commission's distributor, that they needed: a woman, non-partisan, an architect, with some professional standing."[16] She felt that, by joining the work of the parliamentary committees, she would be able to increase the effectiveness of her previous activities as a designer.

> At the time, we still naively believed that much could change for the better and that it was important to get involved. No one imagined that the so-called "real socialism" under Soviet rule during our lifetime could collapse, but perhaps it could be given a "human face." Hence there were a number of people, some prominent, not connected with the regime, who thought it was appropriate to get involved in the work of the parliament.

– she justified her and her colleagues' decision (Piechotka & Piechotka, 2021).

With the advent of the post-Stalin thaw, the communist authorities began to promote slogans of "democratization of life" (Chrobaczyńska-Plucińska, 2019,

Artist or worker? Architect in the socialist country   43

p. 66). Parliament was to reflect the preferences of society to a much greater extent than before. Among the candidates for deputies, educated people were pushed, representing various social groups, who were often non-partisan activists known and appreciated in the region or who enjoyed an exceptional professional position. Andrzej Basista wrote that the SARP "made sure that this seat [in the parliament – note BC] was occupied by architects of high professional standing" (Basista, 2001, p. 46). Not surprisingly, among the deputies were Halina and Zygmunt Skibniewski, Maria Piechotka, Jerzy Hryniewiecki, Adolf Ciborowski (who was also a member of the Council of State), and Bolesław Kardaszewski. In view of this, was the voice of the environment, through its representatives, heard at the highest levels of government? The bassist left no doubt in this regard. "However, one cannot delude oneself that the prominent positions held by the architects allowed them to play a significant role in professional issues; they could at most intervene in individual issues, certainly not fundamental ones." An analysis of the transcripts of the parliamentary speeches of individual deputies-designers unfortunately confirms his thesis.

In the early 1960s, Jerzy Hryniewiecki raised the issue of the status of architecture and the profession of architecture several times. Unsuccessfully. "In Poland, it seems, if it goes on like this, there will remain only 'ship architecture' or 'landscape architecture.' Well, say ship architecture, it's understandable, because it's an export issue" (*Transcript of the 26th . . .*, 1964, p. 127) – he said with his usual irony. He stressed that the contemporary (bad) condition of construction is the result of living beyond our means during the years of socialist realism. "We had a demolished Poland, and we found an unplastered one . . . we wasted years of technical progress and learned to waste human labour most recklessly and waste materials most recklessly" (*Transcript of the 26th . . .*, 1964, p. 128).

Fighting against questionable austerity programs and struggling to improve the quality of the surrounding space formed a large part of the MP's activities. Maria Piechotka repeatedly referred to the economic aspects of mass construction. "It is probably a matter of course," she said, "that the correct way to master the technical and economic problem of mass construction in the face of reduced resources and increased tasks is to look for reserves and savings first of all at the base of the investment process by putting certain essential elements of it in order" (*Transcript of the 16th . . .*, 1962, p. 75). Among the key aspects that, in the opinion of the architect-scholar, urgently required reorganization were the "inadequate regionalization of the supply of building materials and elements nationwide," underdeveloped typification and unification. She stressed that a "proper pricing policy is necessary. According to the analysis, prices in many cases do not correspond to the actual production costs of materials, elements and products, as well as the outlays associated with construction workmanship" (*Transcript of the 16th . . .*, 1962, p. 76). It seems interesting that Piechotka did not shy away from ideas involving reducing expenses by . . . burdening tenants with them.

The issue of achieving savings, allowing more construction by passing the cost of certain elements on to the user, is certainly a matter worth considering

44   *Architecture and Architects in Socialist Poland*

. . . To whom and according to what criteria will sub-standard housing be allocated – this is a question that is frequently and anxiously asked at our meetings with voters.

(Transcript of the 16th . . ., 1962, p. 81)

The problem, therefore, was not the design and construction of sub-standard and substandard housing, but the issue of distribution! The deputy's doubts were allayed from the height of the parliamentary rostrum by the chairman of the Building, Urban Planning and Architecture Committee, Stefan Pietrusiewicz, who, although he conceded her point, at the same time clearly suggested that the objections of the architect were due to a misunderstanding. "I agree on the issues of the direction of the search for savings in housing, and which, as Comrade Piechotka herself stated, are being implemented in construction," he began his statement, only to add in a moment that "there are not the two ways Comrade Piechotka spoke of. No one has so set the task that savings should be sought only in the part of housing construction, the so-called 'austerity' construction" (*Transcript of the 16th . . .,* 1962, p. 109–110).

A dozen years later, similar reactions were encountered by Bolesław Kardaszewski, who, during the deliberations of the Parliamentary Committee on Construction and Building Materials, tried to prove that the separation of the concepts of "quantity" and "quality" was a road to nowhere, and that the prevailing large-panel technology needed to be improved in terms of transport and material intensity, and to increase the flexibility of the various systems. In response to his paper, Deputy Minister Leszek Kalkowski said that the system in use is efficient, and prefabricated products are of good quality.

Mr. Kardaszewski presented a thesis, which implies that design should not be adjusted to the technical capabilities of the contractor, but that the contractor should meet the requirements of the presented design. This thesis may entail dangerous consequences for the proper construction cycle, as it does not take into account the realities available to the contractor.

– deputy Henryk Hałas added (*Transcript of the meeting . . .,* 1978).

In addition to the obvious shortcomings of the system highlighted by the MPs-architects, it is worth noting the characteristic cluelessness within the profession. Legislators, contractors, manufacturers, and, as a last resort, users were blamed. Never the architects. Maria Piechotka, discussing austerity in multifamily housing, tried to defend such solutions as an indirectly lit kitchen and described the overall deterioration of the functional layout as "an undoubtedly painful procedure" (*Transcript of the 16th . . .,* 1962, p. 81), but one to which tenants would get used to over time (as with all innovative solutions). Back in the 1950s, deputy architect Zygmunt Skibniewski stigmatized the issue of lack of knowledge of basic behaviour. This is how he described his own observations from one of Warsaw's housing estates:

I recently walked through the Muranów Estate. There is a lot of right criticism of this estate, its architecture, its facilities, its unfinishedness. It is

Artist or worker? Architect in the socialist country   45

very much a legitimate criticism. But it must be said that last year and just recently, this season a great deal has been accomplished there in the area of finishing buildings, plastering, cleaning up courtyards, arranging green spaces, etc. I am recently in one of these courtyards, I look and see: the sandbox is very decent, but the children are riffling . . . and not playing in the sandbox.

(Transcript of the 34th . . ., 1956, p. 263)

He recalled that the mothers of these children were standing nearby, to whom he pointed out the misbehaviour of their kids. In response, he was told that children should play where they want. Skibniewski's attitude was (and still is) relatively common among architects, who blame any shortcomings of their own projects on the incompetent people who use them.

The influence of architects on the situation of the Polish construction industry was most often limited to advocating changes and complaining about the status quo. Political activity, despite the noblest intentions of those who undertook it, usually did not bring tangible results. Architecture was not a priority area of interest for prominent party activists, as evidenced, for example, by the fate of the Urban Planning and Architecture Committee, first absorbed by the powerful construction industry, and then completely dissolved. Undoubtedly, Andrzej Basista was right when he stressed that, in the Polish People's Republic, the architects' ability to influence the reality created by the party authorities was an illusion.

Notes

1 Tadeusz Barucki, conversation with the author, Warsaw, 09.11.2012.
2 Tadeusz Barucki, conversation with the author, Podkowa Leśna, 03.09.2013.
3 Tadeusz Barucki, conversation with the author, Podkowa Leśna, 03.09.2013.
4 Aleksander Franta, conversation with the author, Chorzów, 09.12.2014.
5 Stanisław Spyt, conversation with the author, Cracow, 29.03.2019.
6 Tadeusz Barucki, conversation with the author, Podkowa Leśna, 03.09.2013.
7 Andrzej Owczarek, conversation with the author, Łódź, 28.05.2021.
8 Wiesław Gruszkowski, conversation with the author, Gdańsk, 29.01.2014.
9 Wiesław Gruszkowski, conversation with the author, Gdańsk, 29.01.2014.
10 Władysław Hennig, conversation with the author, Rzeszów, 11.07.2014.
11 Bogdan Wyporek, conversation with the author, Warsaw, 06.08.2020
12 Marian Fikus, conversation with the author, Poznań, 30.07.2013.
13 Wiesław Gruszkowski, conversation with the author, Gdańsk, 29.01.2014.
14 Władysław Hennig, conversation with the author, Rzeszów, 11.07.2014.
15 Władysław Hennig, conversation with the author, Rzeszów, 11.07.2014.
16 Maria Piechotka, conversation with the author, Warsaw, 14.11.2012.

References

Act of March 7, 1950 on preventing the liquidity of workers in professions or specialties of particular importance to the socialized economy, "Journal of Laws of 1950," no. 10(107). https://isap.sejm.gov.pl/isap.nsf/DocDetails.xsp?id=WDU19500100107.

46   Architecture and Architects in Socialist Poland

Barucki, T., *Fragmenty stuletniej historii 1899–1999: relacje, wspomnienia, refleksje: w stulecie organizacji warszawskich architektów* [Fragments of a Centennial History 1899–1999: Reports, memories, reflections: On the centenary of the organisation of Warsaw architects], Warsaw: SARP, 2000.

Barucki, T., *Ogólnopolska Narada Architektów* [National Meeting of Architects], Warsaw: SARP, 1956.

Basista A., *Betonowe dziedzictwo. Architektura w Polsce czasów komunizmu* [Concrete heritage. Architecture in communist Poland], Warsaw-Cracow: PWN Scientific Publishing House, 2001.

Basista, A., *Ideowy model studiów architektury* [Ideological model for the study of architecture], "Architektura" 1969, no. 1.

Bielecki, C., *Gra w miasto* [Playing the city], Warsaw: Fundacja Dom Dostępny, 1996.

Chrobaczyńska-Plucińska, E., *Posłanki na Sejm PRL II kadencji (1957–1961). Cechy socjopolityczne i aktywność poselska* [Women deputies to the Sejm of the Polish People's Republic for the second term (1957–1961). Sociopolitical features and parliamentary activity], "Czasopismo Naukowe Instytutu Studiów Kobiecych" 2019, no. 2(7).

Framework programs of master's degree programs for architecture majors, Warsaw 1966, Archive of New Files, ref. 2/317/0/14.2/2059.

Gurawski, J., *Z cyklu "Sylwetki"* [From the series "Silhouettes"], "Architektura" 1982, no. 1.

Herbst, K., *O problemie psiej budy, czyli jak zdjąć gorset. Rozmowa z Krzysztofem Herbstem* [On the problem of the dog kennel, or how to take off the corset. A conversation with Krzysztof Herbst], "Miasto" 1984, no. 11.

Kardaszewski, B., *Z kręgu doświadczeń lat 1976–1997* [From the range of experiences of 1976–1997], "Przestrzeń. Magazyn Planowania Przestrzennego" 1998, no. 1(6).

Karpiński, Z., *Wspomnienia* [Memories], Warsaw, 2018.

Kucza-Kuczyński, K., *Zawód – architekt. O etyce zawodowej i moralności architektury* [Profession – architect. About professional ethics and the morality of architecture], Warsaw: Warsaw University of Technology, 2004.

Lisowski, B., *Stan istniejący i postulowany w architekturze końca XX wieku* [The existing and desired state of architecture at the end of the 20th century], Cracow: Cracow University of Technology, 1990.

Marian Fikus + Jerzy Gurawski, "Architektura" 1982, no. 1.

Mycek, T., *Spotkania z mistrzami. Portrety 63 architektów polskich* [Encounters with the masters. Portraits of 63 Polish architects], Warsaw: Nask-Service, 1998.

Nawratek, K., *Ideologie w przestrzeni – próby demistyfikacji* [Ideologies in space – attempts at demystification], Cracow: TAiWPN Universitas, 2005.

Piątek, G., *Niezniszczalny. Bohdan Pniewski – architekt salonu i władzy* [Indestructible. Bohdan Pniewski – architect of salon and authority], Warsaw: W.A.B., 2021.

Piątek, G., *ZAPA Gdańsk. Pionierzy wolnego rynku* [ZAPA Gdańsk. Pioneers of the free market], "Architektura-murator" 2007, no. 9.

Piechotka, M. & Piechotka, K., *Maria i Kazimierz Piechotkowie – wspomnienia architektów* [Maria and Kazimierz Piechotka – memories of architects], Warsaw: Dom Spotkań z Historią, 2021.

Piniński, Z., *Architekt: kryzys czy metamorfoza zawodu? (propozycje kształcenia architekta)* [Architect: crisis or metamorphosis of the profession? (proposals for the education of the architect)], "Architektura" 1971, no. 2.

Skalimowski, A., *Sigalin, towarzysz odbudowy* [Sigalin, comrade of reconstruction], Wołowiec: Czarne, 2018.

Sołtan, J., *Rozmowy o architekturze* [Conversations about architecture], Cracow: Academy of Fine Arts, 1996.

Sprawozdanie Zarządu Głównego i wypowiedź ustępującego Prezesa SARP [Report of the general board and statement by the outgoing President of SARP], "Komunikat SARP" 1961, no. 4–5.

Springer, F., *Wanna z kolumnadą. Reportaże o polskiej przestrzeni* [Bathtube with colonnade. Reportage about the Polish space], Cracow: Karakter, 2020.

Artist or worker? Architect in the socialist country 47

Syrkus, H. & Syrkus, S., *Architekt i uprzemysłowione budownictwo* [Architects and industrialized construction], "Architektura" 1948, no. 8–9.

Syska, A. & Jaworski, P., *Granice transformacji. Poszukiwanie nowej formuły zawodu projektanta* [Frontiers of transformation. Searching for a new formula of the design profession], [in:] *Polskie Las Vegas i szwagier z Corelem. Architektura, moda i projektowanie wobec transformacji systemowej w Polsce* [Polish Las Vegas and brother-in-law with Corel. Architecture, fashion and design vis-à-vis the systemic transformation in Poland], ed. L. Klein, Warsaw: Fundacja Kultura Miejsca, 2017.

Szafer, T.P., *Współczesna architektura polska* [Contemporary Polish architecture], Warsaw: Arkady, 1988.

Transcript of the 16th meeting of the fourth session of the Parliament, Warsaw, 21.12.1962.

Transcript of the 26th meeting of the sixth session of the Parliament, Warsaw, 25.02.1964.

Transcript of the 34th meeting of the tenth session of the Parliament, Warsaw, 09.11.1956.

Transcript of the meeting of the Parliament committee on construction and building materials, BPS 446/VII term, Warsaw, 13.07.1978.

Tyszkowski, J.L., *Współczesna metoda kształcenia architektów* [Contemporary method of training architects], "Architektura" 1971, no. 11.

Warszawska Szkoła Architektury 1915–1965. 50-lecie Wydziału Architektury Politechniki Warszawskiej [The Warsaw School of architecture 1915–1965. 50th anniversary of the faculty of architecture at the Warsaw University of Technology], eds. J. Zachwatowicz et al., Warsaw: Warsaw University of Technology, 1967.

Wierzbicki, J., *Polemika z A. Kijowskim* [Polemic with A. Kijowski], "Komunikat SARP" 1974, no. 5–6.

Wujek, J., *Mity i utopie architektury XX wieku* [Myths and utopias of 20th-century architecture], Warsaw: Arkady, 1986.

Złowodzki, M., *Józef Tadeusz Gawłowski*, "Nasza Politechnika" 2010, no. 1.

Żmudzińska-Nowak, M., *Architektura i urbanistyka* [Architecture and urbanism], [in:] *Reflektory. Interdyscyplinarne spojrzenie na dziedzictwo architektury Górnego Śląska drugiej połowy XX wieku* [Reflektory. An interdisciplinary look at the architectural heritage of Upper Silesia of the second half of the 20th century], eds. M. Żmudzińska-Nowak, I. Herok-Turska, Katowice: Silesian Library, 2017.

Żórawski, J., *O budowie formy architektonicznej* [About the construction of an architectural form], Warsaw: Arkady, 1973.

3 Iron curtain or nylon curtain?

3.1 Foreign literature and journals

"The Iron Curtain," which divided post-war Europe into two camps, capitalist and socialist, was a barrier that was difficult to break through. Difficult does not mean impossible. Besides, its nature changed during the different periods of the so-called Eastern Bloc. During the Stalinist era, it was undoubtedly necessary to speak of an "iron curtain," a barrier through which no one and nothing would get through without the permission of the Communist authorities. After the dictator's death, however, it unsealed to such an extent that, by the end of the 1950s, one could, following György Péteri, speak of a "nylon curtain" (Crowley, 2018). Following this metaphor, one should note the properties of the Nylon Curtain-semi-transparency and semi-permeability. People on the other, socialist side of the Curtain were thus able to derive knowledge about living standards, consumer goods, and so on in the West. Through its semi-permeable shell, new ideas reached socialist countries such as the Polish People's Republic. Their carriers were the media (journals, books), as well as the personal contacts of those who were given a taste of Western reality.

In the case of architecture and architects, the process of crossing the Iron (Nylon) Curtain barrier may have taken place on three levels: personal contact with the West during tours, internships, and professional work; confrontations with Western design thought through international architectural competitions; and indirect contact through reading foreign magazines and books or texts on Western architecture printed in Polish magazines and books. The first two themes will be discussed in subsequent subsections, while this one is an attempt to outline the role of the Association of Polish Architects, and above all the role of the media, in the international contacts of architects from socialist Poland.

The Association of Polish Architects (SARP) was reactivated as early as November 1944 in Lublin, which had been liberated from German occupation. Less than two years later, in June 1946, the first issue of the bulletin "Komunikat SARP" was published in Warsaw (a continuation of the pre-war publication with the same title). The priority, in terms of both the content of the periodical and the activities of the Association itself, was national affairs, headed by the post-war reconstruction of Poland. At the same time, efforts were made not to neglect building environmental awareness of the development of architecture outside the country. In 1947, as part

DOI: 10.4324/9781003603153-4

Iron curtain or nylon curtain? 49

of the SARP discussion club established by the Association, a series of lectures on the architecture of various countries was held: the Soviet Union (its author was the Soviet architect Aleksey Sidorov), Sweden (Gustaf Lettström), or Switzerland (Hans Schmidt). Polish designers also shared foreign experience and knowledge with their colleagues. Stanisław Jankowski presented the problems of contemporary English architecture, Jan Minorski presented Russian architecture, and Adam Krzyszkowski presented the architecture of the United States. Relative pluralism ended in 1949 with the adoption of the doctrine of socialist realism and the political "tightening of the course." From then on, the only direction in which Polish architects could look was east and the Soviet Union. This state of affairs persisted until 1955.

The same evolution of the content presented could be seen in the monthly magazine "Architektura," published by the SARP General Board. The magazine regularly made attempts to internationalize Polish achievements in the field of architecture (including by printing short resumes in English, French, and Russian), as well as to introduce domestic designers to interesting foreign issues. Thus, in 1948, they were able to learn about the urban planning of Stockholm (Krzyszkowski, 1948) or the problems of developing the Tennessee River Valley. Still in the combined August–September issue of the same year, an extensive account of the first congress of the International Union of Architects in Lausanne was published. However, this was the last text treating architecture from behind the Iron Curtain published by "Architektura" in the following six years. At the end of 1948, speeches by Soviet architects at the aforementioned Lausanne congress were printed, while any other papers were omitted. This was a clear indication of where Polish designers should get their inspiration from and where they should look for guidance. The subjects of the articles published in "Architektura" between 1949 and 1955 included Soviet architectural publications, contemporary architecture of socialist countries, urban planning of the USSR, and housing construction there. Interestingly, relatively often these were translations into Polish of articles by foreign authors. When in 1952 "Architektura" published a series of fourteen articles presenting selected problems of architecture in socialist countries (mainly European, but also, e.g., North Korea), most of them came from representatives of the countries in question.

In 1950, at the invitation of the Union of Soviet Architects, a trip of Polish architects and engineers went to the USSR (Barucki, 2000, p. 141), and an account of the trip was published in the pages of the monthly magazine. Not only such architects as Jan Minorski, one of the staunchest advocates of Socialist Realism, but also the greats of Polish architecture – Bohdan Pniewski and Romuald Gutt – shared their impressions with readers. In addition, in 1952, a book was published by Katarzyna Hryniewiecka, "In Soviet Cities. Impressions of Polish architects and engineers from a tour of the USSR." In turn, in 1954, in the January–February issue of the "Bulletin of the Institute of Urban Planning and Architecture," which was attached at the time to the monthly magazine "Architektura," the first pages included an account of the trip of Polish architects to the German Democratic Republic (GDR).

In light of the pro-Soviet (or anti-Western) policy of the political authorities and the related attitude of the architectural community, the International Meeting of

50 *Architecture and Architects in Socialist Poland*

Architects and Local Government Activists, which took place in Warsaw in June 1954 and was described in the pages of "Architektura," was extremely interesting. This was the second edition of the event, the first having been held two years earlier on the occasion of the inauguration of the capital's Konstytucji Square. It was attended by more than 200 people, architects, and local government activists, representing 26 countries. Among them were representatives of both socialist countries – the Soviet Union, Romania, China, East Germany, or Hungary – and capitalist countries, including England, Belgium, Denmark, Norway, Brazil, Chile, and West Germany. The subject of the session was the issue of the post-war city. The organizers distinguished three key areas of discussion: reconstruction of the destroyed city; expansion of the existing city; and construction of the new city. It would seem that these topics were extremely topical less than a decade after the end of World War II. This was indeed the case, but one should not forget the propaganda mission of the entire event, which seemed to be as important (or perhaps more important) as the international exchange of ideas. Foreign visitors Warsaw, Nowa Huta, Auschwitz, Nowe Tychy, and Cracow. Their opinions about socialist Poland were very positive. "Architektura" quoted architect Guido Görres from Hamburg, who admitted that until his arrival he had been living under a misconception about socialist Poland, and blamed his own ignorance on insufficient information and the flood of outright false information that was being disseminated in the West (Majorek, 1954).

However, the International Meeting of Architects did not become a breakthrough in the contacts of the Polish community with non-socialist countries. The editors of the monthly magazine "Architektura" still limited information from abroad to reports from the so-called Eastern Bloc. Practically, every time they were treated as a model and a kind of guideline for Polish designers, as was the case with the description of the architecture of the Leningrad subway or the published conclusions of Moscow architects and builders. However, the first changes in editorial policy could be seen as early as 1955. Although still in the February issue an important place was occupied by Zygmunt Skibniewski's account of the All-Union Conference of Soviet Builders in Moscow and extensive excerpts from the paper delivered during it by Nikita Khrushchev, information about Danish design appeared in the "Chronicle" inserted on the last page of the magazine. A month later, architect Adolf Ciborowski shared his reflections on his visit to Great Britain. At the same time, the editors tried to maintain a balance in the selection of foreign topics. Thus, in April, the latest developments in the field of architecture from Romania were presented, in May – a cross-sectional picture of prefabricated construction in Western countries, and a month, later the latest developments in this field in the Soviet Union were described. With the growing Thaw, the courage grew among editors and authors to write about what was, if not forbidden, then unwelcome under Stalinism. At the end of 1955 and the beginning of 1956, readers of "Architektura" were able to read about both the problems of construction in polder areas in the Netherlands, the construction of Olympic stadiums in Rio de Janeiro, Mexico City or Budapest, as well as residential construction of brick blocks according to methods developed in the USSR and Soviet

Iron curtain or nylon curtain? 51

technologies of finishing work on facades. Finally, in March 1956, a settlement with socialist realism by Adam Kotarbiński was published in the pages of the monthly. It was followed by articles on glass and plastic masses used in construction in the United States and residential architecture in Norway and England. The regular column "Chronicle" published mentions of new and interesting constructions erected in the United States, England, Holland, and Italy. The turn to the West was not slowed down even by the powerful obituary of Bolesław Bierut, who died in March 1956 (for the record, his death was also one of the impulses for further policy softening, both domestic and foreign). Of course, this did not mean, because it could not mean, any loosening of Poland's relations with the Soviet Union. Subsequent issues described, among other things, the sports centre on Moscow's Luzhniki, but architect Jan Minorski, who had recently glorified Soviet Socialist-Realist architecture, was already writing about the current situation of French architecture. Added to this were such texts as a note from a trip to Rome or a report from the French construction enterprise Raymond Camus and Company by Helena Syrkus. Thus, the most important Polish magazine devoted to architecture found a kind of "golden mean" – in addition to information on important phenomena from across the western border, information on the architecture of socialist countries appeared regularly, but no centre was clearly overrepresented.

In addition to texts treating new technical solutions or completed buildings, "Architektura" also published information on foreign publications. Most often these were brief mentions, although there were also longer reviews, such as a review of a book entitled "Bäder" published in February 1961.[1] So what did (or rather – what could) Polish architects read in the 1960s and 1970s? It seems symptomatic that Polish publishing houses published virtually no theoretical texts by Western architects. Thus, among the books published in the post-war years, one looks in vain for works by Le Corbusier (with the exception of the pamphlet edition of "Modulor"), Walter Gropius, or Kenzo Tange. The glorious exception was the 1968 edition of Siegfried Giedion's fundamental work "Space, Time and Architecture – the Birth of a New Tradition," although here, too, it should be noted that Polish readers received the text nearly 30 years after its release. This was by no means due to the fact that translations of foreign texts were not published as a rule. On the contrary, "Architektura" or "Komunikat SARP" more than once reported on Western publishing novelties appearing on the market. However, these were either studies of a general and popularizing nature (e.g., "Three Colors of Mexico" or "Scandinavian Romanesque: monuments of architecture and art of Denmark, Norway and Sweden"[2]) or discussions of specific construction or design problems (among others, T. Coppel and J. J. Coulon "Tubular Scaffolding – Theory and Practice," H. Hossdorf "Model Statics," or C. Siegel "Structural forms in modern architecture"[3]). The publishing house "Arkady" in the late 1970s began publishing a series "Architecture and Architects of the Modern World" – small-volume booklets with a large number of black-and-white photographs concerning such figures as Le Corbusier, Gropius, Tange, and Aalto. However, the authors were mainly Polish, or alternatively – architects from brotherly Hungary. Of the important positions of Western authors, we should single out the books published in 1979 "Revolution in

52 *Architecture and Architects in Socialist Poland*

architecture: theory and design in the "first age of the machine" by Reyner Banham and "History of European Architecture" by Nikolaus Pevsner.

As one can easily see, an architect in socialist Poland had access to books from behind the Iron Curtain, but these were mostly historical or strictly technical studies. If he wanted to learn about current theoretical considerations, then he was usually doomed to search on his own. He could be helped by the Association of Polish Architects, whose branches sometimes bought Western magazines such as "Architecture d'Aujourd'hui," "Domus" or, oriented more strongly towards construction, "Bauen und Wohnen" or "Baumeister." Despite this, one can see a certain backwardness of Poland in relation to the West on the level of architectural theory. Therefore, one can agree in part with Andrzej Basista, who wrote in 2001 that "enchanted by fashion" Polish architects were reaching for the patterns of late modernism, which were developed in a different time, place, and context, and therefore, in his opinion, copied them unreflectively. He blamed this on the period of Socialist Realism (1949–1956) when contacts with Western design thought and theory were completely halted (Basista, 2001, p. 178). However, Basista overlooked the fact that architects in socialist Poland had very limited access to theory, which was the foundation of the trends of the time. Focused on other aspects, the publishing market was not conducive to the development of discussions on the principles of the new architecture. The situation changed in the early 1980s when new trends became the subject of lively discussion in both specialized and popular media.

In 1982, Polish Television aired the program "30 minutes with architecture," which included an interview with Charles Jencks, at the time the most translated foreign author of texts on architecture. His ground-breaking in many aspects work "Post-modern Architecture" was published by the Arkady publishing house in 1987, although parts of it had already been known to the wider public for several years from excerpts published in the press (Drzewiecki & Kłosiewicz, 1982). Slightly earlier, in 1986, a book by Jakub Wujek with the telling title "Myths and Utopias of 20th Century Architecture" (Wujek, 1986) was published. The author, who began his professional career in the 1960s, designing the modernist edifice of the Wybrzeże Theater in Gdańsk together with Lech Kadłubowski and Daniel Olędzki, uncompromisingly exposed the "errors and distortions" of the modern movement. At the same time, however, he warned against, in his opinion, too easy displacement of " 'new' religion" by "post-new" religion (Wujek, 1986, p. 7–8). Wujek's pluralist vision of the architecture and urbanism of the future was essentially anti-modern and was part of a broad trend of critical publications aimed at outlining new perspectives. For the most part, they were based on a negation of modernism, which in a way followed from the very concept of postmodernism, as Diane Ghirardo rightly pointed out (Ghirardo, 1999, p. 28). "The 20th century was marked by the cult of creativity. To be original at all costs, to create something completely new, to surprise with unexpected form and scale – this became an obsession," Czesław Bielecki wrote years later in his book "Head. User's Manual" (Bielecki, 2016, p. 169). Nearly three decades earlier, at the end of the 1970s, he attacked modernists who had brought about a rupture in the development of architecture in the interwar period (Bielecki, 1978). In a similar vein, were architects

Iron curtain or nylon curtain? 53

Tadeusz Zipser (Zipser, 2014) and Dariusz Kozłowski (Węcławowicz-Gyurkovich, 1998), and Henryk Drzewiecki revised the modernist credo, stating that "form does not result from function, it RESULTS FROM CULTURE [emphasis original]" (Drzewiecki, 1983, p. 41).

The platform for the exchange of ideas was primarily the architectural press, which readily published translations of important texts by foreign authors such as Robert Venturi, Leon Krier, and Christopher Alexander, as well as critical reflections by Polish authors. Adam Miłobędzki emphasized that "Architektura," whose publication was briefly halted during martial law, had a postmodern face after 1982, which was determined by such figures as editors Jeremi Królikowski and Jacek Zielonka (Karpińska & Leśniak-Rychlak, 2016, p. 45). The Warsaw-based monthly remained the most opinionated periodical in the world of Polish architecture, but it was not the only industry medium. In the mid-1980s in Cracow, Romuald Loegler made efforts to reactivate "Architekt," a magazine with traditions dating back to the early 20th century. "I felt it was my responsibility to ensure that the message about the existence of the architectural profession did not become detached from tradition. Believing that past generations have added values to our history that we should know about," – he recalled the genesis of the venture.

> "Architekt" stopped going out in 1932. It brought together people of great talent, knowledge and commitment to building the Polish landscape. I thought that if we don't recreate something that gives us continuity and the opportunity to refer to the achievements of past generations, we break a certain educational link for art historians, architects, students.

It ended with only three issues, but Loegler believed that certain goals he had set for the publication had been achieved.

> Continuity was expressed not only by the name itself, the title, but also the external form. So that each of the young people who took "Architekt" in their hands could see that we did not fall from the moon. That we have behind us a cultural and architectural experience that makes us richer with the experience of past generations.[4]

Was the fact that the existence of "Architekt" was only a short-lived episode determined by the lack of interest in architectural issues? Loegler stressed that the monthly magazine was meant to be a communication platform between specialists and society, in a country where "30 some million people had no contact with the architectural community."

The look to the past and emphasis on the continuity of the evolution of architecture as art, postulated by the Cracow editorial board, was part of the leading trend of the Polish variety of postmodernism. Even before 1980, "one can observe a spontaneous growth of interest in local form" (Piątek, 2016, p. 39). At the same time, attempts to refer to the discourse conducted on the other side of the so-called "Iron Curtain" often produced dubious results and exposed backwardness. So, was

54 *Architecture and Architects in Socialist Poland*

Lidia Klein, cited in the introduction to this chapter, right when she accused Polish postmodernism of being secondary to the West?

Czesław Bielecki considered this feature one of the main sins of domestic architecture.

> Our profession went through a time of tremendous intellectual fever after May '68 . . . Out of all this great intellectual turmoil, a few very significant currents were born, and all architects went through these currents. In 1988, when I was released for the second time to the West, I asked Joseph Rykwert why people [in the West] don't talk about Christopher Alexander's "A Pattern Language." He replied that it had simply already entered intellectual circulation, it had entered design thinking, and it wasn't being talked about.

Bielecki already in the 1980s placed great emphasis on knowledge of the canon of contemporary architectural theory. Without this knowledge, we remained a province unreflectively duplicating solutions developed by the centre. "It seems that there are these dozen or so books in the world such as Collage City, A Pattern Language, Jane Jacobs, Venturi, which, if they are not put into intellectual circulation, we will simply always only duplicate certain trends."[5] It is worth noting the efforts of Andrzej Bruszewski, who became editor-in-chief of "Architektura" in the second half of the 1970s, to "internationalize" the most popular Polish magazine treating architecture (Karpińska & Leśniak-Rychlak, 2015, p. 69). Translations of important studies appeared in the pages of the monthly, and attention was paid to publishing news. However, this did not significantly change the overall picture.

Some summary of Bielecki's reflections may be the statements made by Barbara Gadomska and Andrzej Karpowicz in an article bearing the telling title "The big world dealt with the superstructure, and we still could not get to grips with the base" (Karpińska & Leśniak-Rychlak, 2015). Derived from Marxist philosophy, the scheme well captured the essence of the problems faced by national publications publishing materials on architecture. Programmatic issues were not infrequently relegated to the background by such mundane issues as technical aspects related to the proper quality of printing or material shortages, which were also mentioned by Romuald Loegler. The relatively narrow circle of potential readers also remained a problem.

The disputes that took place "in the big world" seemed distant and incompatible with the daily concerns of a designer in the declining communist era.

> Discussions about trends and directions were held by a narrow circle of architects – by no means all of them, because not all of them were at all interested in theoretical and aesthetic divagations, especially since hardly anything could be applied in the coarse reality of the time.

3.2 Polish architects in the Western world

The repeal of the Iron Curtain during the post-Stalin thaw made it possible for Polish citizens to travel abroad. Such travel was subject to a number of restrictions,

Iron curtain or nylon curtain? 55

ranging from the difficulty of obtaining a passport, through a series of official formalities, to a limit on the amount of foreign currency allotted (and the difficulty of buying it legally). Despite this, Andrzej Basista wrote, "as a professional group, architects, along with other people of the arts, were among the people most often traveling abroad" (Basista, 2001, p. 57).

Contacts of architects from socialist Poland with the capitalist Western world (and the countries of the global south) had various forms – from tours organized by "Orbis," through individual trips,[6] and delegations to learn about new technologies,[7] to trips for paid work on behalf of state foreign trade agencies, primarily Polservice.[8] The first foreign trips of the selected architects took place in 1955, with destinations in France, Switzerland, Sweden, and Italy, respectively (Basista, 2001, p. 56). A year later, in the fall, there was a bus trip through Czechoslovakia and Austria to France and Italy. It was organized by the Association of Polish Architects. Dozens of architects were able to see both historical monuments and the latest works of architecture, such as Le Corbusier's Marseille Unit. The significance of the trip was evidenced by the fact that the monthly magazine "Architektura" devoted an article to the trip, and a small-volume book was published in 1957, where, in addition to a concise text by Tadeusz Barucki, there were dozens of photographs taken during the trip. The architects, upon their return, were now able to "look at their projects, their city, their workshop, their country and . . . [had] the opportunity to compare" (Barucki, 1957, p. 5). In 1957, another quite substantial trip of 57 students and employees of the Faculty of Architecture of the Wrocław University of Technology went to the West (*Tadeusz Zipser. Passport files . . .*). In the following decades, the number of foreign trips of domestic designers steadily increased. The trips were of different natures and can be divided into three basic groups: trips of a tourist nature (group and individual); trips to earn money; and trips for professional purposes (among them were consultations, conferences, etc.). The last two seem particularly interesting.

In the early 1960s, a joke circulated in SARP circles that more Polish architects work in Paris than in Warsaw (Basista, 2001, p. 56). Although there are no fully reliable figures on the scale of labour migration at that time, it was a relatively common phenomenon. Of course, it is impossible to determine the exact number of either those architects who permanently left the borders of socialist Poland or those who returned to the country after some time. One can only rely on security service files containing passport applications of individuals and individual memories and stories.

Some remained abroad for the rest of their lives – such as architect Andrzej Wujek (brother of Łódź designer Jakub Wujek) in France. Others treated emigration as a temporary state. The former sometimes stayed in the West illegally, going on organized tours and then separating from the group (this is what Andrzej Wujek did). The latter took advantage of scholarships and invitations from family or friends living abroad. Marek Budzyński went to Denmark on a scholarship in 1970. He stayed there for two years working, among other things, in the architectural studio of Sven Högsbro, where he created a design for a complex of 120 single-family houses in Niverød. Although the concept did not live to see realization, it became the impetus for Budzyński's further deliberations, which resulted

56 *Architecture and Architects in Socialist Poland*

in the so-called "group parceling" (Gzowska & Klein, 2013, p. 15). It combined the advantages of communal and individual activity. The centralized authority was to create a framework (such as communications, communications, energy, water, etc.) for local activities implemented on the basis of self-government and direct democracy (construction of housing complexes and associated developments). When Budzyński returned to Poland and headed the team designing the Ursynów Północny (North Ursynów) housing development in Warsaw, he had to verify his assumptions. It quickly became apparent that in highly centralized People's Poland, "group parceling" could not be implemented.

The aforementioned Jakub Wujek went to the West for the first time already in 1958, they will be in their third year of study at the Faculty of Architecture at the Gdańsk University of Technology. The trip to the Federal Republic of Germany was a reward for him and nine other students. The young people were deployed in the homes of private individuals who agreed to host them for a short stay. This is significant because thanks to the friendship thus made, Jakub Wujek went to Finland a few years later. In 1963, his mentor from his student stay in West Germany extended an invitation to the young Polish architect, and on top of that provided him with the opportunity to work in the atelier of Finnish architect Osmo Lappo. Such an invitation from a permanent resident was necessary to obtain a passport and permission to leave in the Polish People's Republic. In addition, the expatriate had to declare how he was going to finance his stay abroad. Uncle's role at first was that of an assistant, but after only three months, he was promoted and became one of three designers in Osmo Lappo's office. Among other things, he was a co-developer of the Niittykumpu housing development Espoo. As important as the projects and realizations (and, in light of Wujek's later activities, perhaps even more important) were international acquaintances and lessons learned from observing Western reality. The German architect Jakob Schulze-Rohr, whom he met in Osmo Lappo's studio, invited Jakub Wujek to West Berlin and the Federal Republic of Germany in 1973. Despite completing the formalities, however, the architect had problems obtaining a passport, as the Security Office expressed doubts that he would not follow in his brother's footsteps and decide to stay in the West. Uncle had to make a number of statements to finally obtain permission to leave. The Security Office officer who interviewed him noted that Jakub Wujek declared that the Polish People's Republic offered him far greater opportunities for creative development than the capitalist France of his brother, who "is a workman." The report concluded with the remark "Possible operational benefits negligible" (*Jakub Wujek. Passport files . . .*).

Architects leaving for the West were objects of particular interest to the Communist Security Service. This is evidenced by the passport files collected in the archives of the Institute of National Remembrance (IPN). The resumes of individuals (and also, as the case of Jakub Wujek showed, their families) were scanned quite thoroughly. In addition, interviews were held to assess whether a particular architect could be used for operational purposes. In the vast majority of cases, the conclusions were similar – architects did not make good agents. Wojciech Zabłocki, who made a name for himself as a designer of sports facilities (and an

Olympic medallist in fencing), had an "exploratory interview" in 1963, but the security service abandoned further recruitment due to the architect's attitude (*Wojciech Zabłocki. Passport files* . . .). Despite this, his file was retained and he was treated as a "service contact." The files collected in the IPN archives do not indicate that this contact was ever used later. Sometimes, architects decided to take a gamble with the security apparatus. They cooperated, promised materials, and then confessed that they "found nothing interesting" (such a note appeared in the passport file of a figure with the pseudonym "Waza"). Among those who acted in this way was Józef Zbigniew Polak, whose story is so complicated that it escapes common notions about foreign travel in communist Poland and the role of the security service in enabling/disabling such trips. There were a number of threads in the Polak's biography that were difficult to reconcile – on the one hand, he fought in the ranks of the Home Army, and on the other, he conquered Berlin in the ranks of the communist Polish Army. On top of that, after the war, he fought against the "bands," as the authorities at the time called anti-communist militias. When he sought permission to travel to Belgium in 1958, he was persuaded to cooperate with the Security Office. Eventually, the Polak agreed, allowing him to travel to the West. Soon after his return, however, problems began. Subsequent applications for permission to travel abroad were rejected (five times). Only an appeal to the Ministry of Internal Affairs made it possible to travel to the United States.

Architects who did not have such a complicated resume as Józef Zbigniew Polak had to convince the authorities of the legitimacy of their departure, but it was not uncommon for them too to receive a negative decision. Architect Jerzy Kurmanowicz divided his time between Poland and Austria. He first went to Vienna in the mid-1960s at the invitation of his uncle. He found employment with the design office of Leo Kammel. He worked as an assistant co-designing the design of schools and clinics. In the following years, despite invitations sent by Kammel and arguments that the trip would benefit him and his socialist homeland profession-ally, Kurmanowicz was not allowed to cross the border. The authorities felt there was a risk that the architect would remain in Austria permanently (he had a sister in the United States). Even a statement in which the architect firmly disassociated himself from "citizens who see their future in one of the 'Western' countries" had no effect (*Jerzy Kurmanowicz. Passport files* . . .). Only with the political changes in Poland did the contacts made abroad in the 1960s pay off. In 1984, Kurmanow-icz joined the team designing the largest teaching hospital in Europe at the time – Vienna General Hospital (AKH Allgemeines Krankenhaus der Stadt Wien). From then on, he was in the country sporadically, but, as can be judged mainly for family reasons, he did not decide to emigrate fully (Figure 3.1).

The West was tempted with a wide range of opportunities, salaries incompara-bly higher than those at home, and an escape from socialist greyness and perma-nent shortage of consumer goods to a capitalist paradise. Yet this paradise hidden behind the Nylon Curtain was either lost on closer acquaintance, or the Polish architects, longing for their homeland, could not quite find their way there. Accord-ing to many accounts, significant differences in the conditions for practicing the architectural profession did not always fall to the disadvantage of the socialist

Figure 3.1 Architect Jerzy Kurmanowicz and his wife Helena (also architect) in Leo Kammel's atelier in Vienna.

Source: Helena Kurmanowicz's home archive.

country. Józef Zbigniew Polak, despite some success in the United States, did not for a moment consider staying permanently in America. The architect worked at the Office of the City Architect in Chicago in the early 1970s. Polak recalled that he relatively quickly earned a high professional position, but when, however, he proposed solutions that were too expensive in the opinion of his superiors, it was pointed out to him that "such big assumptions can be made in communism. In our country we count every cent."[9] During work on the design of Chicago Center Plaza XXI, "remarks were clearly made that I am designing a communist urbanism of the center" – he wrote in materials collected by the Security Office. In such a situation, Polak resigned. "It's me, then, who is returning to communism," he allegedly replied to the comments of his American superiors. As a "farewell," he wrote in the Polish press "that when Chicago's hosts do not think about humanizing the city's urban planning, it will become a 'stone desert' doomed to a slow death"(*Józef Zbigniew Polak. Passport files . . .*).

Oskar Hansen may have been similarly motivated to Józef Zbigniew Polak. He too decided to return to his communist-ruled homeland. His first trip to the West was before the Stalinist closure of the borders, and in 1948, he received a scholarship from the French government, which allowed him to stay in Paris and stand from the studio of Pierre Jeannerret. Then there was London and the CIAM Summer School in 1949. He returned to Poland from there because "At the time, after

Iron curtain or nylon curtain? 59

my observation of Jeannerret's relationship with the so-called Clientele, compared to the design opportunities in Poland, even for students, after my London observations, it did not seem like freedom to remain here" (Springer, 2013, p. 76). Years later, painter Wojciech Fangor told Hansen that the painter had more freedom at home than he had in the seemingly free West. What he meant, of course, was creative freedom, not restricted by the rules of the free market and capitalism.

Polish architects who went to the West usually experienced culture shock at the first moment. It was not even about colourful advertisements, a dozen or so TV programs, and store shelves stocked like Pewex or Baltona stores, but mostly about working conditions and organization. A real gulf separated state-owned design companies and studios operating on the free market as private ateliers.

Cracow architect Romuald Loegler first left in 1973. He already had, in addition to his university experience, worked in a cooperative design office. Nevertheless, he admitted that working in Professor Karl Schwanzer's atelier "was such a very cold shower."[10] Everything was new, different from Poland, "starting with the very formula for organizing the work of an architect in a large office (the Vienna atelier employed 70 architects)." The institution of a multi-discipline moloch (such as the state design offices in socialist Poland) was not known at all. Moreover, the line between urban planning (or city planning) and architecture was not so clear in communist Poland. In the whole structure of the office, however, the most surprising thing for the young Cracow architect was the organizational structure.

> Of course, the professor was above everything. And then there was a team of six people who did the conceptual designs themselves. This team, under the direction of the design head of the atelier and the professor himself, was responsible for the development of the atelier, intellectual input into architectural concepts and competition solutions.

Loegler was one of those six people.

> We had assistants within this group. One was an Egyptian and the other a Czech. This Czech was responsible for making sure that the concepts created by the others, including me, were in line with technical realities and regulations such as local zoning, utilities, roads.

In a word – he was attaching bold visions and fantastic concepts to the realities of a specific order and investor. "It was, most generally speaking, a colossal difference in the organization of the office" – summed up Loegler, who during his time in Vienna worked, among other things, on the design of a university in Riyadh. From the point of view of didactics and design methods, the experience gained from Schwanzer's studio is still rated as particularly important by Romuald Loegler today.

> The professor assigned topics to architects and left the office for various reasons. When he was building the Austrian Embassy in the city of Brasilia,

60 *Architecture and Architects in Socialist Poland*

> I was given the task of designing 3 office buildings with a total of 10,000 m2 of office space. On top of that, there were service rooms, parking lots and a social area.

On his way out, the professor commanded that, during his absence, the Polish architect was only allowed to use a pencil (or crayon) and his own hand. Under no circumstances, he was allowed to reach for a ruler or eccentric.

> We had a wall in the office, 17 meters long, which was used to display all sorts of sketches. For two weeks I filled it with concepts of various solutions to just one topic – three office buildings for a certain large company,

– Loegler recounted. "It was incredibly instructive. It made you realize that there are no final settlements and decisions, that I drew it, it's good and it's over. There is only an analytical, creative process. Free thought that was being released."[11] Many years later, the reflections on the architect's work initiated in the Vienna office resulted in an exhibition at the Palace of Art in Cracow, "From Free Thought to Consolidated Form." "One had to free oneself from all tools. To have only oneself at one's disposal and one's hand and one's own imagination" – he recalled the Viennese experience.

A path that is more important than the destination it leads to. A quest that is a value in itself. Romuald Gutt understood it, Le Corbusier understood it, and Loegler understood it too. But why is conceptual work, which should be the starting point of any project, so rarely appreciated in domestic design practice? "When I returned from Austria, I began to wonder why, in the climate of our design offices, in our atmosphere of practice, in this machine of design state offices, there was no time to consolidate thoughts around a given theme . . . in order to give the quality, the beauty that we so admired in Western architecture." Returning from Austria, Loegler was at the same time doomed to return to the reality that was framed by the structure of the state-owned studio. "I returned to the state-owned office, because there was no other structure."[12] However, he was not about to give up on the prospects that were outlined before him in Professor Schwanzer's atelier. Together with his colleagues Jacek Czekaj, Piotr Drozd, and Marek Piotrowski, they formed an informal author's group, which, with an increasingly bolder and louder voice, began to raise issues of aesthetics as an inalienable part of the dialogue between the creator and the viewer of architecture at various professional meetings. One of the first results of their activities was the exhibition "Spatial Module? Aesthetics? Architecture?" in 1978. In the introduction to the catalogue, architect Professor Witold Korski wrote "The absence of all norms rarely leads to complete freedom, while it often leads to an absurd mess. This is not the goal of architecture."

3.3   International architectural competitions

With the Gomułka's thaw, access to international competitions opened up. Tadeusz Barucki, who held the position of General Secretary of the Association of Polish

Iron curtain or nylon curtain? 61

Architects at the time, recalled that previously this had been impossible "for very mundane reasons such as the secrecy of mail or the very issue of sending plans." The first post-war international competition in which Polish designers participated manifested itself in Socialist Poland under rather peculiar circumstances. In the late 1950s, Barucki was on a visit to his family in London. By sheer coincidence, he noticed in the press an announcement from the Uruguayan embassy about a competition to design a monument to President Jose Batlle y Ordonez in Montevideo. With the newspaper under his arm, he went to the embassy to ask if, as a representative of the Polish architectural community, he could obtain the relevant materials and spread the word about the competition in Poland. The Uruguayans had no objections. The problem, however, turned out to be the communist party apparatus. It took a lot of trouble for Barucki to convince the representatives of the communist authorities that "it's just a monument," and all works would be sent by the Association of Polish Architects and controlled by the Customs Office. In the end, permission was given as an exception, on a trial basis. The results surprised everyone – the Poles won two honourable mentions, and the project of architect Bogdan Banaszewski was designated for implementation. Emboldened by the first success, Barucki decided to forge the iron while it was hot. In 1959, an architectural competition was announced for a Cultural Centre in the Congolese town of Leopoldville. Although the procedure was much more complicated than before, this time the authorities readily agreed. And again it was a success! Józef Zbigniew Polak's concept was awarded second place, while Jadwiga Grębecka and Tadeusz Kobylański were awarded third place. The first prize was not awarded, but Polak's work made a great impression on the chairman of the jury, Richard Neutra, who decided to make a special trip to Warsaw, reportedly just to see the environment in which designers who create such outstanding competition works grow up

The numerous international successes of Poles have been a mystery to many. In Rio de Janeiro, the Institute of Brazilian Architects invited Tadeusz Barucki to explain the phenomenon of architects from the country on the Vistula River, which no one had heard of before, and who suddenly began to take leading places in international competitions. The question, however not meaningless, did not receive a clear answer. Barucki believed that the successes were the result of a unique combination of several factors: innate talent, the influence of a solid pre-war school of urban planning, and daily coexistence with various trades within large state design offices. Not without significance was also the fact that competitions were an escape from the constraints of everyday work, a kind of "valve" giving an outlet for creative forces. Stefan Müller's assessment of this situation is different. With his usual sarcasm, he explains it . . . by an excess of free time. "In the 60s, 70s, a person would sit at home, or hold a half liter of vodka and drink that vodka, or just think. There was time to think because there was nothing to do." Of course, domestic designers "were no dumber than a Frenchman, a German or a Japanese. But the Japanese guy had a lot of work to do, and the Polish guy was bored. In view of this, he made competitions," Müller provoked.[13] Regardless of whether Barucki or Müller (or perhaps both) are right, the dry numbers speak for themselves. In the 1960s alone, Polish architects won more than 50 prizes and awards in international competitions – a result that, both then and now, must inspire amazement and admiration. At that time, the International Union of Architects organized 34 competitions. Poles won 31 awards and honours in them! (Barucki, 2000, p. 339).

Subsequent decades were not as bountiful in success. In the 1970s and 1980s, less than 40 awards and prizes fell prey to architects from Poland, about 40% of what they had previously won in the 1960s alone.

Among the competitions were those for small-scale architectural projects, furniture, or monuments, as well as for spectacular foundations. Most were organized by Western countries, but Polish architects also competed (and were successful) in international competitions in the Soviet Union or Yugoslavia, as well as in the Middle East (Iraq, Syria). The first prizes were won, as already mentioned, in 1959, when Polish designers received an honourable mention in a competition to design furniture in Cantu, Italy, two more in a competition for a monument to Jose Battle y Ordonez in Montevideo, Uruguay, and second and third prizes in a competition to design a community centre in Leopoldville, Congo (Figure 3.2). The latter was particularly interesting. The international jury, chaired by Richard Neutra, appreciated the work of the team led by Józef Zbigniew Polak, awarding it an honourable second place (the first was not awarded). The architects presented a concept of architecture that takes advantage of local climatic conditions, including

Figure 3.2 Project awarded in the competition for the Leopoldville centre (Belgian Congo) by the team led by Józef Zbigniew Polak.

Source: "Architektura" 1959, no. 10.

Iron curtain or nylon curtain? 63

high temperatures and ample sunlight, for a system of natural ventilation. Also, the hanging design of the overhangs with significant spans was the result of a search for the most suitable and economical system with such large temperature fluctuations. Air circulation issues also became the axis of the concept prepared by the team of architect Jadwiga Grębecka, whose work was awarded the third prize. In addition to them, other architects from Poland (Janusz Ballenstedt, Zbigniew Parandowski) competed in the competition but were not recognized by the jury.

In subsequent years, the number of architects participating in international competitions steadily increased. The number of awards and prizes also increased. Among the most interesting projects of an international character, in which Polish designers successfully participated, one can also include the competition for the design of an experimental housing estate in Moscow (1961). The goal of the organizers was to develop a model for the implementation of housing construction in areas of the USSR with similar geographical conditions to the capital. Polish architects took part in the competition in relatively large numbers, and among the works submitted were designs by a Cracow team led by Tadeusz Ptaszycki (winner of one of the second prizes), the team of Maria and Kazimierz Piechotka, or the Warsaw team led by Tadeusz Zieliński. Four years later, in 1965, a duo of Warsaw architects, Jan Bogusławski and Bohdan Gniewiewski, won second prize in a competition to design the National Theater in Budapest. The same architects had somewhat earlier achieved significant success in a major international competition held in the West, winning first prize in 1964 for the design of the National Theater of the Opera in Madrid. The jury, which included Gio Ponti and Pierre Vago, appreciated the succinctness of the means of expression and the monumentality of the composition of the edifice, in front of which stood four sculpted monoliths, covered with mosaics dedicated to the great artists of theatre and music. Another Polish team, consisting of Wojciech Amanowicz, Ireneusz Rolek, and Wojciech Szymański, received an honourable mention. Subsequent successes cemented the reputation of communist architects. Thus, when a competition was organized in Italy in 1964 for the design of a natural treatment plant in Montecatini, architect Mieczysław Gliszczyński and technologist Andrzej Madejski were invited to participate as specialists in the field and authors of several of the most modern plants of this type in Poland. This resulted in a special prize (first place was not awarded).

It can be said without much exaggeration that the 1960s were a string of continuous international successes for Polish architecture. After all, how else to describe the situation when Marian Fikus, just a 25-year-old architecture graduate, won first prize at the VII Biennale of Contemporary Art in São Paulo (1963) in the category of Architecture and Theatre Technology. The young designer presented a design for a pantomime theatre, which was originally supposed to be sent to Brazil as a student work. Only that there was a mistake at the Association of Polish Architects, which was responsible for the formal side of the submissions, and the project was submitted in the "adult" category. This is at least how Marian Fikus himself described the circumstances of his success. His later colleague and supervisor from the state design office in Poznań, Jerzy Buszkiewicz, won an honourable mention in the 1965 competition for the design of a hotel complex in San Sebastian, Spain

64 *Architecture and Architects in Socialist Poland*

(it is worth mentioning that Buszkiewicz was then on a scholarship in London). This was one of three awards won by Poles at the time. Polish architects achieved an equally favourable result a year earlier in Israel. In the competition for the design of the Tel Aviv – Yafo city centre, among the six awarded projects was the work of a team from Cracow led by Barbara Perchal and architects from Warsaw, led by Józef Zbigniew Polak. Interestingly, the second prize also went to a Pole, Jan Lubicz-Nycz, who, however, acted as a representative of the San Francisco office, where he lived and worked. He was one of the many architects who either decided not to return to the socialist country after the end of World War II or, in later years, decided to flee to the West.

Success in international architectural competitions seems a telling testament to the high level of professional preparation and creativity of Polish architects in the 1960s. Interpretations, such as Stefan Müller's statement, cited at the beginning of this subsection, which explicitly suggested that designers from socialist Poland had no competition because their colleagues from the capitalist West were busy making money, seem unfair. More importantly, they do not also stand up to confrontation with figures. One need only look at a major international competition announced in 1968, the subject of which was the design of the headquarters of international organizations and a conference centre in Vienna. It attracted 272 entries, most of which – 45 – were by Austrian architects. Notably, 38 works were submitted from the United States, 32 from Great Britain, and 13 from Japan (Bieda, 1971). The contribution of Polish architectural thought was 19 projects submitted to the competition. Although none of them was honoured with a prize (the winning project was the work of César Pelli from the United States), the data presented here is proof that Western architects entered international competitions as eagerly as their colleagues from behind the Iron Curtain.

At least as internationally significant were the 1966 competition for the spatial and functional concept of the city of Espoo in Finland and the competition for the design of an administrative and social centre in Amsterdam, announced a year later. The former attracted 171 authors and author teams from all over the world, who decided to face the challenge of designing a satellite of Helsinki for 90,000 inhabitants. The scope of the study ranged from a general plan to a proposal for a development and traffic concept, ending with the architecture of the main administrative, cultural, and service centre, the centrepiece of which and the most essential element for the design of this part of the city was the design of the city hall. The first prize was won at the time by young architects from Warsaw (Jan Chmielewski, Janusz Kazubiński, and Krzysztof Kuraś) (Figure 3.3). The latter competition, which was described in the literature as a competition for a city hall in Amsterdam, was, as Lech Kłosiewicz described it in the pages of the monthly magazine "Architektura" "quite an architectural riddle" (Kłosiewicz, 1969). The answer was to be one of 803 concepts. Among them were as many as 52 works from Poland. In the end, the winner was a Viennese, Wilhelm Holzbauer, but the jury awarded the first prize to architect Jerzy Buszkiewicz, who competed together with Ewa Pruska-Buszkiewicz, a visual artist (and privately his wife). The formalist composition of the building consisted of simple blocks, which, like blocks, were stacked on top of

Iron curtain or nylon curtain? 65

Figure 3.3 Project of the city of Espoo in Finland. Project by Jan Chmielewski, Janusz Kazubiński, and Krzysztof Kuraś awarded the first prize in the international architectural competition in 1966.
Source: "Architektura" 1968, no. 4/5.

each other to create an openwork composition. The individual blocks were to be "draped" with the Amsterdam skyline, which, in retrospect, should be evaluated as a harbinger of postmodernist tendencies in architecture. In such a composed block, was "crammed" (as Buszkiewicz himself put it) the required functional program. The modernist principle that "form follows function" had seemed passe for some time (Figure 3.4).

The 1970s began with perhaps the most famous architectural competition in the second half of the 20th century, the subject of which was the Center for Modern Art on the Plateau Beaubourg in Paris. A total of 681 entries were received from all over the world. Among the jurors were a number of prominent architects, including Philip Johnson and Oscar Niemeyer (Jørn Utzon, who was also supposed to be one of the judges, unfortunately did not participate due to ill health). They awarded the first prize to Richard Rogers and Renzo Piano's design, which was to usher in the era of high tech in architecture. Leaving the winning concept aside, it is worth noting the reception of the competition in Poland. Again, as in many of the previously mentioned cases, Polish architects eagerly participated, with works submitted by, among others: Zbigniew Gądek and Konrad Wierzbicki, Jakub Wujek and Zdzisław Lipski, Witold Cęckiewicz together with Stanisław Deńko and Wacław Seruga, Andrzej Frydecki and Stefan Müller, Jerzy Petelenz and Jan Krug, and Marian Fikus together with Jerzy Gurawski. Unfortunately, none of them received even an honourable mention. The Polish architectural community was disappointed, as much by the lack of even the slightest success as by the jury's dubious verdict, in their view. Konrad Wierzbicki wrote that "The students of Mies and Gropius acted here to Wright's principle, choosing the most mediocre work of mediocre – the best, because it corresponds to the tastes of the majority" (Wierzbicki, 1972). In

66 *Architecture and Architects in Socialist Poland*

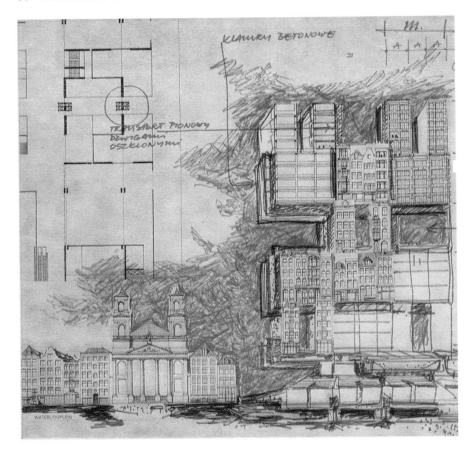

Figure 3.4 Submission awarded in the competition for the city hall in Amsterdam designed by Jerzy Buszkiewicz and Ewa Pruska-Buszkiewicz.
Source: "Architektura" 1969, no. 11.

these words, one can feel the bitterness of the loser, but, at the same time, they are a symptom of the growing discord between the new trends present in world architecture and the views of a not insignificant part of Polish architects. Perhaps, this should be attributed to their decreasing activity competition and fewer and fewer awards. After all, the 1970s and then the 1980s were barely a poor reflection of the 1960s, the "golden decade" of Polish architecture on the world stage.

3.4 Polish architects in the Middle East and North Africa

An important direction of foreign activity of Polish architects under socialism was the Middle East and Africa. The competition for the Leopoldville centre, mentioned in the previous section, was just one of a whole series of projects prepared in the countries of the Global South, both as part of "brotherly aid" and work trips. In 1960, Polservice was established, an institution responsible for sending abroad specialists in various fields of economic life to countries with which the Polish People's Republic had signed technical assistance agreements. From that point on, labour exports developed on a much larger scale, reaching several thousand people a year. In the late 1970s and early 1980s, it was about 3,500 experts in various fields. As many as a third were architects and urban planners (Barucki, 2000, p. 346). Initially, Polservice's expatriate contracts allowed two-year stays. However, it soon became apparent that with the specifics of the architectural profession and the investment cycle, this was too short a period, so the validity of the residence permit abroad was extended.

The contract trip brought a number of benefits to both the socialist state and the architects themselves. The latter, in addition to tangible financial benefits, received the opportunity to get to know other cultures, broaden their horizons in terms of new trends in architectural design (it should be remembered that, in the countries of the Global South, they often worked with French or British architects), and realize their creative potential. Warsaw architect Jerzy Sobiepan, who himself worked abroad for a long time and cooperated with Polservice, believed that architects abroad were not constrained by norms, bans, orders, agreements, and "many similar matters often influencing the distortion of the project" (Barucki, 2000, p. 346). On top of that, Polish designers were free from the constraints that dictated workmanship in their socialist homeland. They only had to reckon with the investor, which, however, was a minor burden. So naturally, the architects were able to develop their full creative potential. Sobiepan's opinion may have seemed surprising insofar as the stories of other architects abound with descriptions of problems with contractors or the local architectural and construction administration. The discrepancies therefore remain to be explained by different individual experiences and the peculiarities of the construct that is memory.

The first group of Polish specialists was contracted shortly before Polservice was established. In the second half of 1959 and early 1960, Iraqi authorities accepted a group of experts. Although initially there were no architects or urban planners among them, they joined after only a few years. The beginning of Polish–Iraqi cooperation in the field of architecture and urban planning took place in 1962, during the visit of the then-chief architect of Warsaw Adolf Ciborowski to Baghdad. As Ciborowski recalled, the Iraqi capital was then "a city of a thousand and one construction sites" (Stanek, 2020, p. 182). During his lectures, he presented to the Iraqi audience the achievements of Polish architecture and urbanism from the first decade after the end of World War II, pointing out the possibility of their implementation on the Tigris and Euphrates. The Iraqi government was planning intensive urbanization, industrialization, and modernization of the country, so the experience of the Polish People's Republic may have seemed an adequate reference. An indirect and deferred effect of Ciborowski's lectures was the arrival in Iraq of architect and planner Tadeusz Ptaszycki, the chief designer of Nowa Huta. His expertise in overall city design was to prove invaluable in Baghdad. The work of a team consisting of architects from the Cracow design office Miastoprojekt

68 Architecture and Architects in Socialist Poland

and working under Ptaszycki's direction was carried out in three stages. A Basic Map ("Zoning and Land Use") was developed between 1965 and 1968. This was followed by the Comprehensive Development Plan (years 1971–1973), and the final stage was the development of detailed plans for selected areas of the city, in 1973–1974 (Stanek, 2020, p. 183–184). The activities of Polish architects and their contribution to the urbanization and modernization of Iraq went beyond design. To some extent, they shaped a new generation of local architects, as exemplified by the professional activity of Jerzy Baumiller, who in the late 1960s taught at the Department of Architecture at Baghdad University.

At the same time that Tadeusz Ptaszycki's team began work on the Baghdad plan, another Polish architect, Jerzy Główczewski, prepared an urban design for the city of Aswan in the United Arab Republic (the state that existed between 1958 and 1961, formed by the merger of Syria and Egypt). The monthly magazine "Architektura" described the plan, developed in 1964–1965, as an interesting and positive example of international cooperation. It was emphasized that the Republic was a regional leader in the proper use of urban planning, which was especially important given the enormity of the design tasks resulting from the economic plans established. This was not an isolated case of the participation of Polish architects and urban planners in the modernization processes that have taken place in Africa since the 1960s. Many of the nations liberated from the yoke of colonialism turned to socialist countries for economic cooperation. The relationship was a two-way street, for the Soviet Union and its satellites saw such activities as the realization of the ideological tenets of the system, as well as an opportunity to expand their influence on the globe. However, architects from socialist countries were not the only ones who created the new face of Kenya or Ghana. Designers from the metropolitan states and their collaborators from other European countries were still active in the former colonies. Architects Jacek Chyrosz and Stanisław Rymaszewski went under contract with Polservice to Ghana, ruled by President Kwame Nkrumah, who made no secret of his aspirations for the country to become a local leader. Chyrosz and Rymaszewski, working in the office of the Ghana National Construction Corporation under the direction of Vic Adegbite, prepared the design of the sprawling International Trade Fair complex in Accra in 1967 (Figure 3.5).

Polish architects and urban planners have worked on developing plans for cities in Libya, Algeria, or Nigeria. They designed public facilities and housing developments (including in Libya). In the case of the latter, the designers' contribution was not limited to the implementation of ready-made solutions known from Europe, but to the creation of new systems suitable for local specifics. When the Polish People's Republic established technical and economic cooperation with Algeria in 1977, the agreement also applied to the field of construction. In the same year, a seminar on industrial methods in residential construction was organized in Algiers, in which Warsaw architect Maria Piechotka participated, presenting a paper on the open system of large-panel construction. This was the first in a series of trips to North Africa and the beginning of a collaboration that lasted several years. The purpose of Piechotka's next trip was to provide technical advice and act as a consultant. She was assisted on the spot by another Warsaw architect, Ryszard Karłowicz, who had been in North Africa for some time. Algeria, in Maria

Figure 3.5 Trade Fair Center, Accra, Ghana, designed by Vic Adegbite, Jacek Chyrosz, and Stanisław Rymaszewski.

Source: "Architektura" 1969, no. 4.

Piechotka's accounts, appeared as a country at a lower level of civilization, where construction is disorganized and chaotic. Attempts to introduce European standards in this area were occupied with enormous efforts. Eventually, however, the ECA system was developed – Elements Compatibles Algeriens (Piechotka & Piechotka, 2021, p. 345), which, due to political complications (both in Poland and Algeria), was never implemented.

In addition to Africa, both northern and sub-Saharan, a special area of activity for Polish architects was the Middle East. The aforementioned Baghdad plan and the work of Tadeusz Ptaszycki, Jerzy Baumiller, and Andrzej Basista in Iraq were just one episode of cooperation with Arab countries. It turned out to be more durable than the communist system, as it lasted from the mid-1960s until the 1990s and beyond. The result was a series of projects and realizations, often very significant and prestigious buildings. In 1974, a team of Cracow architects under the

70 *Architecture and Architects in Socialist Poland*

direction of Jan Meissner received first prize in a competition for the National Library in Damascus. Second place went to a Syrian–German team headed by a professor from the local Faculty of Architecture. As Marek Dunikowski, then a fresh graduate of the Cracow University of Technology, recalled, behind-the-scenes machinations began to eliminate the Polish team. Luckily, there was no upheaval, and Jan Meissner and his team led the design work and later the author's supervision in the construction of the library. The monumental, brutalist edifice was completed in 1984, becoming another vestige of the presence of Polish architects working in Syria during the rule of Hafez al-Assad. Under the firm hand of the prime minister and then president, the country continued the modernization course initiated in the 1960s and had ambitions to be a leader, if not of the entire Middle East, then at least of the Levant countries. A period of prosperity was underway. New investments were made with the help of Western engineers and architects, who were eagerly invited to Damascus. This brought to Syria, among others, Stanisław Niewiadomski, who took the position of general designer of the campus of a new university – Al-Baath University in Homs. Along with him came a team of Polish designers responsible for the architecture of individual buildings (Klimowicz, 2010, p. 75). They collaborated with Syrian architects, who continued the assumptions of the original concept in the later stages of the investment process (Klimowicz, 2010, p. 78). Niewiadomski worked in the Middle East as a designer and consultant for the General Company for Engineering and Consulting Company. While in Syria at the same time, another Warsaw architect, Wojciech Zabłocki, was employed by Military House Est.

Zabłocki, who travelled to the Middle East in 1982, recalled that the Syrians wanted to build a lot of sports facilities. Government officials and architects organized a reconnaissance of prominent sports centres. They held discussions with designers and necessarily wanted to hire "someone from Europe." There was one major problem, however, because, according to Zabłocki, none of the well-known designers wanted to come and design locally, in Syria. They preferred to design at home and only send relevant drawings and instructions. Meanwhile, the Syrians wanted foreign architects to work on-site with local architects, who could learn from them and observe their design methods. Such conditions, however, were not fundamentally different from how Polish architects in the Global South functioned under Polservice. In addition, the Syrians already had experience in cooperation with representatives of the Polish People's Republic, for in the mid-1970s Polish specialists developed the master plan and implementation plans for the new city of Dummar, a satellite of Damascus. Thus, in the early 1980s, a delegation from the Military House Est office visited the Office of Studies and Projects for Industrial Construction in Warsaw, and then Wojciech Zabłocki, who specializes in the architecture of sports facilities, together with designer Stanisław Kuś, went on a similar reconnaissance to Damascus.

Zabłocki and Kuś's first project was a major sports centre in Aleppo. The Poles were responsible for a sports hall for 10,000 spectators and an Olympic swimming pool. Interestingly, despite hiring architects from Europe, the Syrians wanted the centre to have features of local construction. So, Zabłocki spent his free time wandering the streets of Aleppo with a sketchbook in hand, searching for the "spirit of the place" (Zabłocki, p. 101). The largest project that Zabłocki worked on during his stay in Syria was a sports centre built in Latakia for the 10th Mediterranean Games. In 1983, the Polish architect won an international competition to conceptualize the massive 160-acre complex, which included a stadium, swimming pool, and sports halls, among other things (Zabłocki, 2007, p. 101–102) (Figure 3.6). The problem during implementation turned out to be circumstances of a "political" nature, as the martial law prevailing in Poland severely limited Zabłocki's ability to consult the project with the constructor Wiktor Humięcki, who was in Warsaw. In the end, however, everything ended successfully. The Mediterranean Games were held in magnificent new facilities, and Wojciech Zabłocki and his family were invited to the inauguration ceremony. As mentioned earlier, foreign architects working in countries such as Syria were expected to act as mentors and consultants for local designers. The history of the competition to design the National Library in Damascus clearly shows that it was not without personal conflicts, however. Zabłocki was no different. Years later, he recalled that "in Aleppo it started well, but ended badly. There was a very ambitious young Syrian architect who constantly had a different opinion. I got fed up with the constant melee and finally decided that I would leave Aleppo."[14] That designer was Fauzi Khalifa, author of the overall plan for the centre and designer of two stadiums.

Despite further successes, won competitions, and successful realizations, Zabłocki decided to return to Warsaw. He did not change his decision even when

Figure 3.6 Sports hall in Latakia, Syria, designed by Polish architect Wojciech Zabłocki.
Source: SARP Archive.

72 *Architecture and Architects in Socialist Poland*

another lucrative proposal appeared. Although the stage of large public investments was over in Syria, one of the directors of the company where Zabłocki worked, a man with extensive contacts in political spheres, urged him to go to Libya, to Muammar Gaddafi. All the paperwork was prepared, but Zabłocki refused – "I said enough is enough and I want to live in Warsaw with my family."[15] Zabłocki's Syrian achievements were not limited to sports facilities. He also took part in the revitalization of Damascus' historic districts, as well as residences. In the villas he designed, Zabłocki tried to combine modern design thinking with local building traditions, based on the use of local materials. He attached great importance to maintaining a harmonious balance between architecture and nature. A prime example of this was the rock-cut cave-influenced holiday villa in Latakia designed for Basil as-Asad, the president's son. The architect himself described it as "pure 'organics,'" architecture modelled on the natural forms of animate and inanimate nature. In contrast, another of the residences, a striking villa located in Damascus, was a clear reference to Arab building traditions of the 13th century.

Knowledge of architectural history and awareness of the value of historic buildings were extremely valuable contributions of Polish architects traveling to the Middle East. A native of Wrocław, Krzysztof Wiśniowski remembered his first impressions of Kuwait, Dubai, or Abu-Dhabi when he first arrived on the Arabian Peninsula. At that moment, the sea of sand was crisscrossed by single black strands of asphalt highways, and grey patches of unassuming buildings loomed on the horizon. Only the Jumeirah Beach Hotel, designed by Tom Wright of WS Atkins, stood out in Dubai. The rest was "completely flat." Years later, Wiśniowski recounted that "it was fantastic and I liked it terribly. Unfortunately – oil, money. . . . Only small fragments of old Kuwait remain."[16] Petrodollars, which decades later lured Zaha Hadid or Sir Norman Foster to the Arabian Gulf, prompted Polish architects to travel to the Middle East in the 1970s and 1980s.

Wiśniowski left for Kuwait in 1977. The management of the Wrocław-based company where he worked on a daily basis agreed that out of a team of four, which besides Wiśniowski included Andrzej Bohdanowicz, Ryszard Daczkowski, and Edward Lach, only two designers would be allowed to take advantage of the invitation that came from Kuwait. Thus, in 1976, Lach and Daczkowski were wooed, and a year later, they were changed by Wiśniowski and Bohdanowicz. On the Arabian Peninsula, the duo of Wrocław-based designers began working on residential development concepts at the Shiber Consult and Industrial and Engineering Consulting Office. The Kuwaitis pursued a similar concept to the Syrian authorities, stipulating that foreign architects could only work within local project offices. Wiśniowski, together with Bohdanowicz, designed the Sabah al-Salem housing development intended for middle- and low-income tenants (Stanek, 2020, p. 281–282). The concept, as originally conceived, referred to local architecture. The architects introduced a traditional atrial layout and divided the five-story houses into a "day" zone – at the ground level – and a private, "night" zone – located on the first floor. The entire complex was composed as a dense mosaic of repetitive houses located along narrow, shaded streets, thus constituting a modernized variant of the historical development of the Sharq neighbourhood (Stanek, 2020, p. 282–283). Wiśniowski, as he himself emphasized, had worked as an assistant in the Department of History of Urban Construction at the Faculty of Architecture at the Wrocław University of Technology before his trip and was well acquainted with "the building traditions of the various regions in the Mediterranean, including Arab construction, which must meet certain conditions in terms of privacy, light, ventilation system, etc." "This knowledge helped me in my work. Especially in the design of the Sabah Al-Salem estate," he recounted, while emphasizing that for a generation educated in the spirit of modernism, the problem of combining tradition and modernity was an extremely important, and not at all easy, issue. "This was already the period of postmodernism," recalled Wiśniowski.

> We were all alumni of professors from Lviv, Vilnius, pre-war modernists. And yet there [in Arab countries] is a local architectural climate. We had to decide to what extent should international architecture be present in our projects? Should there be local, traditional elements, etc. in it?[17]

When Wiśniowski and Dworzecki had to leave Kuwait and return to Poland, one of the architects who replaced them in their work on the Sabah Al-Salem estate was a colleague from Wrocław, architect Wojciech Jarząbek. He too paid attention to the historical context, as well as social aspects. He stressed that the new development complex was "good for older Kuwaitis, "who were unable to adapt to the new reality, where their clay atrium houses were being demolished. So enclaves were proposed where they would feel comfortable."[18]

The first trip to Kuwait was the beginning of a longer collaboration for the Wrocław architects with investors from Arab countries. Wojciech Jarząbek designed the Al-Othman Center and Fintas Center in Kuwait, and Krzysztof Wiśniowski (with his wife Anna Wiśniowska and Leopold Chyczewski) was an author of the bus station in Baloush (1984–1986) (Figure 3.7) and several public-use buildings

Figure 3.7 Bus station in Baloush, Kuwait. Architects Krzysztof Wiśniowski, Anna Wiśniowska, and Leopold Chyczewski.

Source: Krzysztof Wiśniowski's home archive.

74 *Architecture and Architects in Socialist Poland*

in Kuwait (e.g., Port Authority Headquarters). Wojciech Jarząbek stressed that the increasingly difficult political and economic situation in Poland made the trips an escape to a better world. The piling-up difficulties in the homeland and the associated feelings of growing frustration made the trip to the Arabian Gulf appear as an exciting professional adventure. The architect admitted years later that he experienced a couple of periods of professional enthusiasm during his career as an architect. The first was the realization of the Nowy Dwór housing estate in Wrocław in the second half of the 1970s. The second was when he went to Kuwait.

Notes

1 A review about the book by Dr. B. Fabian entitled "Bäber,"
2 Tuulse A., *Scandinavia Romanesque: monuments of architecture and art of Denmark, Norway and Sweden.* Introduction to the Polish edition written by Stanisław Piekarczyk [translated by W. Jeszke, edited by S. Hołówko], Warsaw: Arkady 1970.
3 Coppel T., Coulon J. J., Pipe Surfaces – Theory and Practice. Translations and comments: E. Kodelska, Z. Niemiatowski, A. Niemiatowski, Warsaw: Arkady 1972; Hossdorf H., *Model statics.* [translated from German by K. Grabczyński, M. Krawczyk, R. Czarnota-Bojarski], Warsaw: Arkady 1975; Siegel, C., Structural forms in modern architecture. [translated by E. Piliszek], Warsaw: Arkady, 1964.
4 Romuald Loegler, conversation with the author, Cracow, 30.04.2019.
5 Czesław Bielecki, conversation with the author, Bartoszówka, 27.04.2019.
6 For example, Danuta and Daniel Oledzki's trip around Europe (Germany, France, and Spain).
7 For example, J. Wyżnikiewicz's trip to West Germany.
8 For example, W. Jarząbek's trips to Iraq and Kuwait.
9 Józef Zbigniew Polak, conversation with the author, Warsaw, 02.10.2014.
10 Romuald Loegler, conversation with the author, Cracow, 30.04.2019.
11 Romuald Loegler, conversation with the author, Cracow, 30.04.2019.
12 Romuald Loegler, conversation with the author, Cracow, 30.04.2019.
13 Stefan Müller, conversation with the author, Wrocław, 04.07.2013.
14 Wojciech Zabłocki, conversation with the author, Warsaw, 03.04.2019.
15 Wojciech Zabłocki, conversation with the author, Warsaw, 03.04.2019.
16 Krzysztof Wiśniowski, conversation with the author, online, 12.02.2021.
17 Krzysztof Wiśniowski, conversation with the author, online, 12.02.2021.
18 Wojciech Jarząbek, conversation with the author, Wrocław, 24.04.2019.

References

Barucki, T., *Architekci autokarem* [Architects by bus], Warsaw: SARP, 1957.
Barucki, T., *Fragmenty stuletniej historii 1899–1999. Relacje, wspomnienia, refleksje* [Fragments of a Centennial History 1899–1999. Reports, memories, reflections], Warsaw: SARP, 2000.
Basista, A., *Betonowe dziedzictwo. Architektura w Polsce czasów komunizmu* [Concrete heritage. Architecture in communist Poland], Warsaw-Cracow: PWN Scientific Publishing House, 2001.
Bieda, K., *Międzynarodowy konkurs na projekt siedziby organizacji międzynarodowych i centrum konferencyjnego w Wiedniu,* "Architektura" 1971, no. 2.
Bielecki, C., Ciągłość w architekturze [Continuity in architecture], "Architektura" 1978, no. 3–4.
Bielecki, C., *Głowa. Instrukcja użytkowania* [Head. User manual], Warsaw: Zwierciadło, 2016.

Iron curtain or nylon curtain? 75

Crowley, D., *Modernizm realny około 1981 roku* [Real modernism around 1981], [in:] *Teksty modernizmu. Antologia polskiej teorii i krytyki architektury 1918–1981* [Texts of modernism. An anthology of Polish architectural theory and criticism 1918–1981], vol. 2, Cracow: Instytut Architektury, 2018.

Drzewiecki, H., *Ruch nowoczesny w architekturze sakralnej: nowość a tradycja myśli klasycznej* [The modern movement in sacred architecture: novelty and classical thought], [in:] *Seminarium SARP nt. architektury obiektów sakralnych. Kazimierz Dolny, 20–21 listopada 1982 rok. Wydawnictwo poseminaryjne* [SARP seminar on the architecture of sacred buildings. Kazimierz Dolny, 20–21 November 1982. Post-seminar publication], eds. R. Girtler, K. Kucza-Kuczyński, J. Miazek, J. Pełka, Warsaw: SARP, 1983.

Drzewiecki, H. & Kłosiewicz, L., *Pluralizm jest dobry na wszystko. Z Charlesem Jencksem rozmawiają: Henryk Drzewiecki i Lech Kłosiewicz* [Pluralism is good for everything. Charles Jencks is interviewed by Henryk Drzewiecki and Lech Kłosiewicz], "Architektura" 1982, no. 2.

Ghirardo, D., *Architektura po modernizmie* [Architecture after modernism], Toruń–Wrocław: VIA, 1999.

Gzowska, A. & Klein, L., *Postmodernizm polski. Architektura i urbanistyka. Z architektami rozmawiają Alicja Gzowska i Lidia Klein* [Polish postmodernism. Architecture and urbanism. Architects are interviewed by Alicja Gzowska and Lidia Klein], Warsaw: 40 000 Malarzy, 2013.

Jakub Wujek. Passport files, IPN Ld 533/2998.

Jerzy Kurmanowicz. Passport files, IPN Ld 533/19861.

Józef Zbigniew Polak. Passport files, IPN BU 763/19986.

Karpińska, M. & Leśniak-Rychlak, D., *Od gorsetu socbiurokracji do służby niewolników bez panów. Z Maciejem Miłobędzkim rozmawiają Marta Karpińska i Dorota Leśniak-Rychlak* [From the corset of socbiocracy to the service of slaves without masters. Maciej Miłobędzki is interviewed by Marta Karpińska and Dorota Leśniak-Rychlak], "Autoportret" 2016, no. 3(54).

Karpińska, M. & Leśniak-Rychlak, D., *Wielki świat zajmował się nadbudową, a my wciąż nie mogliśmy się uporać z bazą. Z Barbarą Gadomską i Andrzejem Karpowiczem rozmawiają Dorota Leśniak-Rychlak i Marta Karpińska* [The great world was busy building the superstructure, and we still couldn't get to grips with the base. Barbara Gadomska and Andrzej Karpowicz are interviewed by Dorota Leśniak-Rychlak and Marta Karpińska], "Autoportret" 2015, no. 3(50).

Klimowicz, J., *Prace polskich architektów w Syrii w latach osiemdziesiątych XX wieku: Stanisława Niewiadomskiego i Wojciecha Zabłockiego*, "Kwartalnik Architektury i Urbanistyki" 2010, vol. 55.

Kłosiewicz, L., *Międzynarodowy konkurs na projekt ratusza w Amsterdamie*, "Architektura" 1969, no. 11.

Krzyszkowski, A., *Aktualne problemy urbanistyczne Sztokholmu*, "Architektura" 1948, no. 1.

Majorek, A. *Międzynarodowe Spotkanie Architetków*, "Architektura" 1954, no. 9, s. 228–230.

Piątek, G., *Bardzo długa transformacja* [A very long transformation], "Autoportret" 2016, no. 3(54).

Piechotka, M. & Piechotka, K., *Maria i Kazimierz Piechotkowie – wspomnienia architektów* [Maria and Kazimierz Piechotka – memories of architects], Warsaw: Dom Spotkań z Historią, 2021.

Springer, F., *Zaczyn. O Zofii i Oskarze Hansenach* [Leaven. On Sophia and Oskar Hansen], Warsaw: Karakter, 2013.

Stanek, Ł., *Architecture in Global Socialism. Eastern Europe, West Africa, and the Middle East in the Cold War*, New Jersey: Princeton University Press, 2020.

Tadeusz Zipser. Passport files, IPN Wr 521/62501.

Węcławowicz-Gyurkovich, E., *Postmodernizm w polskiej architekturze* [Postmodernism in Polish architecture], Cracow: Cracow University of Technology, 1998.

76   *Architecture and Architects in Socialist Poland*

Wierzbicki, K., *Plac Beaubourg w Paryżu. Refleksje pokonkursowe* [Beaubourg square in Paris. Post-competition reflections], "Architektura" 1972, no. 5–6.

Wojciech Zabłocki. Passport files, IPN BU.

Wujek, J., *Mity i utopie architektury XX wieku* [Myths and utopias of 20th-century architecture], Warsaw: Arkady, 1986.

Zabłocki, W., *Architektura* [Architecture], Olszanica: Bosz, 2007.

Zipser, T., *Zygzakiem przez symbole czyli Samouczek drwala znaleziony na Saharze* [Zigzag through the symbols or the Lumberjack's tutorial found in the Sahara], Wrocław: Muzeum of Architecture, 2014.

4 National in form, socialist in content

4.1 Between "old" and "new" times – architecture before 1949

The year 1945 and the end of World War II represented a time of revolutionary changes for Poland and Poles. They affected almost all aspects of life and social activities. It is worth noting, however, that, initially, the new communist reality did not bring significant changes in the ideological and conceptual search for domestic construction in relation to the situation before the outbreak of war. The overriding goal guiding both the authorities and society was the reconstruction of the country destroyed during the war effort, in view of which politics (at least initially) did not seem to enter too much into the areas of architects' activities. As already outlined in Chapter 1, in the first post-war years, the private construction sector functioned, and private initiative was encouraged. Although a nationalization law was passed as early as 1946, the nationalization of enterprises carried out under it was initially quite limited in scope (Basista, 2001, p. 11–12). In terms of formal solutions, architects continued the achievements of pre-war schools of architecture, both avant-garde and conservative.

Back in 1945, architect Maciej Nowicki, who later became famous as the creator of the J. S. Dorton Arena in Raleigh, North Carolina, developed several architectural and urban planning concepts for new developments in downtown Warsaw (Figure 4.1). In terms of urban planning, they were based on the assumptions of the modern movement, while architecturally they were close to the style of architecture of the late 1930s. Wide thoroughfares and extensive green squares were to be surrounded by edifices with clear vertical articulation. In addition, the silhouette of the capital was to be enriched by a plume of skyscrapers.

As for the realizations of the first post-war years, a special role among them was played by the seats of power and public buildings. The former were mostly based on the "modernized classicism" of the 1930s, while the latter were the aftermath of the achievements of the Polish and international avant-garde from the CIAM. Erected in 1947–1951 in Warsaw, the Ministry of Communications building designed by Bohdan Pniewski belonged to the first group. It consisted of a 17-story building with a characteristic tapering body (the first post-war skyscraper in the capital), a lower five-story structure, and a low-rise rotunda with column galleries. Facades of classical proportions faced with stone. In 1949–1952, Pniewski designed the

DOI: 10.4324/9781003603153-5

78 Architecture and Architects in Socialist Poland

Figure 4.1 Concept of the new centre of Warsaw designed by architect Maciej Nowicki in 1945.

Source: Museum of Architecture.

expansion of the Sejm building. Here, too, he used forms and details firmly rooted in the traditions of classical architecture but put through the prism of the designer's own personality. At the same time, it should be remembered that the final design of the seat of the Polish parliament was created after the proclamation of socialist realism, and it is difficult not to find in it the spirit of architecture "national in form and socialist in content." Pniewski was not the only one of the leading pre-war architects who maintained a high professional standing in the new, communist Poland. Romuald Gutt designed the office building of the Central Statistical Office in Warsaw (1947–1949) in the early post-war years. In an interesting way, he combined monumentalism appropriate for the headquarters of a public institution with the achievements of the avant-garde, such as the reinforced concrete skeletal structure, the elevation of the block on pillars, and the Y-like plan.

The combination of monumental forms and modernist simplicity was a solution applied to the design of public buildings, with particular emphasis on the edifices of government agencies or party buildings. In 1947, a competition was held to

National in form, socialist in content 79

design an edifice for the then-leading Polish Workers' Party (Skalimowski, 2010, p. 12). The winner was a team of three Warsaw architects: Wacław Kłyszewski, Eugeniusz Mokrzyński, and Jerzy Wierzbicki (known as the "Warsaw Tigers"), presenting an impressive combination of classical principles of composition and modernism. The building was completed in 1952 – already as the seat of the Central Committee of the Polish United Workers' Party. At the same time, the so-called "district of ministries" in Warsaw was being realized (it was its concept that Maciej Nowicki sketched back in 1945) (Cymer, 2018, p. 45). The individual buildings included in it presented different approaches to both modernity and the tradition of classical architecture, depending on the person of the creator. Since the buildings were designed by different architects (including Stanisław Bieńkuński and Zbigniew Karpiński), we can find both more faithful quotations from history and references to it based on general principles of composition or even a certain general impression. Warsaw architect Marek Leykam, co-author of the headquarters of the Supreme Chamber of Control, which he designed together with Jerzy Hryniewiecki in 1946, excelled in the latter. The clear tri-division of the simple mass, elevations punctuated by rows of windows set in massive stone or concrete frames, and repetition pushed to the limits of monotony, created an impression of solidity and seriousness without losing its modern character. Prefabricated deep window frames were used by Leykam in a department store in Poznań completed in 1954. The cylindrical form, ten stories high, was covered with an even grid of reinforced concrete frames. Both the dimensions (which stood out from the historic buildings of Poznań's downtown) and the uniform, modern form were met with criticism in the mid-1950s (Figure 4.2). The period of the reign of the Socialist Realism doctrine was not conducive to this type of realization. Many architects found this out and were forced to modify their designs (and sometimes even finished buildings). The winning design for the skyscraper of the Textile Industry Headquarters in Łódź was created by architect Jan Krug in 1948 and presented formal features similar to the designs of Leykam, Bieńkuński, or Karpiński, based on the use of prefabricated elements. However, it soon became apparent that both the composition of the facade and details (to more "classical"), finishing materials (to stone), and the shape of the massing had to be changed. Dozens of buildings in various cities underwent similar treatments. This even applied to buildings whose construction had been (or was about to be) finalized. The Central Department Store (CDT), built in Warsaw on Jerozolimskie Avenue, was designed by Jerzy Romański and Zbigniew Ihnatowicz in 1947–1948. A reinforced concrete frame structure was used, which allowed the facade to be completely glazed and the first floor to be freed up. The roof included a terrace, which further emphasized the links of CDT's architecture with international modernism and Le Corbusier's five principles of modern architecture. Such credentials, however, were not to be welcomed after 1949, and even before the building was completed in 1951, efforts were made to persuade the architects of some of the solutions, suggesting, among other things, the abandonment of glazed facades. In the end, Romański and Ihnatowicz did not succumb to pressure, and the CDT building became one of the most important projects representing the avant-garde trend and erected in the first years of People's Poland.

Figure 4.2 "Okrąglak," a modernist department store in centre of Poznań designed by Marek Leykam.

Source: Photograph by the author.

It was part of the resurgent urban infrastructure, which was being rebuilt from wartime destruction. This included cultural facilities, such as modern, free-standing cinemas, six of which were built in Warsaw between 1948 and 1950, including the Moskwa (Moscow) cinema (architects Kazimierz Marczewski and Stefan Putowski), completed in 1950, and the Praha cinema (architects Jan Bogusławski and Józef Łowiński), located on the right bank of the Vistula River.

National in form, socialist in content 81

An extremely important area of activity for architects and urban planners in post-war Poland was housing construction. In this field, it was necessary not only to rebuild the stock destroyed during the war but also to expand it significantly compared to the pre-war state. For two decades of its existence, the Second Republic undertook a series of measures (with scant effectiveness) aimed at satisfying the social "housing hunger." Socialist People's Poland set itself the goal of catching up with all the civilization backwardness of the previous era, and one of the priorities was housing, as evidenced by a text by President Bolesław Bierut. In the "Six-Year Plan for the Reconstruction of Warsaw," he wrote that "for the first time in the history of Warsaw, the working population will receive en masse its comfortable, bright, dry, aesthetically pleasing, duly heated apartments, taking full advantage of all those amenities that modern civilization places at man's disposal" (Bierut, 1950, p. 181). The first new housing estates that were built in Poland after World War II continued the traditions of the mêlée vanguard and cooperative construction. Between 1945 and 1948, a married couple of Warsaw architects, Barbara and Stanisław Brukalski supervised the creation of the first post-war residential colony of the Warsaw Housing Cooperative in Żoliborz. Before the war, the Brukalskis were among the leading figures of the Polish avant-garde, while the colony itself was built based on designs they developed during the German occupation. In 1948, however, the communist authorities abolished the housing cooperative (Leśniakowska, 2003, p. 156). Henceforth, a company ZOR, established by a government decree, was responsible for the implementation of projects such as housing estates. Among the projects developed under ZOR was the Koło II housing development in Warsaw, the work of another pair of avant-garde architects, Helena and Szymon Syrkus (Figure 4.3). Completed in 1949–1951, the project was a testing ground for prefabrication, as the buildings were constructed from rubble concrete blocks produced in situ. The architecture and urban planning of the estate, however, were a development of the Syrkus' pre-war experience. Even before the construction was completed, the Warsaw press was dissolving in admiration of the buildings, which "equipped with gas, bathrooms, and central heating meet the requirements of modern construction, except that they retain a beautiful form. They will also differ from the apartments of other estates in that they have beautiful flooring made of light, smooth beech staves. Each staircase will have a hall with an artistically crafted interior. In each hall, a telephone will be installed in a special cubicle for the use of tenants. The entire estate will be surrounded by the greenery of the nearly 20-hectare park that will soon be established here. In addition, the courtyards of individual colonies will be decorated with flowerbeds, lawns, pools, and ponds." (Weber, 1949). Enthusiasm was also shared by the architects themselves. Characterizing the situation of the Polish construction industry in the first post-war years, the prominent architectural theorist Adam Kotarbiński described it as a "creativity of designing at an exaggerated level, stimulated by fantasy and hopes," which was to be embodied in the near and distant future (Kotarbiński, 1967, p. 32). The optimistic mood was relatively quickly subdued by subsequent decisions of the authorities – the aforementioned liquidation of the cooperative movement and

Figure 4.3 Koło Housing Estate in Warsaw – a continuation of pre-war modernist ideas. Architects Helena Syrkus and Szymon Syrkus.
Source: Museum of Architecture.

private activity and nationalization of individual contracting and design enterprises (Basista, 2001, p. 13–16).

The influence of the pre-war avant-garde on architecture and urban planning in post-war Poland was not limited to projects and realizations. The new reality also redefined the role of the architect and the specifics of his profession. In the late 1940s, Helena Syrkus, writing about architects, used the term "design contractors." This seemingly innocent term was, in fact, a reflection of views whose roots went back to the 1930s. Their exponent was, among others, the architect (and after the war the head of the construction ministry and Minister of Urban and Rural Construction) Roman Piotrowski. Before the war, Piotrowski became known as a declared communist, one of the most radical and leftist members of the Association of Polish Architects. At the time, he worked as an architect at the BudoZus enterprise subordinate to the Social Insurance Institution (ZUS), designing the Social Insurance Institution's housing colony in Żoliborz, Warsaw, or the ZUS office building in Gdynia. He aroused extreme emotions in the community, as with a callousness characteristic of technocrats he tried to strip the profession of architecture of its artistic envelope. Already in the 1930s, he prophesied that "the profession of architect will disappear . . . just like the profession of saddler or blacksmith" (Wujek, 1986, p. 200). He did not change his views in the post-war

National in form, socialist in content 83

reality. At the SARP Delegates' Convention in 1947, in his typical uncompromising manner, he called on his fellow architects to give up their artistic attitude to the profession and condemned the uncommitted attitude (Skalimowski, 2012, p. 44). This was an announcement of the new policy of the authorities towards the environment (Baraniewski, 1996, p. 235). "The planned economy frees the architect from the bane of doubts whether his efforts expressed in architectural and urban planning ideas will not remain only in the sphere of intentions never realized" (Piotrowski, 1948, p. 36), he wrote in 1948 in the pages of "Architektura." The reality of the socialist state, however, showed that the unrealized intentions were far more numerous than the materialized ones.

4.2   The architecture of "Stalinist empire style"

The deliberations of the National Meeting of Party Architects, which took place on 20–23 June 1949 in Warsaw, left a permanent mark on the image of Polish architecture in the second half of the 20th century. By a decision of the authorities, "socialist architecture in content and national in form" was proclaimed, which, following the model of solutions introduced in the Soviet Union back in the 1930s, was to be the style in force in People's Poland from now on. Thus, any hopes that free, unfettered creativity would flourish in the communist country were dispelled. At the same time, the greatest threats to the development of socialist architecture were identified: "formalism, nihilism and constructivism as manifestations of bourgeois cosmopolitanism, narrow traditionalism reflecting nationalist tendencies, too narrow-minded economism" (*Rezolucja Krajowej* . . ., 1949, p. 162).

Some of the greatest advocates of socialist realism on Polish soil were architects Edmund Goldzamt and Jan Minorski. The former spent several years in Moscow as aspirant (doctoral studies), and there became acquainted with the ideas of the new style. During one of the visits of the chief architect of Warsaw, Józef Sigalin, to Moscow, he had the opportunity to introduce him to the idea of national art in form and socialist in content. In May 1949, Goldzamt returned to Poland, where, in early June, he was received by Bolesław Bierut. He later recalled that the president was "disgusted with the position of the architects of the constructivist left" (Baraniewski, 1996, p. 236). Goldzamt himself stigmatized both "pseudo-modernist tendencies" and the facade, eclecticism, and "simplistic prescriptions of Socialist Realism" (Goldzamt, 1956, p. 410). The new times posed new tasks for architecture, which were included in the Resolution of the National Meeting of Party Architects, the formation of which took place in Warsaw, in the building of the Central Committee of the Polish United Workers' Party on 20–21 June 1949. Architecture became "the ideological weapon of the party" (Minorski, 1950, p. 214).

> The influence of the concepts of the bourgeois west on our architecture consists in an attempt to cross out its individuality, independence and contact with the life of the Polish popular masses. On the other hand, exploiting the Soviet experience means only adopting a method that will allow our

84 *Architecture and Architects in Socialist Poland*

architecture to find its own national, Polish face – Golzdamt said in the opening paper of the aforementioned meeting.

What was architecture really supposed to be, "socialist in content, and national in form"? The words of Lenin, whose pleasure was ". . . in socialist painting the realism of Courbet, in literature Balzac, and in architecture Greek classicism" (Basista, 2001, p. 20), were difficult to apply to the realities of Poland in the early 1950s. Architectural historian studying architecture under socialism, Aleksandra Sumorok wrote that although "the shortest, most frequently cited" definition, defining socialist realism as "socialist architecture in content and national in form," was known to "explain little in fact" (Sumorok, 2017, p. 62), the "ready-made formulas and solidified slogans" that had been worked out in the USSR since the 1930s were implemented in the countries of Central and Eastern Europe that had fallen into the Soviet sphere of influence. Thus, under the dictates of politics, a new tradition was created within the socialist reality (Włodarczyk, 1986). Its character was based on the achievements of the past and was to convey "universal, timeless values" (Sumorok, 2017, p. 63). "The time has come for architecture based on the best of the national tradition," he – summed up the specifics of Socialist Realism by Cracow architectural historian Michał Wiśniewski (Wiśniewski, 2019–2020, p. 139). When in 1952 Adam Kotarbiński defined the postulates that socialist-realist architecture should meet, he mentioned the creative element it contained. "Inspiration should not be equated with imitation," he wrote. He postulated that one should reach out to "familiar forms" and traditions from "the precinct of the closer cultural circle" (Kotarbiński, 1952, p. 4–5).

As Aleksandra Sumorok wrote, the façade of 80% of the buildings decided whether they belonged to Socialist Realism (Sumorok, 2017, p. 67). The functional-spatial layout of buildings did not differ significantly from the solutions used in earlier eras. Hence, a significant number of buildings erected in Poland between 1949 and 1956 are "buildings that were constructed under Socialist Realism" rather than "Socialist Realist buildings." The urban planning of this period can be looked at similarly. The doctrine of socialist realism indicated the need to reject the principles of the Athens Charter, to return to the traditional urban composition, frontage development, and axial layouts. Based on these recommendations, among others, the spatial layout of the Marszałkowska Residential District (Marszałkowska Dzielnica Mieszkaniowa – MDM) in Warsaw or Nowa Huta near Cracow was designed (these cases are discussed in more detail in the next subsection). But not every new neighbourhood was an MDM, and not every new urban complex was a Nowa Huta. In most cases, efforts were made to maintain an impression of compactness by locating free-standing building blocks parallel to the streets, while in the interiors of quarters, free ("modernist") building layouts were often chosen.

The building that became somehow identical to the concept of socialist realism in Poland was the Palace of Culture and Science in Warsaw (Figure 4.4). It was built as a gift from the Soviet Union and a symbolic sign of Poland's membership in the Soviet sphere of influence. The project was designed by Russian architect Lev Rudnev, a graduate of the Academy of Fine Arts in St. Petersburg and author

Figure 4.4 Palace of Culture and Science in Warsaw designed by Soviet architect Lev Rudnev. A gift from the fraternal Soviet nation and a symbol of Stalin's power over Poland.

Author: Zbyszko Siemaszko. Source: NAC (National Digital Archive).

of the M. V. Lomonosov Moscow State University building, among others. It was on such projects as Moscow skyscrapers that the Palace in Warsaw was to be modelled. The skyscraper located in the centre of the capital, which was to organize its space anew, was erected in place of 19th-century rental tenements, which could be perceived as a symbolic action, the replacement of the old, capitalist world by the new, communist world. The Polish side, which was represented in the preparations for the investment by Józef Sigalin, among others, had precise expectations of the project – it was to dominate the skyline of Warsaw, and its architecture was to represent national forms. In order to provide Rudnev with the right credentials, a tour was organized, during which the Soviet architect saw the most important monuments of Cracow, Toruń, Kazimierz Dolny, or Zamość. The result was a design for a Soviet-type skyscraper, with an elaborate stylobate section consisting of four pavilions and side wings, as well as a tall tower section topped with a spire. At the same time, the corner annexes were a distant echo of the alcoves of a traditional Polish noble manor house. In the forms of the finials, one could find references to the tower of the town hall in Zamość, while the attics crowning the various parts of the building were the attics of Mannerist townhouses from Kazimierz Dolny. To this was added monumentalism derived from the St. Petersburg school of architecture and socialist content in the form of supernatural sculptures depicting

86 *Architecture and Architects in Socialist Poland*

personifications of science, fine arts, working people, and athletes. Added to this were sculptural images of the poet Adam Mickiewicz and the astronomer Nicolaus Copernicus (interestingly, except for the latter, all the sculptures were brought from the USSR). The foundations of the Palace of Culture began to be poured in July 1952, and the ceremonial inauguration of the edifice took place on 22 July 1955. The predictions that the new edifice would be an inspiration and point of reference for Polish architects did not come true. It did not become one, because less than a year after the completion of this monument to socialist realism, socialist architecture in content and national form was officially condemned.

Before this could happen, however, Polish designers searched for an appropriate formula that would allow them to create forms that both satisfied their sense of aesthetics and conformed to the tastes of the authorities. This was most true of the architecture of power, the edifices of party committees, or government agencies. The forms of public buildings erected in the era of socialist realism were dominated by neoclassical elements, although many architects and artists considered the Polish Renaissance to be the most "national" style. However, the position of the political authorities, who tried to imitate Soviet Socialist Realism as faithfully as possible, decided (Stefański, 1982, p. 54). Among others, the headquarters of local party committees in Kielce, Białystok, and Rzeszów were designed in this spirit. In the capital, on the other hand, the building of the Ministry of Agriculture (1951–1955, architects Jan Knothe, Jan Grabowski, Stanisław Jankowski) was built – a pompous establishment, the main accent of which was the monumental colonnade connecting the two wings of the building. Slightly different, more "modernized" forms were used by architects Stanisław Bieńkuński and Stanisław Rychłowski in the design of the Ministry of Finance (1953–1956), referring, for example, to the art-deco trend, as exemplified by the reliefs placed over the main entrance by sculptor Jan Ślusarczyk. Outside of Warsaw, the headquarters of the District Council of Trade Unions in Katowice, designed and executed in 1950–1954 by a team of architects Henryk Buszko, Aleksander Franta, and Jerzy Gottfried, deserved mention. In the form of this building, there were clear references (taken almost to the limits of quotation) to the Party Headquarters in Warsaw. In fact, the source of their inspiration was not hidden by the creators themselves, who proudly emphasized that this was one of the few socialist-realist buildings that was not a caricature of historical styles (Cymer, 2018, p. 84).

The new regime introduced in Poland in 1945 introduced a number of significant changes in social life. These, in turn, resulted in a series of investments aimed at creating an architectural setting for the new, secular rituals of the communist state. These included community centres, dozens of which were built throughout Poland between 1949 and 1956. Among the most spectacular was the Rzeszów community centre (1950–1953), whose author, Józef Zbigniew Polak, alluded to Polish Neoclassicism from the late 18th century, and whose mass composition was modelled on Warsaw's Palace on the Water in Łazienki Park (Figure 4.5). The silhouette of the Zagłębie Culture Palace in Dąbrowa Górnicza (1951–1958, architect Zbigniew Rzepecki) also showed echoes of Polish neoclassicism – but this time from the first quarter of the 19th century. Similar inspirations guided the designer

National in form, socialist in content 87

Figure 4.5 Community centre in Rzeszów (architect Józef Zbigniew Polak, 1950–1953) represents architecture national in form and socialist in content.
Source: Photograph by the author.

of the Maritime House of Culture in Gdańsk (architect Witold Rakowski), commissioned in 1954, which provided the apex for an interesting discussion on the economic justification of Socialist Realism. Descriptions of the building emphasized the compactness of its mass and monumentalism adequate to its function. They also pointed out the superiority of such solutions over modernism. Criticism of the latter was based as much on aesthetic reasons as on economic ones since a compact mass was supposed to be (according to proponents of socialist-realist design) cheaper to build and operate (Kowalski, 1955). A different, but equally interesting example was a community house in Warsaw's Żoliborz district, designed by Stanisław Brukalski. The first concept was created in 1948 and was a continuation of the author's pre-war activities. Based on it, it was even possible to realize part of the building in its raw state. However, the second part of the building, with the rotunda housing the assembly hall, as well as the facade design, was created later, and the architect, who not much earlier had been a pillar of the Polish avant-garde, created a socialist-realist interpretation of historical forms (Warsaw Baroque). The story of the community centre in Żoliborz seems all the more interesting since it stood on a modernist housing estate of the WSM, designed by Stanisław Brukalski and Barbara Brukalska even before the proclamation of the doctrine of socialist realism.

An important investment of the first decade of the Polish People's Republic was Warsaw's Tenth Anniversary Stadium (Stadion Dziesięciolecia), completed

88 *Architecture and Architects in Socialist Poland*

in 1955 based on a competition design from 1953 (it is worth mentioning that the first plans to build an arena for mass events in the capital dated back to 1945). A team of architects consisting of Jerzy Hryniewiecki, Marek Leykam, and Czesław Rajewski designed a facility capable of holding more than 70,000 spectators, which, despite its considerable size, was skilfully incorporated into the landscape, including by surrounding it with an earth embankment forming the base of the auditorium. Rubble from Warsaw buildings demolished during the war was used in the construction, which gave the stadium additional symbolic significance. The simple, monumental in expression propylae of the main entrance and the sculptural compositions echoed the passing of Socialist Realism. The form of the stands, including the lodge of honour and the press stand, with their forms already heralded the new era.

The end of the reign of the doctrine of socialist realism came in March 1956. It was then that the National Meeting of Architects took place, organized under the slogan "Architects to new tasks in construction." It mainly concerned the prospects and directions of development of Polish design thought and construction practice. However, there was no lack of settlements with the past (Skalimowski, 2011). Among them, the voice of Romuald Gutt, who compared one of Edmund Goldzamt's former speeches to "a prosecutor demanding punishment," resounded strongly and clearly. "Was it an aberration or a scoop?" – he asked (Barucki, 1956, p. 259). Warsaw architect Leszek Kołacz called the papers delivered by Goldzamt and Jan Minorski in 1949 "biased" (Barucki, 1956, p. 266) and pointed to the political bias of the authors, citing words that the former published in the pages of "Nowa Droga" (Goldzamt, 1949):

> The Party line in architecture was developed under the guidance of Comrade Stalin, formulated in a series of resolutions of the Central Committee of the Communist Party of the Soviet Union(b) and speeches by Comrades Molotov, Kalinin, Kirov, Kaganovich, Khrushchev, Bulganin.
>
> (Barucki, 1956, p. 267)

The most important advocates of Socialist Realism, including Józef Sigalin and Jan Minorski, made a self-criticism. Architect Stanisław Jankowski, who collaborated with Sigalin in designing the representative Marszałkowska Residential District, admitted at the outset that he had co-created "the bad MDM." Later, however, he tried to defend himself: "We were under pressure," he said. "I think narrowing this issue to the person of Col. Goldzamt is also narrowing the problem." Zygmunt Stępiński (another MDM co-founder) somewhat coquettishly admitted that, yes, "he may resent . . . the sculptures, the pinnacles, the bands. But the principle of high first floor with mezzanine, fashionable divisions of space remained right" (Stępiński, 1978). He argued that the development around Konstytucji Square, which constituted the most important part of the Marszałkowska Residential District, was inspired by Warsaw tenements of the early 20th century, and not by Goldzamt's or Minorski's directions. Goldzamt himself was absent from the National Meeting of Architects due to health reasons. However, as the proceedings

National in form, socialist in content 89

and individual speeches appeared in print, their editor, Tadeusz Barucki, decided to publish his commentary as well. In it, Goldzamt admitted his mistakes. "I misunderstood the sense of militant party posturing at work in the architectural criticism section," – he wrote. However, he did not hide his regret for his colleagues who condemned him without giving him a chance to defend himself honestly. He stressed that "along with criticism no matter how harsh and painful, but based on honest reporting of facts," there were "personal assaults" (he pointed to Gutt).

More than 70 years after the National Meeting of Architects, the architecture of socialist realism has ceased to evoke negative emotions resulting from criticism conducted from a modernist position. On the contrary, over the years, it has gained recognition, to which postmodernism has undoubtedly contributed. Controversy was (and still is) aroused by the political character of individual buildings, which, like the Palace of Culture, are, in the opinion of many, symbols of Soviet domination and should be removed as such.

4.3 New cities, new estates

The top-down narrative accompanying the first period of building the foundations of socialism in post-war Poland emphasized the dissimilarity of the "new Poland" from the pre-war one. Here, on the ruins of unjust social relations, a new classless society was being born. This society had to be provided with decent living conditions, work, education, and housing. In the face of the enormity of the tasks, the existing urban centres proved to be far from sufficient and also incompatible with the ideological requirements of the new regime. Added to this was the enormous scale of war damage. It was estimated that more than 65% of all industrial plants were demolished, and the buildings of major cities (with few exceptions) were destroyed 45–85% (Juchnowicz, 1986). All of the aforementioned factors meant that a wide field of activity opened up before the authorities (as well as architects and urban planners) to build new settlements, neighbourhoods, as well as new cities.

One of the most important investments of the first Six-Year Plan was the construction of a steelworks complex near Cracow. The decision was made in early 1949, almost exactly a year after representatives of Poland and the Soviet Union signed an economic agreement providing for technical assistance, supply of equipment, and technology. Land south of the city was earmarked for construction. The first concepts were drawn up in 1949, and it was then that the realization of the gigantic undertaking began The Biprohut Metallurgical Design Office, specially dedicated to this investment, was established, and within it – the Nowa Huta Design Office headed by architect and urban planner Tadeusz Ptaszycki. The press wrote about "a happy city of a happy future," and when the implementation of the Six-Year Plan was coming to an end in 1955, 80,000 people already lived in Nowa Huta.

The decision to locate a new socialist city and a huge heavy industrial complex south of Cracow was dictated by a number of reasons – both technical or economic and political. The Cracow region had surplus agricultural labour that could

90 *Architecture and Architects in Socialist Poland*

be redirected to industry. On top of this, there was a large number of highly skilled technical personnel. The proximity of Cracow was to provide Nowa Huta residents with access to social and cultural institutions. The land designated for the construction of the plant itself had good bearing capacity, did not require levelling, and the groundwater was at a relatively considerable depth. Finally, the construction of Nowa Huta in such a location gave the authorities an opportunity to create a centre based on the working masses, the vanguard of socialism, and at the same time in opposition to the aristocratic-bourgeois Cracow (Juchnowicz, 1986).

Nowa Huta was to be a new value located between two dominant features – on the one hand, the silhouettes of the towers of Cracow's churches and the Wawel Royal Castle, and on the other, the panorama of the blast furnaces and smelter chimneys (Ptaszycki, 1953). Its design was an exemplary example of social realist urbanism. The axial composition was based on a radial arrangement of wide avenues converging on the five-sided Central Square, which was undoubtedly inspired by Baroque urbanism. The square was located, characteristically, on the edge of the city. Years later, Jan Zachwatowicz considered this a "spatial error" that was not justified by "neither the layout of communications nor the placement of the industrial plant" (Zachwatowicz, 1968, p. 14). Outlying buildings with historicist forms flanked the frontages. According to the designers' assumptions, non-industrial buildings with administrative, public utility and residential functions were to have national forms – hence, the references to the Polish Renaissance in the forms of the Administrative Center of the Lenin Steelworks (1952–1955) by architects Janusz Ballenstedt, Janusz Ingarden, and Marta Ingarden (Figure 4.6). On the other hand, the unrealized design of the city hall by Tadeusz Janowski, which was to stand on the axis of the main artery (Avenue of Roses – Aleja Róż), was a true collage of Polish historical architecture – it had the tower of the city hall in Cracow, attics from Sandomierz, and a monumental staircase from Zamość. On the other hand, from the opposite side, the composition of Central Square was too close to a house of culture referring to Polish classicism (also not realized).

Years later, one of the architects working on the design of Nowa Huta in Ptaszycki's team, Stanisław Juchnowicz, emphasized that in developing the plan for the foundation of the new city, the pre-war concept of residential development based on small neighbourhood units with an extensive educational and social program.[1] Such declarations contradict the words of Nowa Huta's chief designer, Tadeusz Ptaszycki. His statements echo the tone of revolutionary slogans and constructivist manifestos from the period of communism's great constructions. "The city . . . is taking on production characteristics," and "excessive efficiency" is required of the "young urban organism" (Ptaszycki, 1953). Of course, one should be aware that in 1953, when Ptaszycki wrote these words, admitting to "Western" inspiration meant at least the end of his professional career. Meanwhile, Nowa Huta represented an interesting combination of pre-war experience and new doctrine. Writer Beata Chomątowska mentioned sources of inspiration quite different from those mentioned by Juchnowicz, and pointed out that "the quarters of buildings adjacent to the [Central] Square, cut off from the main streets, differing in the layout of the space and the functions assigned to it, were also based on the Soviet

Figure 4.6 Administrative centre of the Lenin Steelworks in Nowa Huta designed by architects Janusz Ballenstedt, Janusz Ingarden, and Marta Ingarden.

Author: Minderbinder. Source: Wikimedia Commons, CC BY-SA 4.0.

model" (Chomątowska, 2019/2020, p. 130–131). Socialist-realist architecture researcher Aleksandra Sumorok noted the spatial layout of Nowa Huta "fulfills many of the doctrinal postulates" of Socialist Realism (Sumorok, 2017, p. 77). In turn, architecture historian Anna Cymer suggested that the residential development of Nowa Huta, divided into smaller complexes, "may bring to mind the idea of the neighbourhood unit or colony developed in the 1920s in Anglo-Saxon countries" (Cymer, 2018, p. 113), in a way confirming Juchnowicz's words.

This is only an apparent contradiction. Similar solutions were used in Warsaw's MDM, where green courtyards inside the quarters were hidden behind monumental outlying buildings. MDM was, next to the Palace of Culture, the flagship investment of the era of socialist realism in the Polish capital. Although it was not, on the model of Nowa Huta, the construction of a completely new centre, the scope of demolitions, the widening of streets, and the introduction of new buildings on a metropolitan scale made it a radical transformation of the old downtown layout. The architects Józef Sigalin, Zygmunt Stępiński, Stanisław Jankowski, and Jan Knothe worked on the design of the district for 45,000 residents in 1950–1952. The main idea behind the MDM concept was to combine three main functions: capital, housing, and local services (Jankowski & Knothe & Sigalin & Stępiński, 1951). Of course, there was also a clear ideological and political aspect, similar to the one that guided the creation of Nowa Huta just outside Cracow. Socialist poet Adam Ważyk wrote, "The people will enter the Downtown." He wrote that this people would come out of the backstreets and live in the palaces. In a word, in the heart of bourgeois Warsaw, a predominantly working-class district was to be created, and its residents were to inhabit buildings with forms previously available only to the upper classes. The aesthetics of the MDM buildings were an almost textbook example of socialist realism, especially in the case of the buildings located in the central part of the establishment, next to the vast Konstytucji Square, which had the form of an elongated rectangle. It provided a space for the collective rituals of the socialist state, mass celebrations, or parades. The architectural setting for these events was provided by buildings with high first floors with arcades and clearly emphasized tri-division of the body (pedestal, main part, and finial), facades were decorated with attics, pilasters, and monumental reliefs with propaganda content (Figure 4.7). Behind all this, however, were the relatively spacious interiors of the quarters with landscaped greenery, because the Company for Workers' Housing Estates, which was responsible for the investment, was concerned with improving the quality of life of the workers (whom, to be fair, did not live so many in the MDM at all).

Figure 4.7 Konstytucji square in the heart of Marszałkowska Residential District in Warsaw designed by architects Józef Sigalin, Zygmunt Stępiński, Stanisław Jankowski, and Jan Knothe. The socialist-realistic architecture and urban planning were made to host rituals of the new, socialist society.

Source: NAC.

National in form, socialist in content 93

Similar assumptions to the Marszałkowska Housing District can be found in Wrocław (Kościuszkowska Housing District, chief designer Roman Tunikowski) or Gdańsk (Grunwaldzka Residential District – GDM). The Gdańsk example seems interesting insofar as it was one of several attempts to introduce socialist-realist assumptions into the city. An attempt, we should add, rather unsuccessful. In 1952, the local branch of the Association of Polish Architects announced a competition to develop a detailed plan for a section of downtown Gdańsk (Lier, 1954). It assumed the creation of a people's meeting square within the downtown area and the construction of the Central House of Culture as a spatial dominant (Dąbrowski & Kuhnel & Rakowski, 1953). A large part of the works submitted for the competition presented architecture in the Soviet spirit, with a monumental, tall mass of the Gdańsk equivalent of the Palace of Culture and Science. Eventually, the idea of building a new centre near Gdańsk's old town was abandoned. Instead, the model socialist district was to become Wrzeszcz, located further west. Its new face, with squares, a wide thoroughfare, and a soaring skyscraper of a community centre, was designed by young architects from Gdańsk: Daniel Olędzki, Roman Hordyński, and Konrad Pławiński (*Grunwaldzka Dzielnica Mieszkaniowa. . .*, 1953). In the end, the realization of the Grunwaldzka Residential District was limited to residential buildings forming the frontage of the main thoroughfare, with facades decorated with very simplified details of historical provenance. Thus, the socialist-realist character was manifested mainly in the classical principles of urban composition and the tripartition of the masses of individual promises.

GDM was no exception in this regard. Architect Maria Piechotka recalled the years 1952–1954 when she and her husband designed the Bielany I housing development in Warsaw. The blocks of flats, set with their facades along the streets, "recreated the layout of outlying pre-war buildings" and, as Anna Cymer noted, "still had a lot in common with Socialist Realism" (Cymer, 2018, p. 172). The project's author herself made no secret of this fact, stressing that the urban planning and architectural commission analysed whether the buildings were "socialist in content and national in form," which, as it were, automatically obliged the developers to use outlying buildings, composing axes and wide avenues. Even so, she and her husband tried to avoid the exaggerated decorativeness characteristic of the "Stalinist empire style" (as researchers, primarily Russian, have sometimes called socialist-realist monumental neoclassicism). "We believed that the form should be modest, and that 'nationality' is safest achieved by using detailing that refers to Warsaw classicism," Piechotka recalled years later.[2] The Bielany estate was among the investments that the authorities of the time considered particularly important. In the neighbouring district, in Młociny, the construction of the Warsaw Steelworks had begun, and the construction of the plant, which was of considerable importance to the country's politics and economy, "provided the impetus to intensify housing construction in the area" (Lewandowski, 1958). The buildings designed by Maria Piechotka and Kazimierz Piechotka along Kasprowicza Street leading to the Steelworks were to play a special role in the composition of the new district – they flanked the road to the largest industrial plant of the socialist capital (Klewin, 1958).

94   *Architecture and Architects in Socialist Poland*

Perhaps the most interesting neighbourhood of post-war Warsaw was Muranów, built on the land where the Jewish ghetto was located during the German occupation. The first concept, by architect Bohdan Lachert, was created at the Warsaw Reconstruction Office (Biuro Odbudowy Stolicy – BOS) back in 1947. It took into account the use of rubble lying in great quantity in the area, for after the suppression of the ghetto uprising in 1943, German troops methodically demolished building after building. A layer of rubble so thick that its complete removal would take, according to estimates, more than three years with the commitment of considerable forces and resources. So, when construction of the estate began in 1949, it was erected on a rubble pedestal using in situ prefabrication with rubble concrete (Lachert, 1949). Lachert wanted Muranów to be "a testimony to the emergence of new life on the rubble of old social relations, on a site commemorating the unprecedented barbarism of Hitlerism and the heroism of the Ghetto insurgents" (Lachert, 1949). The original plans, based on modernist principles of planning residential complexes, combined high-rise buildings with lower residential buildings. In the end, the former were not realized, while the forms of those designed by the team led by Bohdan Lachert were "socrealized." They were plastered, and rustication, cornices, and baluster balustrades were added. This was the result of the negative reviews that the first buildings in Muranów met with – simple, with facades combining raw brick and concrete prefabricated elements, compared to barracks. They were accused of lacking an artistic concept and carelessness of execution (Wierzbicki, 1952). The brutalist character of Lachert's original concept was therefore hidden behind cornices, pilasters, and attics.

Muranów was not the only case where the former ghetto (and earlier, before the war, the Jewish quarter) became the space on which a new socialist-realist district was built. The same thing happened in Łódź, where a team led by Warsaw-based Jewish architect Ryszard Karłowicz designed the Old Town Estate in the northern part of the city. In Lublin, the People's Assembly Square (now Castle Square) was completed in 1954, with Jerzy Brabander as the main designer. In both cases, simplified historical forms or edged buildings were readily used.

The aforementioned estates or neighbourhoods were realized by the Department of Workers' Estates, which was also responsible for housing complexes associated with new industrial centres, such as Nowa Huta and Nowe Tychy, described earlier. Despite the apparent similarities, Tychy was a thoroughly different city from Nowa Huta. First and foremost, the authors of their master plan, architect couple Kazimierz Wejchert and Hanna Adamczewska-Wejchert, assumed that building a new city for 100,000 residents based on an existing small town was essentially founding a city from scratch. "The concept of it free from the influence of any complications of the existing state and legal relations should be homogeneous, clear and legible," – wrote co-author of the plan Hanna Adamczewska-Wejchert in 1955. Other architects and urban planners were of the same opinion.

Just as the plan of a city, founded in the Middle Ages, was a finite form of composition, so the plan of a city, founded in the twentieth century in the socialist system, should be shaped almost like a theoretical plan, fulfilling all

National in form, socialist in content 95

the requirements set by society (Marczewski, 1956) – they wrote in the pages of the monthly magazine "Architektura."

The master plan envisaged a phased construction of the city, and the settlements included in it were marked with successive letters of the alphabet. Thus, the most severe was settlement A, with a regular urban composition and socialist-realist architecture. It was designed in 1950 by architect Tadeusz Teodorowicz-Talowski of the Silesian University of Technology in Gliwice, a native of Lviv. Interestingly, the competition for the plan of the entire city was announced in 1951, so at a time when the construction of housing development A was already in full swing. That competition was won by the aforementioned Wejchert family, who in later years designed housing estate B (1952–1959) (Figure 4.8). They wanted to preserve the architectural character of a small town. Hence, the buildings had a maximum of three stories, sloping roofs, and arcades. The elevations were varied with balconies, loggias, or bay windows. Despite the fact that the project was created during the dominance of socialist realism, it is difficult to find similarities between developments such as Nowa Huta or MDM and housing estate B, which had an intimate scale, public spaces in the form of small plazas or squares, and softly winding streets adapted to the terrain. Subsequent housing estates in Tychy were built over the decades and represented the changing trends in architecture and urban planning of People's Poland.

Figure 4.8 Housing Estate B designed by Kazimierz Wejchert and Hanna Adamczewska-Wejchert, part of the new town Nowe Tychy. Photography by Henryk Hermanowicz.

Source: City Museum of Tychy.

96 *Architecture and Architects in Socialist Poland*

4.4 Post-war reconstruction of Warsaw

"Only in a socialist city, where the land is owned by the state, is a full functional reorganization of the city possible," wrote in the 1930s. Siegfried Giedion, Karl Moser, and Rudolf Steiger anticipated, as it were, the so-called Bierut Decree and the nationalization of land in Warsaw (Gzell, 2017, p. 23). The aforementioned decree entered into force on 26 October 1945 and stated that "in order to make it possible to rationally carry out the reconstruction of the capital and its further expansion in accordance with the needs of the Nation, and in particular to dispose of land promptly and to make proper use of, all land in the area of the capital city (capital city) of Warsaw shall, as of the effective date of this decree, become the property of the municipality of the capital city of Warsaw" (*Dekret z dnia 26 października* . . .). Plans for the modernization of Poland's capital were made both before the outbreak of World War II and during the German occupation (at that time they were worked on in conspiracy). However, after German troops suppressed the Warsaw Uprising and the methodical demolition of the city that was its consequence, the scale of the challenge proved far greater. When Soviet and Polish troops liberated Warsaw on 17 January 1945, 84% of the built-up area of the part of the city located on the left bank of the Vistula River was razed to varying degrees (9,865 buildings were completely destroyed, 2,973 to a significant degree, and 4,225 to a slight degree) (Datner, 1960).

Even during the war, architect Tadeusz Iskierka created visions of modernist Warsaw á la ville radieuse. "Already in the 1940s, they were treated as curiosities and no one seriously considered their realization" – explained historian Andrzej Skalimowski. The first post-war sketches by Maciej Nowicki also presented skyscrapers and wide thoroughfares, but the sheer articulation of the individual blocks was reminiscent of the official architecture of the 1930s. As the architect Maria Sołtys rightly pointed out, the reconstruction of Warsaw in this, and not another form, was not the result of attitudes formed during Stalinism, but in the pre-war education of architects (Fudala, 2016, p. 25).

On 14 February 1945, the Warsaw Reconstruction Office was established, with Roman Piotrowski as its head. His first deputy was Józef Sigalin. The Urban Planning Department was conducted by Wacław Ostrowski, and the Architecture Department was conducted by Bohdan Lachert. In turn, Jan Biegański and Jan Zachwatowicz were responsible for the Department of Historic Architecture (Sigalin, 1986, p. 75–76). However, it was Sigalin, who instantly earned the rank of major and the title of engineer, and on top of that was a trusted man of President Bolesław Bierut, "remained the power behind the throne of the BOS" (Ajewski, 1995, p. 323). Not only did Piotrowski head the Warsaw Reconstruction Office, but he was also deputy mayor of Warsaw, and from 1951 held the office of Minister of Construction. This staunch modernist thus had the tools in hand to create the modern Warsaw he had dreamed of even before the war. Urban planner Bogdan Wyporek, former president of the Society of Polish Urban Planners (TUP), emphasized that the pre-war Polish capital

was the most intensively built-up urban fabric in Europe! From the 1938 statistical yearbook, we learn that about 40 percent of the apartments in

National in form, socialist in content 97

Warsaw were single-room units. Their average density was 4–5 people. One can imagine what dramatic conditions these tens, hundreds of thousands of people lived in.

Thus, one must conclude,

> Wyporek wrote seventy years after the creation of the BOS, "that regardless of the choice of one or another principles and directions for the reconstruction and restoration of historic buildings, it was simply impossible to recreate and restore the old Warsaw that its pre-war inhabitants dreamed of.
>
> (Wyporek, 2015)

The problem of rebuilding Warsaw, which had been destroyed by the Germans, was widely discussed among Polish architects, urban planners, and monument restorers. The discussion took place shortly after the end of the war and, however tumultuous, was relatively short-lived. Bolesław Bierut in January 1945 reported during a meeting of the Council of Ministers: "Stalin believes that Warsaw should be rebuilt as soon as possible" (Majewski, 2009, p. 30). On top of that, "Stalin categorically opposed" that the Provisional Government be moved to Cracow or Łódź. "Stalin's statement eliminated all hesitation regarding this matter" (Gomułka, 1994, p. 502–503). All that remained to be decided was what form the capital of socialist Poland would take.

At the beginning of 1946, architect and preservationist Jan Zachwatowicz told at meeting of the Warsaw Reconstruction Office that "on the territory of today's Warsaw, pure preservationist concepts cannot be applied" (Majewski, 2009, p. 297–300). It can be assumed that he acted not entirely in agreement with himself, since, as the philosopher Władysław Tatarkiewicz, who conducted secret teaching together with Zachwatowicz during the occupation, recalled, he is supposed to have said, "I will rebuild Warsaw's Old Town, but I will not go there" (Majewski, 2009, p. 72). Zachwatowicz invoked the voice of the public, which "wants to see Warsaw strictly as it was before 1939" (Rymaszewski, 2005, p. 103). He rejected the idea of recreating the Old Town in Gothic forms that no one remembered. He categorically negated the bold but completely unrealistic ideas of erecting a huge pyramid of rubble in the centre of the capital or preserving the Old Town in the form of a permanent ruin as a monument to German barbarism, which was loudly advocated by, among others, the cultural scholar Kazimierz Wyka. When, nearly two decades later, an article was published in "Kurier Polski" with the telling title: in this city, the odds and the wonders went hand in hand, in which the times of reconstruction were recalled, it was accompanied by a sketch of the Monument to the Heroes of Warsaw – a huge mound raised from the rubble. It was described as the "most original" idea for a monument (Nowowiejski, 1975).

In 1947, in the pages of Building Review, Roman Piotrowski presented the achievements of the Warsaw Reconstruction Office with the usual charm of a dense technocrat spilling numbers. "The total loss of cubic capacity in left-bank Warsaw was about 63,500,000 m3, with a value of about 4,175,000,000 zlotys

98   *Architecture and Architects in Socialist Poland*

according to August 1939 prices, which, when converted into current circulating zlotys, adds up to about three hundred billion" (Piotrowski & Terlikowska-Woysznis, 1947, p. 231). He went on to list the following areas that suffered from war damage – communications, education, temples and historic buildings, museums, cinema halls, libraries, and so on. There was no area of social life that did not suffer significant losses (Piotrowski & Terlikowska-Woysznis, 1947, p. 231–232). Such an introduction, according to Piotrowski, was to make it possible to "establish rules for valuing the results of implementation work" assessed by "the amount of enclosed space put into use . . . the amount of population that flowed into the city during the reconstruction period . . . the amount of funds invested in reconstruction" (Piotrowski & Terlikowska-Woysznis, 1947, p. 233). The figures cited by the BOS director were impressive. The success, which was, without doubt, the speed of the work carried out and its scope, would not have been possible without the work of the architects, who unanimously responded to the appeal of the Association of Polish Architects, which was reactivated after the war. Shortly after the liberation of Warsaw, posters appeared on the walls of surviving buildings calling for participation in the reconstruction of the capital. "The Polish architect must fulfil his duty, he must prove himself worthy of the Polish soldier. This soldier has already rebuilt the foundations of the edifice of the Republic – You will rebuild its Capital" (Skalimowski, 2012, p. 43) (Figure 4.9).

What the rebuilt Polish capital was to look like was overseen by representatives of the communist authorities, headed by the president. Bolesław Bierut wrote:

> The new Warsaw cannot be a repetition of the old one, it cannot be a corrected mere repetition of the pre-war collection of private interests of capitalist society, it cannot be a reflection of the contradictions tearing this society apart, it cannot be a show and ground for the exploitation of human labour and the reigning in of the privileges of the possessing classes.
>
> (Bierut, p. 121)

Reconstruction was therefore a political act, as the architects involved realized. The chief apologist of socialist-realist architecture, Edmund Goldzamt, wrote that "the reconstruction of monuments in People's Poland, and especially in Warsaw, has a profound political justification in addition to its cognitive and cultural significance" (Goldzamt, 1956, p. 426). Architecture was also becoming an object of manipulation and censorship by the authorities, as noted by American researcher and architect Duane Mezga (1998) or Michał Murawski (2009). It could not be otherwise, since, as Goldzamt reported, he saw its enormous ideological potential: "Architecture is of interest to the party because it is a particularly momentous form of ideology, and ideology cannot be indifferent to the party . . . Ideology finds in architecture a wonderful form of its embodiment" (Baraniewski, 1996, p. 236–237).

In the process of reconstruction, there was an increasingly bold departure from the prevailing conservation doctrines, in favour of "monument-making" (Majewski, 2009, p. 140). Its effects could be seen in the way of creating the image of both entire urban complexes and individual buildings, in which decorative elements

Figure 4.9 Post-war reconstruction of Old Town in Warsaw by the Warsaw Reconstruction Office (BOS).

Source: NAC.

were sometimes changed to express new content (Miziołek, 2001, p. 171). "Pure" reconstruction, manifested, among other things, in the precise reproduction of historical forms or the use of original materials and technology, gave way to "soft" reconstruction, in which the most important thing was the creation of an appropriate atmosphere (Mezga, 1998, p. 46). There was also a selection of objects to be restored or reconstructed.

> We set different criteria. From a historical point of view, what is important is what characterizes the era and the problems in it. In this sense, perhaps future generations will resent us for not preserving Art Nouveau buildings, and who knows if one such house should not be preserved.

100 *Architecture and Architects in Socialist Poland*

– explained Jan Zachwatowicz (Majewski, 2009, p. 300). Nonetheless, guided by the law's stipulation that a monument is an object "having artistic, cultural, historical value . . . ascertained by a ruling of a state authority" (*Rozporządzenie Prezydenta . . .*), as well as their own convictions, architects, and restorers very rarely preserved eclectic or Art Nouveau buildings.

This was not only the result of the political dislike of the communist authorities for architecture, which was associated with 19th-century capitalism. Gdańsk architect and building restorer Wiesław Gruszkowski admitted years later that, as a student, he believed "that the worst period in the history of architecture was the 19th century."[3] He was echoed by Maria Piechotka, who added that the construction of the second half of the 19th century was seen by former students of Syrkus and Brukalski, who were brought up in the modernist spirit, as a manifestation of architectural tastelessness.[4] In addition, a key aspect was the improvement of housing (Cymer, 2018, p. 16). Basements and outbuildings surrounding courtyard studios did not meet the expectations set for a modern city. In Warsaw on Krakowskie Przedmieście and Nowy Świat, facades were being reconstructed, behind which completely modern interiors were hidden. The composition of the urban layout was unified by reducing the height of buildings, so that the Art Nouveau Savoy Hotel, Wapiński's or Pod Messalką townhouses could not exceed four storeys (Popiołek, 2012). "It is not only about the value of individual buildings, although this too in many cases is high, but about passing on to future generations the image of one of Warsaw's most characteristic streets," wrote Zygmunt Stępiński, who at the Warsaw Reconstruction Office was responsible for the reconstruction of Nowy Świat Street (Stępiński, 1947).

The "to be" or "not to be" of individual buildings was determined by current politics, as well as technical and financial considerations and the extensive modernization plans for Warsaw. Both before 1949 and after the proclamation of the doctrine of socialist realism, a number of works were carried out to improve the city's infrastructure. These included plans to build a subway line, which was to serve not only a transportation function but also an educational and social role. A system of green areas was being created that were also aeration wedges to ensure adequate air movement in the city. Finally, an East-West (Wschód-Zachód – W-Z) route was built, connecting the two banks of the Vistula River via the new Silesia-Dąbrowa Bridge, and then running through a tunnel under Warsaw's Old Town and cutting through the capital's built-up area towards the western industrial districts. The W-Z Route Studio, which included road engineer Henryk Stamatello and architects Józef Sigalin, Stanisław Jankowski, Zygmunt Stępiński, and Jan Knothe, was responsible for the project. The ceremonial commissioning of the new artery took place on 22 July 1949. It not only changed Warsaw's transportation system but also permanently transformed the urban landscape. The construction of the sinkhole under Castle Square made it possible to unveil the view of the Vistula escarpment on the west bank of the river and with it – the Pod Blachą palace, the presbytery of St. Anne's Church, the Sigismund column, and the tenements on Castle Square. The castle itself had to wait until the 1970s to be rebuilt, although the first designs were created in parallel with the reconstruction of the entire Old

National in form, socialist in content 101

Town. The Vistula escarpment, on the other hand, was shaped as green areas, the beginning of riverside boulevards.

During the construction of the W-Z route tunnel, preservationists had to agree to demolish the remains of the so-called Tepper Palace and six surviving town-houses. They were to be reconstructed after its construction was completed. Such a solution was cheaper and faster than undermining and strengthening the historic foundations at the same time (Zachwatowicz, 1981). The tenements were indeed reconstructed . . . except for one. In its place was located the western exit of the tunnel, which could thus be shorter by 70 metres (Cymer, 2018, p. 24). Thus, economic factors proved to be decisive. It was only later that specific solutions took on a political tinge, and rental tenements with historicizing forms became symbols of the "petty bourgeoisie" (Skalimowski, 2018, p. 133). During the reali-zation of the intimate housing estate in Mariensztat (architect Zygmunt Stępiński, 1948–1949), a conscious decision was made not to recreate the pre-war condition. A complex with intimate forms was designed, referring to the times before there were "huge . . . rental houses, whose owners absolutely did not care that the ten-ants lived well." – wrote one of the designers, Zygmunt Stępiński. These relics of 19th-century capitalism "were all demolished unscrupulously, although many of them were technically in a state suitable for reconstruction" (Stępiński, 1972, p. 516). Situations in which the designer recommended preserving Art Nouveau details were rare, as was the case with the tenement at Nowy Świat 7. Stępiński pointed out the well-preserved, impressive portal, the only remnant of the tene-ment demolished during the bombing. He therefore asked the demolition man-ager to leave it and then asked the designer to include the portal in the design of the new facade. For the sake of argument, however, it should be added that "an authentic fragment of an Art Nouveau Warsaw tenement" (Stępiński, 1984, p. 24), as Stępiński referred to the portal, is almost a textbook example of French Neo-Renaissance.

The post-war reconstruction of Warsaw became a pretext – for the authorities – to pursue their own historical policy with the help of architecture and for architects of modernist provenance – to finally deal with the defects of historic urban com-plexes (Piątek, 2020).

4.5 Western and Northern Territories

The post-war history of the so-called Recovered Territories, a term used after the war to describe the northern and western lands granted to Poland under the Yalta Agreement, but before 1939 belonging to Germany, is extremely complicated. The very name indicated that the official, state narrative described them as historically belonging to the Polish state, which can at best be described as a highly selec-tive and biased interpretation of history. Reference was made to a time when the goal of Poland's expansion, ruled by the Piast dynasty, was the west and the lands along the Oder River (Halicka, 2015). Centuries of fighting in the Polish–German borderlands were to find an end with the defeat of Hitlerism in 1945. "History has given us today the only chance to revive Poland within the Piast borders. We are

102 *Architecture and Architects in Socialist Poland*

returning to our lands on the Oder, the Lusatian Neisse and the Baltic . . . We are restoring them to Polishness" – wrote Władysław Gomułka, in the 1960s the first secretary of the Communist Party, in 1945–1949 at the head of the Ministry of Recovered Territories (Gomułka, 1962, p. 329).

However, the development of the newly acquired territories was an extremely complicated task. The scale of destruction in cities such as Gdańsk, Wrocńaw, and Szczecin (as well as in a number of smaller towns in Lower Silesia and Pomerania) was enormous. In addition, "the Soviets treated the Recovered Territories as their war trophies and believed that the goods there were not ours, but post-German, so their rights to them were indisputable" (Torańska, 1985, p. 67), in view of which machinery, livestock . . . virtually everything that could be exported was taken to the Soviet Union. However, the measures taken by the Polish state were not only due to wartime and post-war destruction but also due to the need to materially and culturally "tame" the so-called Recovered Territories, which were a thoroughly alien place for the displaced persons from across the Bug River or the smallholders from Mazovia or Lublin (Torańska, 2015, p. 26). In addition, the communist authorities sought to erase traces of "Germanness" and emphasized the Piast lineage of the area. Architecture was one of the elements contributing to the new identity.

Jadwiga Grabowska-Hawrylak was the first woman architect educated at the Wrocław University of Technology after World War II (diploma 1950). She began her prolific career in the Design and Research Office of General Construction "Miastoprojekt – Wrocław." Initially, she worked on the realization of the Socialist-Realist Kościuszko Housing District, and in 1954, she joined the team responsible for the reconstruction of the demolished town hall and tenement houses within the Old Town Square. Young, mostly inexperienced architects took part in the reconstruction of Wrocław. They had a unique chance to observe how what they had barely plotted on a drawing board a few moments earlier became a portal, a cornice, and a whole building. Their senior colleagues, such as Tadeusz Ptaszycki, later the general designer of Nowa Huta, drew the framework of reconstruction defined by the "master plan." They filled this framework with content. Years later, Jadwiga Grabowska-Hawrylak recalled that working on the reconstruction of destroyed buildings gave a sense of participation in something important, significant for the whole country. However, she admitted that they tried to keep their distance from current politics: "We didn't realize what the times were."[5] Should this be seen as naiveté or ignorance? Or rather, the natural reaction of young people who grew up during the war years and were finally able to start living and working normally, to devote themselves to the work they loved? If not, young Jadwiga Grabowska would not have sacrificed private time to finish projects at night, which often resulted in an overnight stay in the studio. Sometimes, the details drawn out on a 1:1 scale did not fit on the drawing board and it was necessary to spread sheets of paper on the floor. The reward was the opportunity to observe how what had just been a mere sketch on the drawing board became a real building in the city space. In 1958, the townhouses in Wrocław's Market Square, designed by Grabowska-Hawrylak, were put into use. Just 12 years later, they were entered in the register of

National in form, socialist in content   103

monuments as "an example of Baroque bourgeois tenements from the turn of the 16th and 17th centuries." The architects who rebuilt Wrocław (including Jadwiga Grabowska-Hawrylak) became "a kind of ghostwriters," concluded Michał Duda (Duda, 2016, p. 30).

"Searching for the Piast pedigree" often forced architects and conservators to resort to fanciful arguments to convince the authorities of the validity of their actions (Majewski, p. 230). In addition to the historical policy pursued by the authorities of the Polish People's Republic, designers had to face the problem of the specifics of the cultural context.

Cities like Gdańsk were becoming a field of ideological struggle. "Gdańsk was the mistletoe on the Polish tree," – wrote political scientist and publicist Edmund Osmańczyk in 1945 (Majewski, 2009, p. 232). Anti-German sentiments and aspirations to "de-Germanize" the Recovered Territories were extremely strong. So much so that even Jan Zachwatowicz succumbed to them, mentioning the need to "wipe out the raid of Germanness" (Zachwatowicz, 1948). The discussion about rebuilding the historic centre of Gdańsk has been going on since 1946. As in the case of Warsaw (Ciarkowski, 2023), the preservation of the Main City as a permanent ruin and a monument to German barbarism was considered, as well as the construction of a new centre on the shipyard grounds or in the New Port (Perkowski, 2013, p. 326). Already at the beginning of 1948, the matter was basically a foregone conclusion – the so-called Zachwatowicz Plan, which assumed reconstruction (partial) and preservation of the (Polish) atmosphere, was identified for implementation. This was, to tell the truth, the creation of a fantasy, which never existed in such a shape at a particular moment in the past. Few people, however, had objections to a reconstruction strategy outlined in this way. "At a time when elementary things were in short supply: bread and a roof over one's head, historic preservation was not the number one topic of all resolutions, discussions and programs" (Greczanik-Filipp, 1997, p. 18). Perhaps under different circumstances, mistakes could have been avoided, such as the decision made in the fall of 1946 to reduce the Main City to a housing development (Nowakowski, 2013). The subject fell by the wayside as early as 1947 when it was decided that the historic street grid and, as far as possible, the facades of townhouses would be reconstructed within the Main City. Several of the most important buildings were reconstructed in their entirety. Others were adapted to modern requirements, as the "modernists" wanted. This was compounded by unabated anti-German resentment, which sometimes determined what would be reconstructed and how. "Maybe I am a barbarian," Edmund Osmańczyk wrote a year earlier, "but when Professor Jan Kilarski, a distinguished historian of Gdańsk's Polishness, speaks of the impossibility of rebuilding Marienkirche, there is a salty joy in me" (Osmańczyk, 1945) (Figure 4.10).

Architect Wiesław Gruszkowski, among others, was involved in the reconstruction of historic Gdańsk. Sixty years later, he positively assessed the realization of the Main City (although he described the facades of the tenements themselves as pseudo-historic). As an argument reinforcing such an assessment of the state of affairs, he cited the praise and approval of renowned American architect Richard

104 *Architecture and Architects in Socialist Poland*

Figure 4.10 After World War II, Main Town in Gdańsk was nothing more than ruins and piles of rubble.
Source: NAC.

Neutra. During Neutra's visit to Poland, Gruszkowski gave him a tour of Gdańsk. He recalled the tour as follows:

> I had trepidation terrible, because this was one of the five most famous modern architects at the time, a pioneer, a promoter of modern architecture. I think to myself that when he sees these historicisms of ours, he will laugh at us. He was watching, nodding. At the end I say: professor, you see something we had to do here. And he says: dear colleague, this is a simple matter, completely normal. If someone's ancestral portraits go missing, what does such a person do? He orders portraits from photographs or from memory and hangs them on the wall. And here you have portraits of ancestors.[6]

Citing Neutra's opinion can be seen as an attempt by a recognized authority to legitimize his own actions and decisions. It says as much about the architect himself as it does about Gruszkowski's motivation in working on the reconstruction of the Main City.

In Szczecin, few people thought about "ancestral portraits" or attempts to reconstruct the former downtown. The direction for rebuilding the city at the mouth of the Oder River was set by the first post-war mayor of the city, urban planner Piotr Zaremba. He arrived in the city before the end of the war and decided to plant

National in form, socialist in content 105

the red-and-white flag on 30 April on the walls of the almost-undestroyed building of the Szczecin District (transformed into the headquarters of the new Polish authorities). The annexation of Szczecin to Poland was officially announced in an announcement on 7 July 1945. "Our efforts, our work and hardships were not in vain. On July 6 this year. The incorporation of the city of Szczecin by the Republic of Poland took place. Szczecin is Polish!" – it was written. The text ended with the words: "Long live the Republic of Poland and Polish Szczecin! Long live the Government of National Unity." It was signed by "Eng. Piotr Zaremba. Mayor of the City of Szczecin" (Zaremba, 1945). Twenty years later, he recalled the atmosphere of the first post-war weeks and months.

> Seeing the ruins of Szczecin in 1945, feeling the urgent need to carry out the improvised ad hoc works, at the same time we had to find time to think and to calmly consider what path to take. For it was clear that it was precisely the destruction of the war that knocked down the application of new possibilities, and not only in terms of reconstruction, . . . but also in terms of rebuilding and modernizing the city.
>
> (Zaremba & Orlińska, 1965, p. 90)

The result of the measures initiated by President Piotr Zaremba was the "old city," where four-story blocks of flats with sloping red-tiled roofs stood along streets repeating the pre-war layout pattern (Fiuk, 2017b) (Figure 4.11). Adjacent to them were restored monuments that had survived the wartime conflagration – the Castle of the Pomeranian Dukes, the cathedral Basilica of St. James, and the Church of St. John the Evangelist. In this way, characteristic of modernist thinking about a historic city, modernity was combined with the most precious relics of the past. Zaremba himself wrote of the reconstruction strategy adopted in the 1960s as follows:

> The lack of a commercial downtown in Szczecin and the complete destruction of the Old Town force the construction of a new urban center from scratch, without the tendency to use "historic" buildings where they no longer existed in the 19th century. On the other hand, it is necessary to expose the most important monuments, revealing them from haphazard development. This is especially true of the castle hill with the ruins of the Castle of the Pomeranian Dukes, which is the basic accent of the urban landscape.
>
> (Zaremba & Orlińska, 1965, p. 96)

It is worth mentioning that the "total" destruction was not really total, but newspaper articles and literature popularized an incomplete, simplified picture of reality that was supposed to justify the radical decisions taken by the authorities (Fiuk, 2017a, p. 117–118). These included the construction of a wide thoroughfare at the level of the Old Town, which was strongly opposed in April 1948 by Szczecin conservationists and the local branch of the Polish Landscape Society. However, no one cared about their opinion, especially since Piotr Zaremba's modernization

Figure 4.11 New old town in Szczecin. On the site of destroyed tenement houses, new housing blocks were built. Photography by Jerzy Bujnowski.

Source: Janowski M. & Lisek J. & Skłodowski B., *Szczecin 1945 i dziś*, Warsaw: Interpress, 1968.

plans were supported by Jan Zachwatowicz himself. After learning about the development plans for this area of the city, he reiterated what the Mayor of Szczecin had repeatedly said and written – "the unveiling of the Castle and the Old Town escarpment in Szczecin will result in unique effects, bringing out the values of the historic area" (Knap, 2007, p. 77). At the same time, demolition and brick recovery were underway. Piotr Zaremba recalled that, in the course of the work in the Lower Town, he himself often no longer found arguments in polemics with the defenders of the old buildings, and "in succour came the Demolition Division and simply demolished the wobbly walls, thus ending the whole discussion" (Zaremba, 1980, p. 766). Here we come to one of the most controversial threads related to the post-war reconstruction of cities in the Recovered Territories.

Szczecin Mayor Piotr Zaremba recalled the even piles of bricks piled along the streets waiting to be loaded and taken to Warsaw, where they were used to rebuild the destroyed capital. He treated them as an almost natural part of the urban landscape, as the building blocks were obtained with the permission, and often by order, of the authorities. Szczecin was no exception in this regard. Witold Milewski, an architect from Poznań, told of the plundering economy in the Recovered Territories and the demolition or complete demolition of historic buildings in order to

National in form, socialist in content 107

obtain the bricks needed to rebuild Warsaw and other cities in central Poland. This was confirmed by conservator Bohdan Rymaszewski, who wrote about undamaged monuments that were being demolished in order to obtain the materials necessary to rebuild the country (Rymaszewski, 2005, p. 110). In addition, Milewski told of large-scale organized demolitions carried out on an individual level. He remembered how, practically before his eyes, fragments of the medieval city walls surrounding Kożuchów, one of the oldest cities in Lower Silesia, which before the war was called Freystadt, were dismantled. The ideology? Writing history "anew," without the centuries-old relics of German heritage? Milewski saw the reasons for the looting as economic. "Garages and cottages in the area were built out of everything," he recalled. "It wasn't about the Germans, it was about the looting economy."[7]

The oft-mentioned Breslau supplied more than just bricks. From Lower Silesia were also brought pianos for the Cracow conservatory, streetcars to Warsaw, and the printing press on which the "Breslauer Neueste Nachrichten" was previously prepared was given to the capital's editorial office of the "Evening Express" (Thum, 2006). The bricks, however, made the strongest mark in history. To this day, stories are still vivid among residents of the Western Territories about shipments of demolition bricks gliding towards Warsaw (Halicka, 2015). Beata Maciejewska called post-war Wrocław "the largest brickyard in Poland," citing data that could make one wonder: in 1951 alone, the Municipal Demolition Company "excavated" as many as 165 million bricks in the capital of Lower Silesia (Maciejewska, 2013). In the meantime, new companies sprouted up to acquire building materials, often illegally and in cooperation with dishonest representatives of the authorities. The first "brick millionaires" appeared. In turn, the bricks themselves flowed in a wide stream to construction sites in other parts of Poland.

Demolitions did not stop with the so-called thaw of 1956. What is more, a new threat emerged – the dogma of misunderstood modernity. Back in 1956, Stefan Müller and his wife Maria designed the development of the frontage of the market square in Jawor, combining tradition with modern construction solutions. Instead of recreating historical patterns, the architects filled the frontage of the market with low-rise, simple, modernist blocks covered with sloping roofs, with impressive reinforced concrete arcades in the ground floor (Müller, 2010). Years later, Müller called this realization "a minor episode," adding that his boss at the Miastoprojekt design office gave him considerable creative freedom while working in Nysa, Jawor, or Świdnica[8] (Figure 4.12). However, not all architects had such freedom, and not all possessed a sense of historical context to the same degree as Maria and Stefan Müller. In the 1960s, a disturbing phenomenon began to grow, involving the introduction of stigmatized multifamily residential development into the precincts of historic urban centres. It reached its apogee in the next decade, back with the spread of prefabrication in construction (Rymaszewski, 2005, p. 112).

Industrialized technologies were used on a large scale. Standardized four- and nine-story "apartment blocks" ruthlessly invaded Kołobrzeg, Słupsk, or Nidzica. Gdańsk architect Szczepan Baum designed the Old Town housing development in Malbork in 1960. Initially, the local party authorities wanted to force the architect

Figure 4.12 New frontage of the market square in Jawor – a rare mixture of modernity and traditional elements of architectural design. Architects Stefan Müller and Maria Müller.

Source: Photograph by the author.

to introduce sparing construction typical of the era of Władysław Gomułka's rule. There was a real danger that simple, featureless blocks of flats would grow in the shadow of the mighty Gothic castle. Fortunately, the preservationist and the provincial architect supported Baum and strongly protested. Finally, in 1969, construction was completed on the estate, which was an interesting attempt to fit modern architecture into the historical context. The new blocks were located along the course of the old streets, and in the forms of the facades, an attempt was made to reflect the divisions characteristic of the facades of medieval tenements. At the same time, Baum was designing a service complex to be built in the historic centre of Elbląg, a city whose historic centre was completely destroyed in 1945. Fortunately, as he claimed, the realization did not come to fruition. The construction of a huge modernist complex on the site of the former old town would have derailed the possibility of creating a "new old town" for good. It was created by Baum himself, together with another Danzig architect Stefan Phillip (and in close cooperation with the conservator Maria Lubocka-Hoffmann) in the mid-1980s – at a time when architecture had freed itself for good from modernist dogmas.

Criticism of modernist (or rather, pseudo-modern) solutions and the implementation of large-scale residential development within historic districts, however,

National in form, socialist in content 109

began much earlier. As early as 1977, architect and urban planner Hanna Adamczewska-Wejchert said that

> it is known who killed the old city X or put up high-rise buildings in city Y. What the public doesn't know, however, is that the press is acting very erratically, raising shouts of enthusiasm in honor of the first high-rise buildings in Nowy Sącz or Kamieniec Pomorski.
>
> (Stępiński, 1977, p. 42)

Misconceived modernity in architecture and urban planning has led to the degradation of many centres, and the problem has primarily affected smaller cities and towns with historic character.

Notes

1 Stanisław Juchnowicz, conversation with the author, online, 21.11.2012.
2 Maria Piechotka, conversation with the author, Warsaw, 14.11.2012.
3 Wiesław Gruszkowski, conversation with the author, Gdańsk, 29.01.2014.
4 Maria Piechotka, conversation with the author, Warsaw, 11.12.2012.
5 Jadwiga Grabowska-Hawrylak, conversation with the author, Wrocław, 26.06.2013.
6 Wiesław Gruszkowski, conversation with the author, Gdańsk, 29.01.2014.
7 Witold Milewski, conversation with the author, Poznań, 29.07.2013.
8 Stefan Müller, conversation with the author, Wrocław, 04.07.2013.

References

Ajewski, E., *Polska walcząca na moim podwórku. Pamiętnik z lat 1939–1947* [Fighting Poland in my backyard. A diary from 1939–1947], Warsaw: Self-Publishing, 1995.
Baraniewski, W., *Ideologia w architekturze Warszawy okresu realizmu socjalistycznego* [Ideology in the architecture of socialist realism in Warsaw], "Rocznik Historii Sztuki" 1996, no. 22.
Barucki, T., *Ogólnopolska Narada Architektów* [National Meeting of Architects], Warsaw: SARP, 1956.
Basista, A., *Betonowe dziedzictwo. Architektura w Polsce czasów komunizmu* [Concrete heritage. Architecture in communist Poland], Warsaw-Cracow: PWN Scientific Publishing House, 2001.
Bierut, B., *Sześcioletni plan odbudowy Warszawy. Referat na Konferencji Warszawskiej PZPR w dniu 3 lipca 1949 r* [Six-year plan for the reconstruction of Warsaw. Paper at the Warsaw Conference of the Polish United Workers' Party on 3 July 1949], Warsaw: Książka i Wiedza, 1950.
Chomątowska, B., *Pomniki epoki* [Monuments of the era], "Herito" 2019/2020, no. 37–38.
Ciarkowski, B., *Słowo architekta. Opowieści o architekturze Polski Ludowej* [An architect's word. Stories about the architecture of the Polish Republic of Poland], Łódź: University of Łódź Publishing House, 2023.
Cymer, A., *Architektura w Polsce 1945–1989* [Architecture in Poland 1945–1989], Warsaw: Centrum Architektury, 2018.
Dąbrowski, L., Kuhnel, A. & Rakowski, W., *Plan Śródmieścia Gdańska* [Gdańsk city centre plan], "Architektura" 1953, no. 8.
Datner, S., *Zburzenie Warszawy* [The demolition of Warsaw], [in:] *Straty wojenne Polski w latach 1939–1945* [Poland's war losses in 1939–1945], Poznań–Warsaw: Wydawnictwo Zachodnie, 1960.

110   Architecture and Architects in Socialist Poland

Dekret z dnia 26 października 1945 r. o własności i użytkowaniu gruntów na obszarze m. st. Warszawy [Decree of 26 October 1945 on the ownership and use of land in the area of the capital city of Warsaw].

Duda, M., *Patchwork. Architektura Jadwigi Grabowskiej-Hawrylak* [Patchwork. Architecture by Jadwiga Grabowska-Hawrylak], Wrocław: Museum of Architecture, 2016.

Fiuk, P., *Architektura miasta odbudowanego. Wybrane przykłady: Elbląg, Głogów, Kołobrzeg, Szczecin na tle historycznym* [Reconstruction of the city's architecture. Selected examples: Elbląg, Głogów, Kołobrzeg, Szczecin in historical context], Szczecin: West-Pomeranian University of Technology Publishing House, 2017a.

Fiuk, P., *Przywrócenie środowiska miejskiego w Szczecinie. Podzamcze – odbudowa nadwodnej "dzielnicy" staromiejskiej* [Restoration of Szczecin's urban environment. Podzamcze – reconstruction of the old town's waterfront "district"], "Przestrzeń – Urbanistyka – Architektura" 2017b, no. 1.

Fudala, T., *Odbudowa Warszawy i miastobójstwo "małego Paryża." Spór o odbudowę 70 lat później* [The reconstruction of Warsaw and the city killing of 'Little Paris'. The reconstruction dispute 70 years later], [in:] *Spór o odbudowę Warszawy. Od gruzów do reprywatyzacji* [The dispute over the reconstruction of Warsaw. From rubble to reprivatisation], ed. T. Fudala, Warsaw: Museum of Modern Art, 2016.

Goldzamt, E., *Architektura zespołów śródmiejskich i problemy dziedzictwa* [Architecture of inner-city neighbourhoods and heritage issues], Warsaw: PWN, 1956.

Goldzamt, E., *O realizm socjalistyczny w architekturze* [For socialist realism in architecture], "Nowa Droga" 1949, no. 3(15).

Gomułka, W., *Artykuły i przemówienia* [Articles and speeches], vol. 1, Warsaw: Książka i Wiedza, 1962.

Gomułka, W., *Pamiętniki* [Diaries], vol. 2, Warsaw: BGW, 1994.

Greczanik-Filipp, I., *Wspomnienia z odbudowy Głównego Miasta* [Memories of the reconstruction of the Main Town], Gdańsk: Marpress, 1997.

Grunwaldzka Dzielnica Mieszkaniowa [Grunwald Housing Estate], "Architektura" 1953, no. 8.

Gzell, S., *Nowy wspaniały świat: racjonalizm Karty Ateńskiej i jego wpływ na kształt paradygmatów w urbanistyce XX wieku* [Brave new world: The rationalism of the Athens Charter and its impact on the paradigms of 20th-century urban planning], [in:] *Manifesty urbanistyczne. W poszukiwaniu współczesnego modelu miasta* [Urban manifestos. In search of a contemporary city model], eds. T. Majda, I. Moronowicz, Warsaw: Towarzystwo Urbanistów Polskich, 2017.

Halicka, B., *Polski Dziki Zachód: przymusowe migracje i kulturowe oswajanie Nadodrza 1945–1948* [The Wild West of Poland: Forced migration and cultural taming of the Nadodrze 1945–1948], Cracow: TAiWPN Universitas, 2015.

Jankowski, S., Knothe, J., Sigalin, J., & Stępiński, Z., *Marszałkowska Dzielnica Mieszkaniowa* [Marszałkowska Housing Estate], "Architektura" 1951, no. 7.

Juchnowicz, S., *Nowa Huta*, "Architektura" 1986, no. 1.

Klewin, J., *Doświadczenia bielańskie* [Bielany experience], "Architektura" 1958, no. 7.

Knap, P., *Sylweta zapowiadała się tak korzystnie . . . Kontrowersje wokół odbudowy szczecińskiego Starego Miasta (1945–1970)* [The silhouette looked so promising . . . Controversy surrounding the reconstruction of the Old Town in Szczecin (1945–1970)], "Biuletyn IPN" 2007, no. 3(74).

Kotarbiński, A., *Na drodze ku realizmowi socjalistycznemu w architekturze* [On the road to socialist realism in architecture], Warsaw: Ministry of Construction, Urban Planning and Housing. Institute of Urban Planning and Architecture, 1952.

Kotarbiński, A., *Rozwój urbanistyki i architektury polskiej w latach 1944–1964. Próba charakterystyki krytycznej* [The development of Polish urban planning and architecture in the years 1944–1964. An attempt at critical characterisation], Warsaw: PWN, 1967.

Kowalski, J., *Morski Dom Kultury* [Maritime Community Centre], "Architektura" 1955, no. 4.

National in form, socialist in content 111

Lachert, B., *Muranów – dzielnica mieszkaniowa* [Muranów – housing estate], "Architektura" 1949, no. 5.

Leśniakowska, M., *Architektura w Warszawie 1945–1965* [Architecture in Warsaw 1945–1965], Warsaw: Arkada, 2003.

Lewandowski, T., *Bielany*, "Architektura" 1958, no. 7.

Lier, S., *Konkurs na projekt urbanistyczno-artystyczny fragmentu śródmieścia Gdańska* [Competition for an urban planning and artistic design of a part of the city centre of Gdańsk], "Architektura" 1954, no. 7–8.

Maciejewska, B., *Szaber w majestacie prawa* [Plundering under the guise of the law], "Ale Historia" – "Gazeta Wyborcza" supplement, 04.10.2013.

Majewski, P., *Ideologia i konserwacja. Architektura zabytkowa w Polsce w czasach socrealizmu* [Ideology and conservation. Historical architecture in Poland during the era of socialist realism], Warsaw: Trio, 2009.

Marczewski, K., *Nowe Tychy*, "Architektura" 1956, no. 1.

Mezga, D., *Political Factors in the Reconstruction of Warsaw's Old Town*, "Urban Design Studies" 1998, no. 4.

Minorski, J., *O polską architekturę socjalistyczną* [For polish socialist architecture], Warsaw: State Technical Publishers, 1950.

Miziołek, J., *Zabytkowe falsyfikaty* [Antique forgeries], [in:] *Spotkania w willi Struvego 1998–2001. Wykłady o dziedzictwie kultury* [Meetings at Villa Struve 1998–2001. Lectures on cultural heritage], ed. K. Kwiecińska, Warsaw: TOnZ, 2001.

Müller, S., *Wynurzenia, czyli nic* [Digressions, in other words, nothing], Wrocław: Museum of Architecture, 2010.

Murawski, M., *(A)political Buildings: Ideology, Memory and Warsaw's 'Old Town'*, [in:] *Mirror of Modernity. The Post-War Revolution in Urban Conservation*, Docomomo e-proceedings 2, 2009.

Nowakowski, M., *Sto lat planowania przestrzeni polskich miast (1910–2010)* [One hundred years of planning the space of Polish cities (1910–2010)], Warsaw: Oficyna Naukowa, 2013.

Nowowiejski, W., *W tym mieście dziwy z cudami chodziły w parze* [In this city, wonders and miracles went hand in hand], "Kurier Polski," 28–31.03.1975.

Osmańczyk, E., *Gdański finał* [Gdańsk final], "Odrodzenie" 1945, no. 23.

Perkowski, P., *Gdańsk – miasto od nowa* [Gdańsk – city from the scratch], Gdańsk: Słowo/obraz terytoria, 2013.

Piątek, G., *Najlepsze miasto świata. Warszawa w odbudowie 1944–1949* [The best city in the world. Warsaw under reconstruction 1944–1949], Warsaw: W.A.B., 2020.

Piotrowski, R., *Architekt i społeczeństwo* [Architect and society], "Architektura" 1948, no. 8–9.

Piotrowski, R. & Terlikowska-Woysznis, G., *Odbudowa Warszawy 1945–1947* [Warsaw reconstruction 1945–1947], "Przegląd Budowlany" 1947, no. 9.

Popiołek, M., *Powojenna odbudowa ulicy Nowy Świat w Warszawie* [Post-war reconstruction of Nowy Świat Street in Warsaw], Warsaw: Egros & Mazovian Centre for Culture and Arts, 2012.

Ptaszycki, T., *Nowa Huta*, "Architektura" 1953, no. 3.

Rezolucja Krajowej Partyjnej Narady Architektów z dniu 20–21 czerwca 1949 r. w Warszawie [Resolution of the National Party Conference of Architects on 20–21 June 1949 in Warsaw], "Architektura" 1949, no. 6–8.

Rozporządzenie Prezydenta Rzeczypospolitej z dnia 6 marca 1928 r. o opiece nad zabytkami [Regulation of the President of the Republic of Poland of 6 March 1928 on the protection of historical monuments].

Rymaszewski, B., *Polska ochrona zabytków* [Polish monument preservation], Warsaw: Scholar, 2005.

Sigalin, J., *Warszawa 1944–1980. Z archiwum architekta* [Warsaw 1944–1980. From the architect's archive], vol. 1, Warsaw: PIW, 1986.

112 Architecture and Architects in Socialist Poland

Skalimowski, A., *Dom Partii* [House of the Party], Warsaw: Neriton, 2010.

Skalimowski, A., *Partyjny kolektyw i jego eksponenci. Bezpośrednia ingerencja kierownictwa PZPR w organizację odbudowy Warszawy w latach 1949–1956* [Partisan collective and its exponents. Direct interference of the leadership of the Polish United Workers' Party in the organisation of the reconstruction of Warsaw in the years 1949–1956], [in:] *Letnia Szkoła Historii Najnowszej IPN 2011* [IPN Summer School of Contemporary History 2011], eds. P. Gasztold-Seń, Ł. Kamiński, Warsaw: IPN, 2012.

Skalimowski, A., *"Pierwsza szczera narada architektów." Motywy, przebieg i konsekwencje Ogólnopolskiej Narady Architektów z 1956 roku* ['The first open discussion between architects'. Motives, course and consequences of the National Council of Architects in 1956], "Polska 1944/45–1989. Studia i Materiały" 2011, no. 10.

Skalimowski, A., *Sigalin, towarzysz odbudowy* [Sigalin, comrade of reconstruction], Wołowiec: Czarne, 2018.

Stefański, K., *Architektura polska 1949–1956* [Polish architecture 1949–1956], "Kwartalnik Architektury i Urbanistyki" 1982, vol. 27.

Stępiński, Z., *Gawędy warszawskiego architekta* [The tales of a Warsaw architect], Warsaw: KAW, 1984.

Stępiński, Z., *Odbudowa Nowego Świata* [Nowy Świat reconstruction], "Biuletyn Historii Sztuki" 1947, no. 1–2.

Stępiński, Z., *Postawy* [Attitudes], "Architektura" 1978, no. 1–2.

Stępiński, Z., *Sprawa spuścizny kulturalnej i historycznej przy projektowaniu i budowie Trasy W-Z* [Cultural and historical legacy in the planning and construction of the West-East route], [in:] *Pamięć warszawskiej odbudowy 1945–1949. Antologia* [Memory of the Warsaw Reconstruction 1945–1949. Anthology], ed. J. Górski, Warsaw: PIW, 1972.

Stępiński, Z., *Wejchertowie. Wokół miasta, wywiad Z. Stępińskiego z H. Adamczewską-Wejchert i K. Wejchertem* [The Wejcherts. Around the city, interview with H. Adamczewska-Wejchert and K. Wejchert by Z. Stępiński], "Architektura" 1977, no. 3–4.

Sumorok, A., *Zaprojektować socrealizm? W obronie architektury* [Designing Social Realism? In defence of architecture], "Herito" 2017, no. 29.

Thum, R., *Obce miasto, Wrocław 1945 i potem* [A foreign city, Wrocław in 1945 and afterwards], Wrocław: Via Nova, 2006.

Torańska, T., *Aneks* [Annex], Warszawa: Świat Książki, 2015.

Torańska, T., *Oni* [Them], London: Aneks, 1985.

Weber, F., *Dzielnica mieszkaniowa na Kole* [Koło housing estate], "Stolica" 1949, no. 48.

Wierzbicki, J., *Dzielnica mieszkaniowa Muranów* [Muranów housing estate], "Architektura" 1952, no. 9.

Wiśniewski, M., *Płaszcz narodowych dekoracji* [The mantle of national decorations], "Herito" 2019/2020, no. 37–38.

Włodarczyk, W., *Socrealizm. Sztuka polska w latach 1950–1954* [Socialist Realism. Polish Art in the Years 1950–1954], Paris: Libella, 1986.

Wujek, J., *Mity i utopie architektury XX wieku* [Myths and utopias of 20th-century architecture], Warszawa: Arkady, 1986.

Wyporek, B., *Warszawa 1945 i BOS* [Warsaw 1945 and BOS], Warsaw 2015, private archive.

Zachwatowicz, J., *Budownictwo i architektura w Polsce 1945–1966* [Construction and architecture in Poland 1945–1966], Warsaw: Interpress, 1968.

Zachwatowicz, J., *Pomniki kultury polskiej na Ziemiach Odzyskanych – ich losy, ochrona i upowszechnienie* [Monuments of Polish culture in the Recovered Territories – their fate, protection and promotion], "Przegląd Budowlany" 1948, no. 7.

Zachwatowicz, J., *Problemy zachowania historycznych założeń przy odbudowie Warszawy* [Problems with maintaining the historical design of the reconstruction of Warsaw], [in:] *Warszawa współczesna, geneza i rozwój* [Contemporary Warsaw: Origins and development], ed. J. Kazimierski, Warsaw: PWN, 1981.

National in form, socialist in content 113

Zaremba, P., *Odezwa Prezydenta Szczecina z dnia 9 lipca 1945 "Polacy! Szczecina jest polski!"* [Appeal of the Mayor of Szczecin on 9 July 1945: 'Poles! Szczecin is Polish!'], "Biuletyn 'Wiadomości Szczecińskie'" 9 lipca 1945, no. 1(1).

Zaremba, P., *Wspomnienia prezydenta Szczecina* [Memories of the Mayor of Szczecin], Poznań: Wydawnictwo Poznańskie, 1980.

Zaremba, P. & Orlińska, H., *Urbanistyczny rozwój Szczecina* [Urban development of Szczecin], Poznań: Wydawnictwo Poznańskie, 1965.

5 Back to the modernism

5.1 Architecture and modernization policy

The National Meeting of Architects, held on 26–28 March 1956, marked the official end of the reign of socialist realism in architecture, as well as a clear signal to designers, approved by the authorities, indicating potential directions for their work. Politicians spoke of architectural freedom, while architects sought to redefine the concept of modernity. However, already during the meeting, it became clear that both "freedom" and "modernity" could be understood differently, and the following years only highlighted the differences between the positions of individuals and groups.

The meeting was held in the Theatre of the Polish Army House in the Palace of Culture and Science. The importance of the event, not only for the architectural community, can be evidenced by the fact that the Prime Minister of the Polish People's Republic himself, Józef Cyrankiewicz, graced it with his presence. He was not only a passive listener but also took the floor, exhorting, "Let the new period be characterized by freedom of creativity. Let no one be afraid of innovation" (Skolimowska, 2012, p. 88). It might have seemed that, after the dark period of Stalinism, architecture had finally become free of any pressure. "I wanted to emphasize once again that neither the Party leadership nor the Government wants, will not lead Polish architecture by the hand" – declared the Prime Minister (Barucki, 1956, p. 241). Tadeusz Barucki, who was the organizer of the meeting on behalf of the Association of Polish Architects, was particularly memorable for the speech by SARP President Jerzy Wierzbicki, who postulated that the discussion should strive to bring out the richness of thought of each participant. "What worries me is that the resolutions of the Central Committee (of the Party) are passed unanimously," he said. – he added. "But it doesn't worry us!" – replied from the front row Cyrankiewicz. Silence fell in the room, and Wierzbicki froze. The prime minister had made it clear to the architects that the freedom they were so excited about coming would be licensed and controlled by the party authorities

Thus, in March 1956, at the Congress Hall, architecture was combined with politics, and visions of the future – with reckoning towards recent history. The past years of "errors and distortions" were categorically condemned. Many bitter words were said about the absent Edmund Goldzamt or Jan Minorski. Józef

DOI: 10.4324/9781003603153-6

Sigalin offered self-criticism, just as only a few years earlier had been offered by architect-modernists, who renounced their former beliefs in the hope that, within the framework of socialist-realist doctrine, there would be room for them as well.

> I, in my section of work, used the same methods [mentioned in his speech by J. Cyrankiewicz – note BC] and I have no intention of invoking the so-called example from above. I applied them because I thought they were right, I thought I was helping the cause of building Warsaw better that way. . . . But one thing I know for sure is that the methods were wrong, that they harmed not only our construction, but that they broke people. – Sigalin said.
>
> (Barucki, 1956, p. 413)

In addition to settlements that can be described in retrospect as personal, specific omissions and mistakes that characterized the era just past were also scored. Jerzy Wierzbicki already at the very beginning of his speech bearing the telling title "Polish Architects to the New Mass Needs and Tasks in Construction," pointed out that the challenges, facing designers are associated "primarily with the development of typification and the development of the industrialization of construction" (Barucki, 1956, p. VII–XX). He pointed out the distortions of the past. He pointed out that in the period 1945–1949 "under the pressure of quantitative needs at the end of the 3-Year Plan, a tolerant attitude to a steady reduction in the quality of workmanship began," and "The process of lowering the creative potential of the community and moving to schematic design work with the apotheosis of banality began in 1949." At the same time, he pointed out the direction of architecture in the future: "Not a unique building – a masterpiece of building art against the background of shabby, old, disorderly buildings, but the offensive of mass construction against the shabbiness and squalor of our suburbs, towns and settlements – will testify to our times."

Architects threw themselves into the vortex of variously (sometimes misguidedly) conceived modernity with a zeal worthy of a better cause. Pierre Restany described a desire to break cultural isolation and a drive to make up for delays and belong to modernity at any cost. This began a period that many years later architectural historians would refer to as Social Modernism.

The term "socmodernism" (or "socialist modernism") was first used by Adam Miłobędzki in 1994 (Miłobędzki, 2014), who thus described the domestic construction of 1956–1989. Recently, both the term and its definition have begun to raise some doubts and be criticized. At the same time, they continue to be used by researchers and publicists (mainly from Central and Eastern Europe, but not only). In an article in "The Guardian," Naomi Larsson defined it as the architecture of the former Eastern Bloc countries from 1955 to 1991. She cited Dumitru Rusu, a Romanian architect and founder of the B.A.C.U. (Birou pentru Artă și Cercetare Urbană – Art and Urban Research Bureau) studio and web portals promoting the architecture of "socialist modernism." However, the term is not reserved only for post-Stalinist construction in Central and Central and Eastern European countries. For example, Jelena Janković-Beguš wrote about social modernism in Serbian music as a combination of modernist form and socialist ideas (Janković-Beguš,

116 *Architecture and Architects in Socialist Poland*

2017). This short definition seems extremely accurate and, importantly, universal – it can be successfully applied to architecture as well.

Architecture was an important tool of modernization policy in the socialist state. And this was true regardless of whether it happened to represent paseist Socialist Realism or the late modernism of the 1960s. After all, communism was in its very foundations a modernization project, and progress was an immanent feature of the system regardless of the aesthetic doctrines of the day. Among the wide-ranging programs, such as industrialization and housing development, there was also the development of education at all levels. At the level of higher education, the key decisions were the establishment of new academic centres, the development of existing universities, and the related need to expand infrastructure. In the case of primary education, an important moment was 1949 when the illiteracy eradication law was passed, and the education reform of the early 1960s. The latter act coincided with the campaign to build "a thousand schools for the thousandth anniversary of the Polish state." This slogan, thrown around in 1958 by the First Secretary of the Central Committee of the Polish United Workers' Party (PZPR) Władysław Gomułka, became the impetus for the creation of the Thousand Schools Construction Fund, followed by the realization of more facilities. In total, between 1959 (when the first school was opened in Czeladź, Silesia) and 1966 (when the millennium celebrations ended), more than 1,400 schools were built in Poland.

In 1957, the Committee for Urban Planning and Architecture sought to make school construction henceforth subject to generally accepted guidelines for standardization and prefabrication (Cymer, 2018, p. 195). Most of the schools of the millennium were thus built on the basis of repetitive designs containing, in addition to modern classrooms, a few fixed elements (such as outdoor sports infrastructure and gymnasiums). Among them, however, there were also works by recognized architects, distinguished by their original form or original spatial and functional solutions. The first school in Wrocław implemented under the "thousand schools" program was located on Podwale Street and was commissioned in 1960, and its designer was Jadwiga Grabowska-Hawrylak. It was an excellent example of responding to local needs and challenges based on international experience, as the architect followed the guidelines of the "Charter of school construction" promulgated in 1959 by the International Union of Architects. The building had a clear functional layout and refined aesthetics of both interiors and facades, which were finished with slabs of dark terrazzo and white opaque glass (marblite). On the other hand, the school in the Sadyba housing development in Warsaw, designed by Warsaw architect Halina Skibniewska, presented functional solutions that were not standard for the time. The building itself, although designed as part of the "thousand schools" program, was completed much later, and the first students could use the building only in 1971. Nevertheless, it is worth noting that Skibniewska not only developed the school's functional program, adding workshop rooms, a reading room, or studios (also accessible to residents of the neighbourhood), but also adapted the building to the needs of people with disabilities, which was a rarity in the late 1960s and early 1970s. Architecturally and functionally interesting school buildings were built in all major Polish cities. In Łódź, these were buildings designed by Tadeusz Herburt.

Back to the modernism 117

In Katowice – a school on the Koszutka estate, consisting of simple pavilions connected by glass connectors (architect Stanisław Kwaśniewicz, 1958–1961). The pavilion system was also successfully used in Tychy (including the building of the Building Technical School by Andrzej Czyżewski and Maria Czyżewska, 1959) or Nowa Huta (architect Józef Gołąb 1960–1961). However, the aforementioned buildings were glorious exceptions, as most of the school buildings that were constructed from the late 1950s to the mid-1960s were based on stylized designs, presenting restrained and economical architecture, devoid of formal fireworks. The situation was somewhat different in the field of infrastructure for higher education.

"Nineteen cities – up from seven before 1939. – now constitute centers of higher education in Poland, usually concentrating several or more each, and in Warsaw even 13 universities," – wrote in the second half of the 1960s, stressing that the significant increase in the number of students required huge outlays from the state, building new edifices and academic complexes (Zachwatowicz, 1968, p. 59). The first stage of increased investment in Polish universities was in the period just after the war. The next – in the second half of the 1960s, when the following were built: the campus of the Nicolaus Copernicus University in Toruń, created by a design team under direction of Warsaw architect Ryszard Karłowicz (Różański, 1971), plans for the District of Higher Education in Łódź (Samujłło, 1970) and the University of Gdańsk, similar in layout to it, by Witold Benedek and Stanisław Niewiadomski (Benedek & Niewiadomski, 1971), and the Cracow University of Technology, designed by Witold Cęckiewicz's team as a system of interconnected pavilions (Popławski, 1982, p. 210–246). "The key is to program investments for a minimum of 20 years," – stated Karłowicz in a paper at the 1966 Seminar on Higher School Construction in Warsaw, adding that the main principle of shaping university complexes should be "programmatic flexibility of implementation" (Benedek & Niewiadomski, 1971).

Two, often simultaneous and complementary strategies were observed. The first was based on the use of vacant spaces within the inner city (and often the adaptation of the existing stock of buildings), while the second was based on the creation of new university towns located outside the city centre. A combination of these was used in Łódź (Stefański & Ciarkowski, 2018) or Poznań, where the local university and other universities were developing dynamically (Marciniak, 2005). The example of the latter city shows the process of the multi-stage formation of academic centres. At the same time, it is worth noting that, in the capital of Greater Poland, the individual units used different solutions – the Poznań University of Technology and the University of Life Sciences established separate campuses inscribed in the urban structure, while the Adam Mickiewicz University sought to create a science district on the outskirts of the city, the design of which was the subject of a competition decided in 1968. The academic campus was to be located outside the city, in the form of an independent complex combining, in addition to the University, the Academy of Medicine, the Academy of Economics, the Academy of Physical Education, art schools, the Polish Academy of Sciences, and the Central Academic Sports Center, enriched with residential and service facilities (Popławski, 1982, p. 234–237).

118 *Architecture and Architects in Socialist Poland*

The great importance of investments for higher education purposes is illustrated by the fact that in many design offices special units were established to deal exclusively with the problems of academic centres. Architects Lech Sternal, Witold Milewski, and Zygmunt Skupniewicz worked in the Higher Education Studio, created as part of the Poznań-Miastoprojekt (Sternal was the manager). Milewski assessed the team's designs as "marked by the sign of the coarse times," but at the same time constituting "a testimony to our passions and architectural views" (Marcinkowski, 2013, p. 237). "We professed the view that truly modern architecture is construction brought to perfection, Milewski wrote, and recounted that they were among the first in Greater Poland to introduce typification in their projects" (Piątek, 2006b). The projects developed at the Higher Education Studio presented the most important features of late modernism: economy of forms, simplicity, and the use of modular prefabricated elements in facades. This could not please party decision-makers, who, despite the passage of years, seem not to have quite recovered from socialist-realist eclecticism. Milewski wrote that the concepts created by him, Skupniewicz, and Sternal often met with criticism from the authorities. "They complained that nothing here was designed. They said we were practicing brutalism."[1] In 1974, construction began in Poznań on the Collegium Altum, a 15-story skyscraper housing academic facilities connected to a lower, three-story volume of a library, lecture halls, and cafeteria (Figure 5.1). Describing the realization, architect and researcher Piotr Marciniak mentioned the "high-tech inspirations of the authors," which could not be realized in the face of material shortages and the level of workmanship (Marciniak, 2010, p. 185). Transitional problems were, after all, not unusual in the realities of People's Poland. The output of the Higher Education Studio, including the Collegium Novum building, the buildings of the Poznań University of Technology and the Medical Academy, and the Eskulap and Jowita student houses, could have been much richer. In many cases, only a small part of the complexes planned on a grand scale was erected. Among other things, the ambitious project to build a University of Technology campus, which was to be located on the right side of the Warta River, was curtailed. Milewski, Sternal, and Skupniewicz planned an impressive scientific and didactic complex consisting of four (eventually – eight) repetitive nine-storey edifices connected by lecture hall complexes. Only two have been completed – the headquarters of the Faculty of Mechanical Engineering and Electrical Engineering. A similar fate befell the extensive development plans for the Agricultural Academy (now the University of Life Sciences). In turn, the only completed element from the large complex of buildings of the Medical Academy was the Eskulap student house, designed in 1973 by Sternal, Milewski, and Skupniewicz.

In 1974, the competition for the complex of the Adam Mickiewicz University Poznań-Morasko was decided. The winner was a team of architects from Opole, consisting of Marian Fikus, Jerzy Gurawski, and Jan Godlewski, who cooperated with them (Marciniak, 2005, p. 202). The design concept included the development of an area of 300 hectares intended for 24,000 students (Popławski, p. 234–237). The campus was designed as an ensemble built "based on a thoroughfare, which they called the University Esplanade . . . an element that is a meeting place for

Figure 5.1 Collegium Altum – a dominant modernist 15-storey-high skyscraper in the centre of Poznań designed by architects Witold Milewski, Zygmunt Skupniewicz, and Lech Sternal.

Source: Photograph by the author.

all citizens: students, professors, everyone" – Gurawski recounted.[2] In accordance with the then-current trends in the design of academic centres, the architects arranged the functions within a hierarchical urban-architectural structure, harmoniously coexisting with the natural landscape. Despite the support of the authorities, including Chief Provincial Architect Jerzy Buszkiewicz, the investment was not

120 *Architecture and Architects in Socialist Poland*

completed. As Marciniak emphasized, from the original project "Only the compositional skeleton and the spatial and textural structure remained" (Marciniak, 2010, p. 196).

The Poznań University campus was not an isolated case. In Łódź, which became the seat of five universities in 1945, a plan to build a joint campus for the University and the Medical Academy was conceived as early as 1948. Its author was architect Bolesław Tatarkiewicz, with whom, among others, Edmund R. Orlik, the designer of the University Library project, collaborated. It was this edifice, which constituted the most modern library in Poland at the time of its completion in 1960, that was the only project to be built in the first stage of campus development in Łódź. Plans to develop the Higher Education District (Dzielnica Wyższych Uczelni – DWU), as the campus was called, were revisited in the late 1960s. In 1970, architects Bolesław Kardaszewski and Włodzimierz Nowakowski developed a comprehensive urban-architectural concept, which, however, did not gain approval from the authorities. Only its next version, which Kardaszewski and Nowakowski created in the early 1970s together with Anna Wiśniowska, was sent for further work. It already betrayed a completely new, structuralist way of thinking about urban planning and architecture. A "forum" was located in the central part of the DWU, with administrative facilities, the rector's offices of both universities, a common auditorium, and the university library to be located near it. The entire complex was supplemented with recreational areas, landscaped greenery, and service and commercial facilities. The individual complexes were shaped using the basic "pavilion-module" unit and its repetition, as well as a modular system of communication between units (Kardaszewski, 1986). The only element of the District that was successfully implemented, and at the same time, a "prototype" object, setting the direction of the design and implementation of the district, was the building of the Institute of Physics of the University of Łódź, designed in 1971–1974. Throughout the entire period of the Polish People's Republic, the development of the academic centre in Łódź was characterized by inconsistency. In the following decades, urban planning concepts were developed, different from the previous ones, whose only "common" feature was that none was brought to completion, and "each new object was governed by its own laws, fighting for better with its neighbour" (*Z pracowni . . .*, 1973, p. 215).

Against the background of the described cases of Łódź and Poznań (as well as a number of other academic cities, such as Gdańsk, Lublin, Cracow, and Wrocław), the campus of Nicolaus Copernicus University in Toruń stood out. The concept of the whole was "unified, compact and fulfilling all the conditions that should be demanded for a higher education institution," and the architects, under the direction of Ryszard Karłowicz, managed to combine the teaching, sports and entertainment, and residential parts into a coherent functional layout. Located in a scenically attractive area, the complex was an interesting composition, in which nature was intertwined with architecture, which, in turn, was designed to give the impression of being open and friendly. The entrance to the campus was accentuated by the rectorate building connected to the main auditorium with a colourful panneau on the facade (Figure 5.2). Further on, two main compositional axes were delineated,

Figure 5.2 Main auditorium with a colourful panneau on the façade is a "gate" to the campus of Nicolaus Copernicus University in Toruń (chief architect of the whole complex – Ryszard Karłowicz).

Source: Wikimedia Commons, author: Pko, CC BY-SA 4.0.

which led towards the pavilions of individual departments, student houses, or sports areas. The entire project was implemented in three stages: 1967–1973, 1973–1976, and 1976–1980, and different architects were responsible for the designs of the individual buildings included in the Karłowicz master plan. Despite this, it was possible to preserve the coherence and integrity of the entire layout – features that distinguish the campus of Nicolaus Copernicus University in Toruń from other university towns realized in the Polish People's Republic.

5.2 "Prestigious developments"

The concept of "prestigious realizations" in relation to the architecture of the Polish People's Republic was popularized by Andrzej Basista, who, in the pages of *Concrete Heritage*, defined in this way investments of special importance (primarily propaganda) to the central or local authorities (Basista, 2001, s.101). Their occurrence was characteristic for the entire duration of the Polish People's Republic and included buildings of various characters – monuments, public buildings, and housing estates. The analysis of diverse examples allows us not only to characterize the phenomenon of "prestige realizations" but also to draw a picture of political control over artists and their work. This issue seems particularly interesting in

122 *Architecture and Architects in Socialist Poland*

relation to the architecture of the years 1956–1989. While top-down pressure in the Stalinist era was unquestionable, and the fate of individual projects and realizations has more than once been thoroughly characterized, party control in subsequent decades was clearly less noticeable. This did not mean its absence, of course. The concept of "creative freedom," mentioned by Prime Minister Cyrankiewicz at the 1956 National Council of Architects, seemed to be understood by the authorities quite differently from the designers.

"Prestigious" ventures were usually accompanied by greater outlays of resources, but also increased vigilance on the part of the party apparatus. Communist authorities were sometimes a generous patron, but capricious. Working on objects of special importance gave architects a wider than usual spectrum of possibilities but, at the same time, often required a special skill in practicing intellectual equilibrium to avoid potential problems. It is worth looking at how the circumstances of the design and implementation of "prestige objects" changed at different stages of the communist era.

There is no doubt that the Bierut era was a period of particularly intensified control by the state apparatus over architecture and architects. It applied to both prestigious and seemingly less important buildings. The party authorities paid attention to even the slightest manifestations of impropriety. At the same time, there were times when an architect had a certain causal power, capable of causing a stir among those at the top of the authorities. Warsaw architect Tadeusz Mycek recalled that Professor Jerzy Hryniewiecki was the idol of independently thinking young architecture students. "He was our ideal of an architect" – he stated and, as if to confirm his words, cited a story about the construction of a new mountain railroad in the Tatra Mountains. The meeting, chaired by Zygmunt Skibniewski, chairman of the Committee for Urban Planning and Architecture, was attended by members of the Politburo headed by President Bolesław Bierut and architects. Among them was Hryniewiecki, although, as Mycek made clear, he did not belong to the trusted circle of "court architects." He listened to the discussion regarding the investment, which raised doubts among many designers. However, no one dared or could directly express objections. Finally, Hryniewiecki could not stand it: "I would like to point out that this side of the Tatra Mountains was looked at from Poronin by Lenin" – he said, referring to the fact that the later leader of the Bolsheviks in 1913–1914 stayed in Poronin, a small village located in the Tatra Mountains (Mycek, 1998, p. 23). "Bierut reportedly went into a rage. He rejected the project," Mycek recounted.[3]

The 1956 thaw introduced a temporary sense of relative freedom. The comrades at the head of the state had changed. Priorities and the prevailing aesthetics in architecture changed. The rationale guiding party patrons also underwent partial changes. What remained unchanged, however, was the influence of politics on prestige projects.

The realizations that naturally fit the criteria of "prestige objects" were monuments and edifices of great symbolic importance, which are tools for shaping historical policy. Such include the Grunwald Monument and the Wrocław rotunda of the Racławice Panorama. The former object was of particular interest to the first secretary of the Central Committee of the Polish United Workers' Party (PZPR), Władysław Gomułka, because commemorating the victory of Polish and Lithuanian troops over the Teutonic Order achieved in 1410 fit perfectly into the top-down anti-German narrative. The rotunda in Wrocław, on the other hand, posed a serious problem, as the painting to be displayed there depicted the triumph of Poles over the Russian army.

In 1959 Witold Cęckiewicz, in duo with sculptor Jerzy Bandura, won a closed competition to design the Grunwald Victory Monument. The precursor concept was to integrate the architecture of the monuments and museum with the surrounding landscape (Wojciechowski, 2014) (Figure 5.3). The prominence of the investment

Figure 5.3 Grunwald Victory Monument designed by architect Witold Cęckiewicz and sculptor Jerzy Bandura.

Source: SARP Archive.

124 *Architecture and Architects in Socialist Poland*

involved considerable pressure from the authorities, and the monument itself had to be ready for the celebration of the 550th anniversary of the Battle of Grunwald. Cęckiewicz described the circumstances of the monument as follows: "Autumn comes, and in spring the Grunwald Field has to be finished. The field. Literally a field. There are no roads, no utilities."[4] The coordinator of the investment on behalf of the party was Czesław Rajewski, who earlier, together with Marek Leykam and Jerzy Hryniewiecki, co-created Warsaw's Tenth Anniversary Stadium. Thanks to the considerable funds reserved in advance and the enormous amount of work, in the spring of 1960 the most important elements of the entire premise were ready, although the program of competition work was much broader.

Critics emphasized the successful composition of the establishment, stressing that the strength of the Grunwald monument (and other similar realizations created in those years) lay, in the skill of the creators, who struck a "high tone" without falling "into flamboyance or pathetic loftiness." Modern forms were skillfully combined with references to the imagined Middle Ages, which included both the "knight Światowit" (Slavic pagan god of war with four faces) and the decorations by Cęckiewicz, Helena and Roman Husarski and Maria Ledkiewicz in the museum's interiors, where a colourful mosaic depicting medieval warriors was a Polish interpretation of Bayeux fabric (Karpińska, 2015, p. 95). Representatives of the state authorities had custody of the project throughout the investment process, but Władysław Gomułka did not appear on the fields of Grunwald until early July, two weeks before the planned celebrations. His attention was drawn to the monument depicting the menacing faces of medieval knights. He inquired in which direction they were looking (if not east). He was only reassured by the information that their eyes were turned west, towards Germany.

Architects who were given the opportunity to realize objects of symbolic importance had to reckon with the fact that politics, at both the national and international levels, would influence the final result of their work. When Ewa and Marek Dziekoński began construction of the Panorama Racławicka rotunda building in Wrocław, they never imagined that it would take as long as 23 years. Initially, nothing foreshadowed problems. In a competition decided in 1957, the jury awarded the Dziekońskis' concept with the first prize, after which it sent the project for further work. The post-Stalin thaw was quite quickly frozen by the Gomułka tightening of the course, and party decision-makers, fearing a possible reaction from the Soviet authorities, halted work. Although they restarted in 1961, as soon as a reinforced concrete skeleton filled with prefabricated elements stood on the site, work was again halted. The adventures of Panorama's construction were talked about on Radio Free Europe and were lived by Wrocław Street. In the following years, construction was repeatedly resumed and interrupted, and concepts were changed. Finally, the administrative authorities of Wrocław decided to turn the structure into the Wrocław Cultural Center. It was only after the changes forced by the events of August 1980 that the third-ever Social Committee of the Racławicka Panorama was formed and work began (Trębacz, 2007, p. 71). The ceremonial opening of the building took place in 1985, all because the painting by Wojciech Kossak and Jan Styka presented the victory of the Polish army led by Tadeusz Kosciuszko over the

Back to the modernism 125

tsarist army. Admittedly, Catherine II is not Khrushchev or Brezhnev, but Russia is always Russia – in the Central Committee, they preferred not to take any risks.

The history of Cęckiewicz's or Dziekońskis' projects illustrates how important monumental assumptions of monumental character were for the authorities. Art historian Marta Karpińska aptly described them as "scenographies of historical politics" (Karpińska, 2015, p. 83). Just as the Grunwald Monument was part of the anti-German policy of the Gomułka era and the glorification of victory, monuments at the sites of former Nazi camps in Płaszów or Chełmno nad Nerem were part of a "strategy of understatement," contributing to the phenomenon of collective amnesia (Karpińska, 2015, p. 97). A telling example is the latter monument, designed by architect Jerzy Buszkiewicz and sculptor Józef Stasiński, where a passage indicating that the victims were Jews was removed from the work's key inscription.

The years 1956–1969 were a period of building great monuments. In the following decades, realizations of a magnitude similar to those at the Majdanek camp in Lublin (designed by Wiktor Tołkin) or at Treblinka (designed by Franciszek Duszeńko and Adam Haupt) practically did not occur anymore. The attention of the authorities in the 1970s focused on material effects, not the ideological layer. On the other hand, in the architectural landscape of the 1980s, one can notice an almost total absence of public realizations that could be described as "architecture of power" (Nawratek, 2005, p. 118). The last great prestige realization of the Polish People's Republic should be considered the Łódź Hospital-Monument of the Polish Mother's Health Center (CZMP), designed by architect Janusz Wyżnikiewicz and erected in 1982–1988. It seems significant that the realization was written about primarily in the local press. Industry periodicals such as "Architektura" were silent about it despite its exceptional scale and innovative nature, which illustrates that the circumstances were not conducive to interest in large state investments. The history of the hospital began in 1982, when the first secretary of the Central Committee of the Polish United Workers' Party, Wojciech Jaruzelski, decided to endow society with a monument as a tribute to all Polish mothers. This monument was to be a modern gynaecological and obstetric hospital erected in Łódź (Kulik, 2015, p. 97–98). Thanks to the full approval of the highest authorities and substantial funds allocated for the investment, non-standard solutions were possible. The ceremonial opening of the Memorial Hospital of the Polish Mother's Health Center took place on Mother's Day, 26 May 1988. A helicopter from Warsaw, which was flown by party officials headed by the Chairman of the State Council, landed at the hospital's heliport. However, due to the progressive decay of the socialist state, the inauguration of the CZMP was not fully exploited for propaganda and passed without much echo nationally. The time for the realization of the prestigious and grand constructions of socialism was passing irretrievably.

The prestige realizations served not only to reinforce intra-state historical policy and communist propaganda. They were also elements of rivalry – international and internal, conducted between individual cities or regions.

The central authorities saw the potential for prestigious realizations and confrontations of Polish design thought with the West. Especially when native thought emerged victorious from these confrontations. Image-critical investments were not infrequently accompanied by earlier, state-funded trips by architects to observe Western solutions. When architects Arseniusz Romanowicz and Piotr Szymaniak were preparing to develop the final design of Warsaw's Central Railway Station, they were sent to study the latest developments in the West. Similarly, before construction began, "We were sent abroad to watch and check specific solutions and technologies," – Romanowicz recalled (Romanowicz, 2006). Switzerland, France, and Belgium – the station was a priority investment, and the authorities made every effort to make it look as grand as possible. "In the course of construction, Prime Minister (Piotr) Jaroszewicz, who was taking care of it, only asked what further material needs there were and found the money." Was it worth it? The new train station not only received Leonid Brezhnev visiting Warsaw in 1975 with dignity but also garnered praise behind the "Iron Curtain." Arseniusz Romanowicz repeated years later that the slogan in the English press was "Go to Poland and learn how to design railway stations" (Romanowicz, 2006) (Figure 5.4).

Warsaw's Central Station was not the only building erected in the Polish People's Republic that gained recognition abroad. Of course, for the authorities and the architects themselves, the praise coming from the West was much more valuable, but architectural magazines published in the Soviet Union, Bulgaria, or Czechoslovakia from time to time published information about Polish achievements such

Figure 5.4 Warsaw Central Station, one of the prestigious developments of the "Gierek's decade." Architects Arseniusz Romanowicz and Piotr Szymaniak.

Source: Photograph by the author.

as the Przymorze housing estate in Gdańsk or the Supersam shopping pavilion in Warsaw, built in 1962. The latter was also recognized at the 1965 Architecture Biennale in São Paulo, where its creators, architects Jerzy Hryniewiecki, Maciej Krasiński, and Ewa Krasińska, received an honorary award. On an equal footing with the architects, the constructors Wacław Zalewski, Stanisław Kuś, and Andrzej Żórawski should have been honoured at the time, as it was thanks to them that the hanging steel roof structure based on the use of a tensegrity system was created.

The architectural rivalry at the intra-state level was also passionate, although its effects were not as spectacular as the prestigious realizations directed to the West. For local authorities (municipal or provincial), new investments were a way to strengthen their political position and gain public support. Thus, in agreement with companies operating in the region, they built housing estates, community centres, stadiums, and sports halls. Among these can be highlighted the realizations by Warsaw architect Wojciech Zabłocki, who in 1970 and 1972 designed a sports centre in Konin and Puławy. The former city was associated with a massive aluminium smelter and coal mine, the latter with a large nitrogen plant. In both cases, Zabłocki used a roofing structure inspired by the roof of Warsaw's Supersam. Thanks to the patronage of important industrial plants, the investments gained priority status, and the architect himself was able to benefit from non-standard solutions and special treatment. During construction, a very high quality of workmanship was achieved, which was an exception on construction sites in socialist Poland, where sloppiness and shoddiness usually prevailed. Wojciech Zabłocki could even afford to have the clinker bricks that covered parts of the facade fired in shades that perfectly matched his concept. Similarly, the ceramic tiles that were used in the interior (Zabłocki, 2007, p. 31). The finished project has won recognition from the architectural community. "Against the background of the new districts of Konin, the Sports Hall became a valuable element of both the urban landscape and a vivid accent in the silhouette of the city," Jerzy Hryniewiecki wrote in the pages of "Architektura," emphasizing the outstanding importance of the realization and the quality that testified, in his opinion, to the "enthusiastic attitude of the contractors to a difficult task" (Hryniewiecki, 1972, p. 170) (Figure 5.5).

Of course, prestigious realizations were not created only in smaller cities, such as the aforementioned Puławy or Konin. Those buildings that could become showpieces of the country and the city enjoyed special attention from the authorities. For example, in Cracow, such an object was the Cracovia hotel (architect Witold Cęckiewicz, 1960–1965), and in Katowice, the railway station by Wacław Kłyszewski, Jerzy Mokrzyński, and Eugeniusz Wierzbicki (1959–1973) or the Spodek sports and entertainment hall (architects Maciej Gintowt and Maciej Krasiński, design 1960, construction 1965–1971). However, while in first-tier cities such realizations were somewhat normal, in Konin, with a population of just over 40,000 in 1970, it was the only time in history when local authorities were able to carry out investments on such a scale. The decline and gradual depopulation of Poland's smaller cities after the fall of communism seems only to confirm this.

The Palace of Sports in Konin was built even before the administrative reform, which was carried out in 1975. Until then, the country was divided into 22 provinces

Figure 5.5 Palace of Sports in Konin, a relatively small town connected to the huge industrial site. Architect Wojciech Zabłocki.

Source: Photograph by the author.

(in 1946, there were 16, in 1950, their number was increased to 19, and in 1957 – to 22), but in the mid-1970s Poland was divided into 49 provinces. This opened up a wide range of possibilities for architects and urban planners. Władysław Hennig, who at the time headed the Interprovincial Office of Spatial Planning based in Rzeszów, prepared development plans for the new provincial cities of Krosno, Przemyśl and Tarnobrzeg. It was a special moment. The newly created provincial capitals were getting quite a large injection of investment to prepare for these new functions. Hennig recalled that Przemyśl, for example, "always hoped that it would one day be the capital of the province, but Krosno, for example, was not placed so high in any regional concepts."[5] This involved a great deal of work for planners and architects, who had to encase the new administrative system with appropriate infrastructure.

"Never has any era had to deal with such a scale of investment and with this row of needs, which are multiplying with increasingly bewildering speed" (Szafer, 1988, p. 5), wrote Tadeusz P. Szafer. As part of the modernization policy, the authorities of the Polish People's Republic launched a series of measures aimed not only at rebuilding the country destroyed by the war but also at modernizing it (Majmurek, 2010; Leszczyński, 2013). The accompanying structural transformation associated with the migration of the population from the countryside to the cities, in addition to the development of industry, the expansion of cultural and educational institutions, and the growth of the administrative apparatus have significantly contributed to changing the character of both large centres with a long-established metropolitan status and smaller cities.

Back to the modernism 129

Despite the centralized decision-making apparatus and the concentration of financial resources, one can observe a policy with signs of "decentralization" involving new investments that included outlying localities. As historian and sociologist Adam Leszczyński noted, "new investments, built from scratch, were more desirable than cheaper modernization of existing plants" (Leszczyński, 2013).

The same mechanisms applied not only to factories and combines but also to other functions – from housing to cultural facilities (noting that in successive "five years," the priority areas changed). New investments filled the needs of residents, while at the same time building prestige and allowing to redefine local identity. Interestingly, often scaled-up investments, exceeding the budgetary capabilities of the centres in question, were not implemented in the end, but their momentum shows how high hopes were attached to them. An unambiguous message emerges from the narrative – it was not about a specific building, but about a new perspective, prestige, and a higher place in the phantasmagorical race of cities.

5.3 (Critical) regionalism

When two Cracow architects, Andrzej Skoczek and Zbigniew Radziewanowski, analysed contemporary leisure architecture in southern Poland in the second half of the 1980s, they wrote about the widespread retreat from "some devalued ideas of the Bauhaus" and the past "fascination with Le Corbusier's principles, whose personification in the massing of the Marseille's Block has become more evidence against than for" (Skoczek & Radziewanowski, 1987, p. 6). Their work was another voice in the growing criticism of modernism since the late 1960s (Wujek, 1986), which advocated a turn away from the idea of "international style" in favour of a search for a widely understood genius loci (Stępiński, 1977). The starting point for the further development of modern architecture was to obtain its "identifying character of architecture created in conformity with the character of the place" (Skoczek & Radziewanowski, 1987, p. 7). Not without significance was the fact that both Skoczek and Radziewanowski represented the environment of the Cracow University of Technology and the direction that can be described as the "Cracow School of Architecture." Significant influence on its shape (and the views of the authors of the aforementioned book) had Professor Włodzimierz Gruszczyński, co-founder of the Faculty of Architecture assiduously seeking "large-scale forms for new, contemporary tasks, but closely connected with native art and native landscape" (Rączka, 1996, p. 75–76). He instilled in his students the idea of "creating architecture to match the era, yet one's own, Polish" (Skoczek & Radziewanowski, 1987, p. 4). Gruszczyński's influence went far beyond the single publications authored by his former students. His traces can be found both in the projects and realizations of the time and in the discussion of the role of modern architecture in the process of shaping the cultural landscape.

An interesting example of the search for the local face of modernity was the works submitted to an open competition announced in 1954 for the design of a shelter over the Morskie Oko Lake in the Tatra Mountains. The first prize went to a team of young Cracow architects Krzysztof Bień, Leszek Filar, Jerzy Pilitowski,

130 *Architecture and Architects in Socialist Poland*

Andrzej Skoczek, Przemysław Gawor, and Bogumił Zaufal. The project envisaged the construction of a dismembered block covered with sloping roofs characteristic of the region. Walls faced with broken stone pleasantly contrasted with wooden woodwork and large panes of glazing. In the verdict, the jury clearly emphasized that "the architecture, despite its nature of contrasting with nature, results in harmonization with the surroundings" (Skoczek & Radziewanowski, 1987, p. 103). Przemyslaw Gawor and his colleagues were strongly influenced by Professor Gruszczyński and were fascinated by regional construction. When designing the shelter at Morskie Oko, they managed to "get out of 'urban thinking' into the enchanted circle of 'architecture in the landscape'" (Skoczek & Radziewanowski, 1987, p. 102). Gawor pointed out the peculiarities of Podhale modernism and spoke highly of the post-war architecture of Podhale. "What happened in Zakopane with the participation of Zakopane architects, architects who grew up from highland families, highland traditions, was unique," he stressed.

> Anna Górska from Zakopane was the co-author of virtually all the Tatra mountain shelters built at that time. They were designed precisely in such a regional character. And the hostel in Kościeliska and the hostel on Ornak. The last was the shelter in the Valley of Five Ponds, very nice and beautifully located.[6]

In 1963, Anna Górska herself summarized the architectural achievements of Podhale: "A number of such and other technical shortcomings, however, do not obscure the generally positive, creative and innovative value of the realized objects." She singled out several new developments, including the Sports Training Center, by Skoczek, Zaufal, and Stanisław Karpiel. The characteristic hanging canopy in the form of a parabolic hyperboloid, covering the gymnasium, was a unique combination of modernity and tradition: "the original form of the Gymnasium's roof, the strongly protruding eaves and the use of indigenous materials, the regional character of the architecture was achieved" (Górska, 1963).

Years later, Przemysław Gawor pointed out the inadequate presence, in his opinion, of modernism with a regional tone (Kenneth Frampton would probably call it "critical regionalism") in the discussion of 20th-century architecture in Poland. He stressed that an attempt to search for a positive national identity in architecture was the Harnaś resort in Bukowina Tatrzańska, which he designed in 1962 with Leszek Filar and Jerzy Pilitowski (Figure 5.6). This was the moment when mountain regions became an area of increased investment movement – mainly for recreational facilities, hotels, and spas. In the 1960s, a popular trend was planning the development of architecture in areas with special landscape values, assuming that the concentration of new buildings was the only possible way to meet the growing recreational needs in harmony with environmental protection. Its most important representative was Cracow architect Zbigniew Gądek. "Scattered development takes up too much space, which changes its natural character" – he wrote, and proposed erecting buildings in linear and piled-up layouts (Gądek, 1970). According to the concept of tourist development in the Tatra region, Harnaś was to

Figure 5.6 Harnaś resort in Bukowina Tatrzańska in Tatra Mountain – local reception of modernism, designed in 1962 by Cracow-based architects Przemysław Gawor, Leszek Filar, and Jerzy Pilitowski.

Source: Photograph by the author.

be part of a "structural system capturing a full program of holidays for the entire Bukowina" (Szafer, 1972, p. 276–277). In the end, the system was not built, and Harnaś remained the only testament to the ambitious plans. Completed in 1967, the building was a successful combination of local traditions and the universal characteristics of the modern movement. The dynamic, lightweight body of the building appears almost suspended above the slope. The architects planned the construction of a south-facing single-tenant hotel building, which was justified by the assumed directionality of the scenic exposure to the full panorama of the Tatra Mountains and the provision of equal sunlight conditions for the residential rooms. The visible elements of the reinforced concrete structure were left in the texture of natural concrete with visible traces of wooden formwork. At the first floor level, the walls were to be faced with natural stone from a local stream. In the interiors, decorations with a local character were envisaged, such as a composition with a robber theme by Podhale-based artist Józef Galica.

Kenneth Frampton stressed that critical regionalism "requires a more direct dialectical relationship with nature" (Frampton, 2017, p. 18). He considered it expedient to seek a critical point of contact between the global and local values. Contemporary architecture should maintain a distance from both the universalism of international style and sentimental neo-vernacularism. Coming from the Cracow school of Professor Gruszczyński, the creators of Harnaś consistently pursued the ideas that the author of Towards Critical Regionalism (Frampton, 1983) formulated much later.

A project that combined a large-scale investment with an effort to inscribe the architecture in the local (natural and cultural) context was the Ustroń – Zawodzie spa district designed in 1966 by a duo of Silesian architects, Henryk Buszko and Aleksander Franta (in cooperation with Tadeusz Szewczyk) (Figure 5.7). On the hillside, on an area of nearly 200 ha, the complex consisted of a sanatorium and natural treatment facility, as well as 17 rest houses capable of accommodating more than 6,000 people at a time. Despite the considerable scale of the entire establishment, the design team managed to avoid the impression of monotony. A system of variable forms was adopted – from the long, disjointed body of the sanatorium, through two low long pavilions of the natural treatment facilities, to "a complex

Figure 5.7 Pyramid-shaped spa resorts in Ustroń-Zawodzie district, the largest newly designed health and recreation complex in Poland. Architects: Henryk Buszko, Aleksander Franta, and Tadeusz Szewczyk.

Source: SARP Archive.

Back to the modernism   133

of identical rest houses with shapes associated with traditional Beskid roofs." Thus, not only "tower buildings, which are associated with urban development and always carry a huge risk of deforming the natural mountain landscape," were avoided, but also an attempt was made to create a contemporary, modernist interpretation of regional forms. "Almost all views of the blocks gave triangles and fit into the landscape" – Aleksander Franta told about his idea (Barucki, 2015, p. 53). The white blocks arranged on the mountainside can also evoke associations with natural rock forms scattered on the slope, among the forests.

The search for a new regional architecture continued in People's Poland long before the emergence of postmodern ideas. They were a certain continuation of the attempts to develop a "national style," the beginnings of which dated back to the end of the 19th century. During the years of the reign of the doctrine of socialist realism, they were a "refuge" from the necessity of using forms of "Stalinist empire style." After 1956, with the return to modernity in architecture, the combination of local materials and artistic and construction traditions with new technologies and forms and scale characteristic of late modernism resulted in a number of interesting projects and realizations that are local interpretations of the international style.

5.4   New city centres

The modernization policy of the Polish People's Republic involved the rapid urbanization of the country, which was largely agrarian before the war. The intensity of the process was primarily due to the priorities of the centrally planned economy and rapid industrialization at the time. Between 1946 and 1960, when the census was conducted, the number of urban residents increased from nine to more than fourteen million people, which meant that already nearly half of Poles lived in urban centres (Czarnecki, 2019, p. 62–63). The scale of the process forced a number of new investments in housing (which will be characterized in the next section), infrastructure, and facilities with metropolitan functions. At the same time, the dangers of uncontrolled urbanization began to be recognized as early as the second half of the 1960s. One of them was fringe urban sprawl, as described by architect and researcher of modern architecture Tadeusz P. Szafer, who drew attention to the negative effects of urban sprawl in cities of the United States, warning of the risk of a (relatively small) repetition of a similar scenario in Poland. On top of that, wrote Szafer, fringe development often resulted in the loss of coherence of new development with historic central districts, although, as he stressed, it was less pronounced in fully rebuilt cities such as Gdańsk, Szczecin and Warsaw (Szafer, 1972, p. 197).

In 1960, the first stage of a section of the new centre in Warsaw began – the development of the so-called Eastern Wall, a frontage along Marszałkowska Street, in the immediate vicinity of the Palace of Culture and Science and Parade Square. Plans for the development of this part of downtown had already been made. First, in the spirit of socialist realism, efforts were made to develop a suitable setting for the Parade Square in 1953, and then the development of the Eastern Wall was included as part of the Master Plan of Warsaw in 1957. The final design was selected in 1960 as part of a competition, the winner of which was Warsaw architect Zbigniew

134   *Architecture and Architects in Socialist Poland*

Karpiński. Construction began a year later and was completed in 1969. The composition of the new development was based on two traffic axes – a vehicular one (Marszałkowska Street) and a pedestrian one (a new passage running on the inner side of the quarter). Karpiński created an interesting composition of modern buildings of varying sizes and forms. The height dominant were three 24-storey residential skyscrapers with aluminium panelled facades (architects Zbigniew Wacławek and Jan Klewin were responsible for their final form). Added to this were eight eleven-storey residential blocks. All of them were moved away from the main thoroughfare, the frontage of which was formed by a screen of four cuboidal blocks of department stores acting, in a way, as an acoustic screen. Behind the department stores a shopping arcade was created, along which smaller pavilions were built – Zodiak bar, Relax cinema, or light, glazed rotunda of General Savings Bank (Powszechna Kasa Oszczędności – PKO) constituting an accent closing the composition of the Eastern Wall from the south. Various designers were responsible for the design of the various buildings being built as part of Karpiński's master plan (Figure 5.8). One managed to preserve, in accordance with the general designer's assumption, the homogeneity and large scale of the foreground objects and the intimate character of the back interiors. The modernist architecture of the Eastern Wall itself was considered an "anti-symbol" of the Palace of Culture and Science or, more broadly, of the entire period of socialist realism (Sigalin, 1986, p. 143).

At the end of the 1960s, an urban planning competition was held for the design of the City Center of Warsaw and the Western District of the City Center of Warsaw. The winning team included, among others, Bogdan Wyporek and Jerzy Skrzypczak (Rogowski, 1971). The plan called for the construction of skyscrapers in the form of high point buildings and lower service buildings. As Wyporek recounted, the main guidelines of the project were successfully put into practice.

> In accordance with this competition, two tall buildings were built south of Jerozolimskie Avenue – the Marriott and a skyscraper at 8 Chałubińskiego Street, two buildings of the same height. According to the concept, this principle was to go north with similar buildings to create a system . . . Later this principle was changed because the form of these buildings was different. However, despite the different character, in terms of the concept this is a continuation of our project.[7]

Modernization efforts within the centre of large cities were not limited to Warsaw. In Katowice, instead of having a unified spatial concept, the city's image was being modernized by adding more buildings that had been built over time. The focal point was a large traffic circle, which was later named the traffic circle named after General Jerzy Ziętek, in memory of the Silesian governor, to whom the region, with Katowice at its head, owed a number of new investments. Among others, skyscrapers housing offices and hotels were built in its vicinity, as well as the Coal Industry Design Office building. The futuristic shape of the Spodek sports and entertainment hall was also an important part of the composition of Katowice's new centre.

Figure 5.8 Pedestrian passage in the centre of Warsaw, behind the so-called Eastern Wall. Architect Zbigniew Karpiński. Photograph by Zbigniew Wdowiński.
Source: PAP (Polish Press Agency).

Katowice, however, was an exception, as most centres decided on comprehensive measures similar to those undertaken in Warsaw in the 1960s. Sometimes, they did not bear fruit – as in the case of competitions for new centre projects in Wrocław or Cracow. In other situations, the failure of wide-ranging initiatives necessitated measures that can be described as "spotty." In Gdańsk, which was rebuilt after wartime destruction, the discussion about a modern centre near the old city continued uninterrupted since the late 1940s. In 1963, a nationwide competition was even announced for a development project in the area of Rajska and Heveliusza Streets, where the headquarters of the Supreme Technical Organization (Naczelna Organizacja Techniczna – NOT), the Teacher's House, a hotel, a CDT and a fast-food bar were to be built. The project turned out to be one too costly. Even the preparation of a cost-saving variant with a functional program limited only to the Teacher's House

136 *Architecture and Architects in Socialist Poland*

and the Technician's House (NOT headquarters) did not help. In the end, several unrelated buildings were erected. In 1962, architect Szczepan Baum designed the headquarters of the state project office Miastoprojekt-Gdańsk (completed in 1965). Then, in 1969, the same architect, together with Danuta Olędzka, developed the concept for the NOT building, which was completed in 1974. Meanwhile, the 72-metre tall skyscraper of the Central Shipbuilding Industry Construction and Research Center (architects Stanisław Tobolczyk and Jasna Strzałkowska, 1966–1971) was also built, with an interesting core structure and systemic prefabricated facades of tinted green glass.

The realization of the dream of a modern centre worthy of a metropolis not infrequently involved the complete reconstruction of the downtown area and the demolition of existing buildings. Such was the case in Poznań, where architect Jerzy Liśniewicz in 1960 created a concept for a development complex consisting of three 12-storey office towers connected by a two-storey shopping and service centre. The construction of the Alfa (or Centrum – the two names functioned in parallel) complex was preceded by the demolition of the existing tenement houses at the site, some of which were in good technical condition. Although in the 1960s such actions were not unusual and opposition from the architectural community or historic preservationists was marginal, in retrospect, the assessments are not so clearcut. Poznań architect and researcher Piotr Marciniak admitted that Liśniewicz's project was counter-intuitive, but, at the same time, "one can clearly see in it the inspiration of the latest solutions of the time" (Marciniak, p. 154), thanks to which the new centre of Poznań gained a metropolitan character. It should be emphasized that, in popular perception, metropolitanity was derived from the construction of architecture on a metropolitan (and therefore correspondingly large) scale. The same perception of reality was held by the authorities of Łódź, a city that, like Poznań, had no significant high-rise dominants.

In the mid-1960s, Tadeusz P. Szafer, in an article with the telling title "Łódź odmieniona" (Łódź as changed), wrote that it was "the first big city to start arranging its downtown in an organized manner" (Szafer, 1965, p. 8–9). In June 1964, a "competition was announced to develop a general concept for shaping the disposable-service centre of Łódź within the downtown area to be rebuilt" (Przegalińska-Kruger, 1965). A year later, a team led by architect Aleksander Zwierko and urban planner Wacław Bald prepared a concept for the reconstruction of the inner city. Along Main Street (now Marshall J. Piłsudski Avenue), a complex of four tall office buildings connected by lower pavilions with commercial and service functions was envisioned – a solution twinned with Alfa in Poznań or, to a slightly lesser extent, with the Eastern Wall in Warsaw. The whole thing looked impressive and fulfilled Łódź residents' dreams of a modern centre. It was emphasized that here, in the place of demolished inconspicuous old houses, soaring skyscrapers are rising. The new buildings "by the form of their architecture must emphasize their metropolitanity." Study and design work on the development of the centre of Łódź continued in the following years. In 1968, the Society of Polish Urban Planners announced a closed competition for the design of the Downtown Residential District – a complex of multi-family housing within the historic centre of

Back to the modernism 137

the city. Although a residential function was planned, the anticipated scale was as adequate as possible to the centre of the second-largest city in Poland at the time. A project prepared by a team from Wrocław consisting of Ryszard Żabiński, Mieczysław Sowa, Krzysztof Wiśniowski, and Andrzej Nędzi was sent for implementation (*Problem przebudowy . . .*, 1969). The architects designed multi-family buildings of 18–24 storeys in height, with a stem-and-spoke construction. "These were the early days of the Gierek era. There was pressure to realize some spectacular project in Łódź," Wiśniowski recalled years later.[8] Despite this, work on the realization of the Downtown Residential District did not proceed smoothly. First, it was necessary to change the construction system to a less demanding one, and then the custody of the investment was partly taken over by Miastoprojekt – Łódź, where architect Aleksander Zwierko was responsible for its implementation. The final result was a complex of eight buildings completed in the early 1980s, the tallest of which reached 78 metres. However, this was already a time when the public paid more attention to the shortcomings and deficiencies of the system than to the ambitious modernization plans. The colloquial name of the Downtown Residential District, "Manhattan," took on a bitterly ironic meaning.

Łódź was not the only city to modernize downtown by building its "Manhattan." Wrocław, as it was referred to in the post-war years, was a large city, but not a metropolitan one. At the same time, it had large land reserves within the city limits and the downtown area itself, which, in turn, made it possible to weave ambitious modernization plans. One of them was the development of Grunwald Square, an area near the academic campus, which had been haunted by emptiness and isolated outposts of tenement houses since the end of World War II. Such a location made it possible to introduce buildings on a metropolitan scale to Wrocław, which, at the same time, did not compete with the dominant buildings in the Old Town (Gabiś, 2019, p. 390). Jadwiga Grabowska-Hawrylak was responsible for preparing the project and its subsequent implementation. The first concepts, outlined back in 1963, depicted six point blocks connected by two-storey commercial pavilions. As architectural historian Michał Duda emphasized, Grabowska-Hawrylak experimented and "with successive versions of the project, the internal structure, construction and finally the external appearance of the complex also evolved" (Gabiś, 2019, p. 146). The final form of the buildings was a resultant of the use of prefabricated elements, which the designer was somehow obliged to do, as well as the pursuit of a certain originality and a departure from the simple apartment blocks that filled the space of Polish housing estates. "Since we can't yet afford to model each residential building individually – let's try to arrange 'sculptural' compositions from ready-made, serially reproduced elements" (Piątek, 2006a) (Figure 5.9).

Eventually, the buildings reached a height of 16 storeys. Not only was their scale unusual but also their external form. Although the architect was imposed top-down on the construction system based on the use of "H" frames, the form of the prefabricated exteriors was developed by Grabowska-Hawrylak herself. Unusual solutions, however, enforced greater than generally accepted precision in the manufacturing and assembly process, which was feared by the management of the Wrocław General Construction Company, which was responsible for the investment. "Many

Figure 5.9 "Prefabricated gems," as the local press named them – residential towers and commercial pavilions on Grunwaldzki Square in Wrocław designed by Jadwiga Grabowska-Hawrylak.

Source: Szafer T.P., *Nowa architektura polska: diariusz lat 1971–1975*, Warsaw: Arkady, 1979.

officials and architects considered the project impossible to implement" – wrote Michał Duda (Duda, 2010, p. 160). In turn, the Presidium of the Municipal National Council and the management of Miastoprojekt had doubts, which concerned the excessive cost of implementation. Only when prototype prefabricated elements were made in the workshops of the Wrocław University of Technology did the discussions cease and work began. The architect recalled that when the first of the six skyscrapers was ready and the construction of another was underway, however, the Presidium of the National Council decided to halt the work and demolish what had already been erected. Eventually, the unfavourable decision was changed as a result of the intervention of MP-architect Jerzy Hryniewiecki, who personally came to Wrocław to defend the project. Not without significance was also the fact that

Back to the modernism 139

the aforementioned events coincided with Edward Gierek's visit to France. The First Secretary of the Central Committee of the Polish United Workers' Party visited an exhibition devoted to modern Polish architecture, where Wrocław skyscrapers, among others, were presented. Their striking shapes received an exceptionally favourable reaction from visitors. In such a situation, demolition would have been an action whatever improper, and the "minor intercession of a satisfied dignitary" helped to clarify all the contentious issues (Duda, 2010, p. 162). Despite numerous obstacles, Jadwiga Grabowska-Hawrylak's project was realized. However, it was not without minor modifications. The grey, rough brute concrete was not at all the architect's intention. The prefabricated elements were to be white, while the walls behind the balconies, eventually faced with red ceramic tiles, were designed with dark wood cladding. The entire structure was to be overgrown with lush greenery.

The realization lived to see numerous publications at home and abroad (on both sides of the "Iron Curtain"). The domestic press wrote about the "prefabricated gems" (Rogala, 2016, s. 133). "The very fact that the architectural work provoked the environment and, above all, the residents of Wrocław to fierce discussions, I consider my success" – commented the architect (Chmielewski, 1974). Wrocław art historian Agata Gabiś added years later,

This is the only realized vision of metropolitan Wrocław, in which the fascinations and expectations of the post-war generation of architects, educated on the models of pre-war modernism, but very well versed in the latest world trends, were focused as in a lens. Only Jadwiga Grabowska-Hawrylak managed to put into practice the authorial ideas that her colleagues presented on the competition mockups.

(Gabiś, 2019, p. 400)

5.5 Housing estates

The architecture of the communist era is often, but wrongly, identified with gray, monotonous housing estates of large-panel blocks of flats. In turn, the apartment blocks themselves have been considered a "communist invention" erected using technology from the Soviet Union, ignoring the fact that prefabricated multifamily housing was built after World War II throughout Western Europe, while the prefabrication systems themselves were often created, based on licenses from Germany or Denmark. The first house factory, "Fadom" in Bzie Zameckie near Rybnik, was launched in 1969 under a license purchased from the GDR. Moreover, even in cases where "house factories" or finished building elements came to Poland directly from the USSR, they were based on specific patents from behind the Iron Curtain. An excellent example is the Szczecin blocks of flats in the Kalina and Przyjaźni housing estates, fondly referred to as "leningrads" (Wojtkun, 2008) – the result of a Soviet modification of the Camus heavy prefabrication system purchased in France (Zarecor, 2011). The very idea of a housing estate, which in the West took the form of a neighbourhood unit, while in the Soviet republics, it was a microrayon, had a similar "internationalist" character.

140   *Architecture and Architects in Socialist Poland*

As mentioned in earlier parts of this book, housing development was one of the priorities of the authorities of communist Poland. They aimed to build the maximum amount of housing within the budget funds allocated for this purpose. This was guided by several basic rules: each family was to live in an independent apartment (the end of the pre-war angularity, i.e., the sharing of apartments by several families); the kitchen is not a sleeping area; sleeping more than two people in one room is excluded; the design of apartments in basements is prohibited; each apartment is equipped with its own sanitary facilities (Jarosz, 2010, p. 37). These rules, adopted in the early years of the Polish People's Republic, were not always strictly observed. It is enough to mention the concepts of so-called economical buildings, which, following the Soviet model, had common sanitary facilities for all residents of a given floor. It is worth noting, however, that the introduction of regulations in general influenced the cessation of sub-standard housing construction. One of the most important aspects of top-down regulation that most often came up in discussions about housing in socialist Poland was the square footage of housing units. The permissible area of apartments was regulated by norms, which changed over the years. They determined the size of an apartment depending on the number of people who were to occupy it, which number was denoted by the letter "M" (e.g., M2 meant an apartment for two people, which consisted of a room and a kitchen). And there the 1959 normative specified the following square metres: M1 12–20 m²; M2 24–30 m²; M3 33–38 m²; M4 42–48; M5 51–57; M6 59–65; and M7 67–71. In the following decades, area norms gradually increased, but it should be noted in doing so that the lower values were almost always sought to be maintained.

During the 45 years of Polish People's Republic, more than 5 million housing units were put into use. In the decade of the rule of the First Secretary of the PZPR Central Committee, Edward Gierek (1970–1980) alone – 2.6 million (Jarosz, 2010). Despite these undoubtedly impressive achievements, the huge hunger for housing could not be satisfied. Thus, they sought to increase the number of "tangible effects" (housing units) while lowering quality standards. For the investors, which were local and central governments and state-owned enterprises, it was more important than "how to build" to build at all. The first comprehensive vision of the direction of development of multifamily construction in Poland was presented in 1959 as "Theses on Ensuring the Performance of Construction Tasks in 1959–1965 by Typification of Industrial Production Principles" (Czapelski, 2018, p. 93). The primacy of austerity and industrialization and the related typification of construction became increasingly pronounced in the following years. In 1966, another resolution was issued on the development of typification, and four years later, the party authorities accepted the W-70 system, selected in a competition of the Association of Polish Architects, as a model solution for the future. It was developed by a couple of Warsaw architects Maria and Kazimierz Piechotka.

Despite the pressures of austerity translating into design conditions and construction, architects sought to provide the best possible conditions for future residents – if not through the materials or technologies used, then through the architectural and urban quality of the design itself. Polish architects sought to optimize design solutions, guided by an analysis of the needs of the "average user." They looked with

Back to the modernism 141

envy at countries on the other side of the Iron Curtain, where, as Łódź architect Bolesław Kardaszewski claimed, "the architect can get to know future residents already at the design stage" (Wrońska, 1986; Basista, 2001, p. 70–71). We should read these words more as an expression of a rather naive belief in the ideal conditions for practicing the profession in the mythical "West" than as a knowledge – or experience-supported diagnosis of the actual state of affairs. It should be noted that, although the figure of the "inhabitant," i.e., the future occupant of the apartment, remained unknown practically throughout the development of the project and its subsequent implementation, the architects were quite thorough in analysing the needs of potential users. As Tadeusz P. Szafer stressed, "every person is different, has different requirements and different tastes," but it is up to the designer to determine "typical human needs" (Szafer, 1972, p. 29).

The architects used various tools. One of them was consultations with residents, and in the case of investments carried out in stages, evaluated over time. The most famous case when the users' opinion influenced the final shape of the realization was the Warsaw housing estate Sady Żoliborskie (Żoliborz Orchard) designed by Halina Skibniewska. In turn, during the design of Retkinia in Łódź or Ursynów Północny in Warsaw, architects worked with sociologists and psychologists (Pańkow, 2017). The legitimacy of creating multidisciplinary teams and basing design and implementation activities on analysis was emphasized by Skibniewska, who, while a member of parliament, appealed during the 1972 parliamentary session.

> Our society must not only be a recipient, must not only be a user of housing, but also a participant and co-creator of the process of its construction . . . For whom are we building housing? For the users. And in this connection, the most important thing is to determine what kind of users these are, what their needs are and what their aspirations are. We often forget that need is a living, dynamic matter, that it changes.
>
> (Transcript of the 6th meeting . . .)

Halina Skibniewska's best-known project was the Sady Żoliborskie estate in Warsaw (1958–1962) (Figure 5.10). The name itself came from the existing orchards and gardens in the area, which influenced the final form of the estate, as Skibniewska aimed to preserve as many existing trees (including fruit trees) as possible. The humanistic attitude of the architect to the designed space was evident in the strong attitude of her master, Romuald Gutt. The result was an estate not only filled with vegetation but also maintained a friendly, human scale. It must be admitted that Skibniewska hit a unique moment in the history of Polish architecture after World War II. In the wave of the post-Stalin thaw, the original author's designs were accepted, but there was not yet top-down pressure to use prefabrication wherever possible, and rigorous standardization had not yet been introduced. As a result, Skibniewska had some freedom in the disposition of the site. Can Skibniewska be considered a representative example of an architect struggling with the constraints of the system? "She was in the limelight of the authorities of the

Figure 5.10 Sady Żoliborskie housing estate in Warsaw designed by architect Halina Skibniewska.
Source: Photograph by the author.

time and this activity influenced her brilliant professional career," architect Marta Urbańska described her unique position (Urbańska, 2016, p. 98). Arguably, she was able to do more than others and took advantage of this privilege. Jadwiga Grabowska-Hawrylak emphasized that Skibniewska was genuinely involved in social issues. Sady Żoliborskie, the flagship work of the Warsaw architect, owed its unique shape to her persistence and sensitivity. "She recognized that people in wheelchairs, people chained to their beds, people trapped in cells cannot sit around waiting for the system to change! Everyone has one life, here and now. If she can improve their lot, she will." – This is how architect Ewa Kuryłowicz, a former graduate and doctoral student of Halina Skibniewska, described her actions (Urbańska, p. 101). In the end, 23 multifamily buildings were built on more than 5 hectares of former orchards, with varied forms resulting from the adopted square or elongated rectangular plan. The apartments were small, but as flexible as possible, as the architect wanted to be able to change the interior layout as the family structure changed (e.g., the birth of another child). The author of Sady consulted with residents and modified the designs. She defended the quality of the designed buildings even when she was demagogically accused of "preferring people to live under a bridge." However, she, too, did not protect herself from typification, large

Back to the modernism   143

slabs, and top-down restrictions. The first stage of the Sady Żoliborskie project was implemented in accordance with Skibniewska's ideas. In subsequent stages, she had to introduce more and more changes. In the second stage (Sady II), three 11-storey residential towers were planned, but the architect was ordered to add a fourth as a cost-saving measure. It was also not possible to realize the apartments for people with disabilities designed on the first floors of the buildings. In the third stage (Sady III), Halina Skibniewska already had to use "solutions from the catalogue" (prefabricated elements), but the reinforced concrete skeletal structure (the so-called H-frame) still left her relative freedom in shaping the layout inside the buildings. Finally, Sady IV and Sady V were described by Skibniewska herself as follows, "I was implementing foreign designs from a large slab . . . I only tried to shape urban planning from these buildings" (Skibniewska, 1977, p. 26). Even Skibniewska's high professional and political position (she was a member of the Polish People's Republic's parliament, and her husband, Zygmunt Skibniewski, was chairman of the Committee for Architecture and Urbanism for years) could not defend the architect from top-down pressures.

With the passage of time, the technology, scale, and character of the designed estates changed. While prefabrication dominated from the mid-1960s and the buildings were characterized by their age, the second half of the 1950s abounded in realizations of individual character and intimate scale. In this context, those housing estates which, like the Sady Żoliborskie, were realized in several stages, seem to be extraordinary, which makes it possible to observe how external circumstances influenced the form and execution of the project. The story of the Bielany housing estate in Warsaw, designed by Maria and Kazimierz Piechotka, which has already been described in an earlier chapter as an example of the multi-family architecture of the Socialist-Realist era, was similar. Indeed, the first part of the housing estate was built in the mid-1950s and betrayed some features of socialist realism (such as frontage buildings). Subsequent lots, Bielany II, Bielany III, and Bielany IV, were realized gradually until the end of the next decade. As in the case of Sady Żoliborskie, the following stages of Bielany design and construction involved changes in the form of the neighbourhood, the dimensions of the buildings, and the technologies used. The Bielany II housing estate had an intimate character, consisting of oblong four-story blocks arranged parallel to each other, and behind them (as if inside the whole complex), freely distributed "point" blocks of four and five storeys – as well as low, single-storey terraced housing. At the close of the estate from the northeast stood an impressive tall building on the plan of a three-pointed star (the so-called windmill). The coherence of the entire layout was given by the homogeneous finishing of the facades of the buildings faced with silicate bricks. More high-rise buildings appeared in Bielany III – four ten-story blocks, as well as lower buildings with a galleried layout. Piechotkas increasingly used prefabricated elements, which in their case coincided with their professional interest in industrialized technologies in construction. This was particularly evident in the Bielany IV housing development, where five- and eleven-story residential buildings were created from repetitive sections, while the basic building material was a prefabricated large slab (Piechotka & Piechotka, 2021)

144 *Architecture and Architects in Socialist Poland*

The Piechotkas may have considered themselves the chosen ones of fate, for Bielany was realized as they intended (or at least they didn't recall it being otherwise). Meanwhile, the discrepancy between the original idea and its final realization became a common phenomenon in the work of communist architects. Silesian architect Mieczysław Król designed the "Superjednostka" (Compassed Housing Unit) in Katowice primarily with single people and young (by implication, childless) couples in mind. In practice, however, it often happened that young married couples reared offspring and grew old in cramped apartments, with complicated transportation systems and elevators stopping at every third level. Similar "anthouses," as Tadeusz P. Szafer called this type of multifamily housing, were built in large numbers. Among the most famous are the "wave houses" on the Przymorze housing estate in Gdańsk (Figure 5.11).

The estate itself was a development of the winning 1959 competition concept by Tadeusz Różanski and heralded a new stage in the development of multifamily housing in Poland based on large-scale structures. Różanski's design envisaged that 11-story multi-family buildings stretched east-west would be built on the vast land by the Baltic Sea. The area between them was to be filled with greenery, service facilities, and low, five-story blocks running along a north-south axis. The character of the estate was defined by the tall blocks of considerable length (reaching almost a kilometre) and meandering shape, to which they owed their common name – "wavers." Danuta Olędzka, a Gdańsk-based architect, was responsible for

Figure 5.11 One of the so-called "wave buildings" in the Przymorze housing estate in Gdańsk – large-scale mass housing designed by architect Danuta Olędzka.

Source: Wikimedia Commons, author: Artur Andrzej CC 0.

Back to the modernism 145

their architectural design, who proposed to use a transportation system based on glass-covered galleries. Unfortunately, the cost of implementation turned out to be too high. In the end, a revised version of the project was realized, in which the galleries were open and served each floor, and the apartments had a lighted kitchen and in this situation met optimal conditions.

> The apartments were to be relatively small and economical – not as small as in Katowice's Superjednostka, but also not as spacious as in the blocks of apartments that were erected later. Szafer wrote that "the large scale of the 'Przymorze' buildings does not counteract the small residential cells, but on the contrary, clearly accentuates them." Concentration of residential development was, in his opinion, inevitable, but the Gdańsk "wave buildings" proved that it could realize "essential human needs."
>
> (Szafer, 1972, p. 42)

These needs were indeed at the centre of Polish architects' interests, but reality often negatively verified plans built on noble intentions. When a pair of architects, Oskar and Zofia Hansen, created a project for a housing development in Warsaw on Przyczółek Grochowski, they conducted thorough consultations with future residents trying to adapt the designed space to their particular needs. So what if they did not take into account the socialist state's system of housing allocation, which completely thwarted their efforts. The Przyczółek Grochowski housing estate itself was designed in 1963 and built in 1969–1974 and was an attempt to implement the author's concept of the Linear Continuous System (earlier the Hansens had tried to introduce its principles in the J. Słowacki housing estate project in Lublin). LSC, Linear Continuous System assumed the realization of linear settlement systems running from the south to the north of Poland and the shaping of the surroundings based on organic, flexible patterns (the idea of the so-called Open Form). It was an unusual combination of ideas, such as the ciudad lineal of Arturo Soria and Ebenezer Howard's garden city, providing access to urban infrastructure and proximity to nature characteristic of urban areas. The Hansens introduced horizontal segregation of pedestrian and vehicular traffic and linear segregation of the functional zones of the estate. Added to this was the linear concentration of development characteristic of the LSC. The communication system was connected to the residential zone by introducing open galleries running along the buildings and being "overhead streets."

While the concept of the Linear Continuous System and the Przyczółek Grochowski housing estate emanating from it can be described as a total and innovative idea, most of the housing estates built in People's Poland were based on the assumptions of the Athens Charter and the CIAM experience. An excellent example of this was the Millennium Estate in Katowice, designed in 1960 by Henryk Buszko and Aleksander Franta in cooperation with Marian Dziewoński and Tadeusz Szewczyk. The project of the estate, initially envisioned for 27,000 residents (and eventually for 45,000), was developed over the next 15 years. The last buildings were completed in the mid-1980s and were 27-story residential high-rises with forms resembling corn cobs (to which they owed their common name – corn). Before that, multi-family buildings were built with heights ranging from 5 to 25 storeys and varied forms. The buildings were set up freely, but taking into account the directions of the world, so as to gain the best possible exposure of the apartments. They were surrounded by greenery and comprehensively designed infrastructure. Kindergartens, schools, recreational areas, and pedestrian routes were connected in a well-thought-out system to ensure comfortable and safe movement between the various points of the estate.

While Osiedle Tysiąclecia was still an example of designing a development complex in the modernist spirit, the housing development in Warsaw's North Ursynów was an attempt to break the prevailing paradigm (Figure 5.12). The origins of the project date back to 1971, when a competition was announced for a detailed development plan for the North Ursynów area of Warsaw. The winning work created by three young Warsaw architects Ludwik Borawski, Jerzy Szczepanik-Dzikowski, and Andrzej Szkop "continued and transferred to a new scale the best previous achievements in shaping the residential environment" (Szafer, 1979, p. 11). The new grand estate designed by the young and for the young was to be a showcase of the "new deal." The jury's verdict emphasized the freshness of the concept: "The

Figure 5.12 It must have taken decades for a North Ursynów to meet the expectations of the designers and users. Fragment of the North Ursynów housing estate in Warsaw designed by a team led by architect Marek Budzyński.

Source: Wikimedia Commons, author: Radosław Botev, CC BY-SA 4.0.

arrangement of the development with buildings differentiated in plan and dimensions is spatially correct and has led to a 'scale of distinctiveness' perceptible to the residents of the various complexes" (Borawski, Szczepanik & Szkop, 1975, p. 23). The early 1970s also marked the beginning of Edward Gierek's rule as First Secretary of the Central Committee of the Polish United Workers' Party and an attempt to humanize socialism. The design and implementation of the 208-acre housing development in North Ursynów for 38,000 residents was entrusted to a group of young designers who were just entering the world of serious architecture. The oldest, Marek Budzyński (he replaced the prematurely deceased Borawski), was 33 years old. Szkop and Szczepanik-Dzikowski, who were 6–7 years younger, did not yet have diplomas. "We want Ursynów to be not just an anonymous unit of accountability for planners, but a city district with a face of its own" – said the authors on Polish Radio (Borawski & Szczepanik & Szkop, 1975). Having the green light from the authorities, the architects eagerly got to work. Not a year passed, and the concepts for all the buildings in Ursynów were ready. Housing, schools, health centres, service, and commercial and universal facilities were precisely drawn at a scale of 1:200. Years later Budzyński recalled the then "unbelievable speed of action."[9] Construction work began in January 1972, and less than two years later, in November 1974, the first Ursynów residents moved into their new apartments.

The design of Ursynów Północny assumed the rehabilitation of the street, the separation of pedestrian and vehicular traffic, and the introduction of so-called "pedestrian streets." Instead of rigid geometric arrangements of buildings or quarters and frontages, the designers opted for organicity delineated by soft lines of "pedestrian streets." Along them stood blocks made of large slabs with meandering forms and varying heights within a single building. The estate was designed with a full infrastructure, the individual elements of which were connected into functional sequences (e.g., recreational and educational facilities were tied together by green areas).

The authorities' support did not mean the automatic elimination of all obstacles. Ursynów shared the fate of most housing developments in Polish cities in terms of the implementation (or rather – lack of implementation) of the accompanying program. Ewa Dziekońska, who, together with her husband Marek, was responsible for many of the public facility projects under another prestigious communist-era development, Nowe Tychy, recalled that "almost all the projects landed in the closet, because the housing development had to be implemented."[10] Budzyński claimed that, in the case of Ursynów, "the entire social program was realized at most 20%."[11] Stores and services were in short supply. The schools, which were designed after lengthy consultations with two Pedagogical Institutes, did not work as they should have. They were designed in such a way as to function optimally in a single-shift system, while three-shift operation was enforced. The most serious problem, however, turned out to be communication – "Ursynów was supposed to be a district along the subway, but became a district without communication with the city center" (Bartoszewicz, 1994, p. 7). The subway line was launched in Ursynów only in the mid-1990s. In 1983, the Warsaw weekly "Stolica" reported:

148 *Architecture and Architects in Socialist Poland*

"When the first residents moved in here from 1976 to 1977, no one, including those residents, raised an outcry that along the deserted strip of the future Komisji Edukacji Narodowej (KEN – the Commission of National Education) avenue, the construction of the subway had not yet begun, although it was already known at the time that it would soon become an absolute necessity. Today's Ursynów is just such a settlement of disappointed dreams and disappointed dreamers. Contrary to what journalists suggested, architects tried to change the unfavourable state of affairs, but their responses proved mostly ineffective (Roszewski, 1983). Public transportation was initially virtually non-existent. Budzyński himself said in the 1990s that "everything there is unfinished" and compared the district to "a man without a head, one arm, maybe without two legs" (Bartoszewicz, 1994, p. 7). It took another two decades for the district, which was supposed to be an independent, multifunctional organism, to come to life.

Despite a number of shortcomings and implementation problems, the cases described above were positive exceptions rather than the rule. The reality looked decidedly worse. When, in the second half of the 1970s, the Association of Polish Architects conducted an analysis of nearly 200 housing estates built or intended to be built using industrialized methods, the results showed a very unfavourable picture of Polish multifamily housing construction. Notably, 80% of the developments were typical blocks of flats. In 57 housing estates (i.e., more than a quarter of all surveyed complexes) there were only two types of buildings. Buildings with a varied plan or height were recorded in only 26 cases (15%). The question of the urban composition of the settlements was similar. Seventy-five settlements had, according to the criteria adopted in the evaluation, a composition that was completely monotonous and led to topographical disorientation. Only in every second settlement, a clear spatial arrangement was achieved. Many architects were aware of this state of affairs and its causes. Moreover, as early as the 1970s, they warned of the serious consequences of neglect in the area of multifamily housing.

In the mid-1960s, in order to streamline investments, it was decided to subordinate design offices to the construction industry. The architect's control over the implementation of the concept and thus his influence on the final shape of the building was reduced. The entire process was largely subordinated to construction companies, for which simple and schematic solutions were optimal. Wojciech Jarząbek recalled that, during the construction of the Nowy Dwór estate in Wrocław, individually designed prefabricated units were rejected by the contractor. Nevertheless, he carried out the author's supervision. So what if the "whole litany of comments" he prepared were "completely ignored in the protocols" by the contractors and administration?[12] In 1978. SARP's then-president Tadeusz Mrówczyński, author of, among other projects, the Gocław – Airport housing development in Warsaw, provided an assessment of the professional situation of architects that could be considered the voice of the entire community.

> We architects are not, practically speaking, authors of projects, but producers of documentation. The word project, moreover, is disappearing. What's more, we have become just one of the cogs of the documentation-producing

Back to the modernism   149

machine . . . design documentation, which is often changed beforehand in the framework of agreements and approvals, takes its final shape only on paper, because it constitutes a kind of score for the builders . . . which can be interpreted at will.

(Szafer, 1988, p. 7)

Contractors had a say not only in the construction of individual buildings but also in the way entire neighbourhoods were laid out. "The layout of the space is most often schematic, adapted to the track of the cranes," MP-architect Bolesław Kardaszewski said in 1976 during a session of the Parliamentary Construction Commission (*Transcript of the meeting of the Parliament committee . . .*). Kardaszewski was also echoed by Halina Skibniewska, who in 1980 drew MPs' attention to the piled-up unsolved problems of the construction industry.

> In recent years, attention has turned more to contractors, less to investors, and insufficiently to users . . . there has been widespread criticism of the scale of development, convenient for contractors so-called "antebellum" and "skyscraper" buildings, symbols of a kind of apparent prestige, but in reality high costs and social disadvantages.

The situation did not inspire optimism. "It seems that precisely in the field of housing we have not made as much progress as in other areas of our lives" (*Transcript of the 3rd meeting . . .*). Statements by planners and politicians indicate that the housing situation appeared to be a choice between "to be" and "to have." At least, this is how it was portrayed by party decision-makers, who, in their search for savings, gave up many elements that constitute the value of architecture. Besides, they often identified the sources of problems not where they actually lay. In 1972, MP Jan Mariański, later director of the design office Miastoprojekt – Gdańsk, looked for a recipe to improve the situation of the Polish construction industry in raising the quality of executive work and simplifying the bureaucratic system:

> The elimination of any unreliability in the work of the foreman, worker or engineer, the elimination of excessive forms, forms and writings, the social condemnation of slackers and do-nothings will lead to the rapid implementation of tasks. We should constantly strive for the only sanctified value to be the result of wise and diligent work.

(Transcript of the 8th meeting . . .)

Reality, however, often presented a different picture. It is worth recalling at this point once again Kardaszewski, who wanted "the social (working) class once underprivileged . . . to live in magnificent, bold, close-to-human architecture." One of the attempts to realize these ideas was the multi-family residential buildings erected in downtown Łódź on Zamenhoffa Street. They were appreciated by both the public and the architectural community (second-degree award from the Minister of Construction and Building Materials Industry, 1984), but despite this, the

150 *Architecture and Architects in Socialist Poland*

designer repeatedly expressed his dissatisfaction with the level of workmanship. "Perhaps I should sing a paean of praise to the construction company . . . I should be grateful. But I'm not. The building was botched and it couldn't have been any other way," said an embittered Bolesław Kardaszewski in 1986 in an interview with the Łódź weekly "Odgłosy" (Wrońska, 1986).

With the passage of time, interest in "block housing" has contributed to some extent to their partial rehabilitation. As late as 2001, Andrew Basista wrote that "it can be presumed that the volume built under market economy conditions could be immeasurably larger," and the resulting "effects would certainly be better"(Basista, 2001). Less than two decades later, his optimism may have seemed somewhat naive. The new housing complexes that were realized under the conditions of a free market economy are often evaluated critically. Modern multifamily construction presents a wide spectrum of individually designed masses and elevations, but "in reality, incredibly standardized apartments are being built in Poland" (Kępiński, 2019), and the place of norms has been taken by . . . the creditworthiness of future tenants.

Notes

 1 Witold Milewski, conversation with the author, Poznań, 29.07.2013.
 2 Jerzy Gurawski, conversation with the author, Poznań, 12.08.2020.
 3 Tadeusz Mycek, conversation with the author, Warsaw, 24.05.2013.
 4 Witold Cęckiewicz, conversation with the author, Cracow, 08.01.2015.
 5 Władysław Hennig, conversation with the author, Rzeszów, 11.07.2014.
 6 Przemysław Gawor, conversation with the author, Cracow, 12.04.2019.
 7 Bogdan Wyporek, conversation with the author, 06.08.2020.
 8 Krzysztof Wiśniowski, conversation with the author, online, 12.02.2021.
 9 Marek Budzyński, conversation with the author, Warsaw, 16.09.2014.
10 Ewa Dziekońska, conversation with the author, Tychy, 05.02.2021.
11 Marek Budzyński, conversation with the author, Warsaw, 16.09.2014.
12 Wojciech Jarząbek, conversation with the author, Wrocław, 24.04.2019.

References

Bartoszewicz, D., *Architekt marzeń państwowych. Z Markiem Budzyńskim rozmawia Dariusz Bartoszewicz* [The architect of the state's dreams. Dariusz Bartoszewicz interviews Marek Budzyński], "Magazyn Gazety," 17.06.1994.

Barucki, T., *Ogólnopolska Narada Architektów* [National Meeting of Architects], Warsaw: SARP, 1956.

Barucki, T., *Zielone konie – Henryk Buszko, Aleksander Franta, Jerzy Gottfried* [The Green Horses – Henryk Buszko, Aleksander Franta, Jerzy Gottfried], Warsaw: Salix Alba, 2015.

Basista, A., *Betonowe dziedzictwo. Architektura w Polsce czasów komunizmu* [Concrete heritage. Architecture in communist Poland], Warsaw-Cracow: PWN Scientific Publishing House, 2001.

Benedek, W. & Niewiadomski, S., *Uniwersytet Gdański* [Gdańsk University], "Architektura" 1971, no. 6.

Borawski, L., Szczepanik, J. & Szkop, A., *Ursynów Północny w Warszawie* [North Ursynów in Warsaw], "Architektura" 1975, no. 1–2.

Chmielewski, M., *Wrocławska sensacja. Nagroda SARP 1974* [Wrocław sensation. SARP prize 1974], "Trybuna Ludu" 1974, no. 240.

Back to the modernism 151

Cymer, A., *Architektura w Polsce 1945–1989* [Architecture in Poland 1945–1989], Warsaw: Centrum Architektury, 2018.

Czapelski, M., *Moduły i wieżowce. Polscy architekci wobec przemian w budownictwie mieszkaniowym 1956–1970* [Modules and skyscrapers. Polish architects and the transformation of housing construction 1956–1970], Warsaw: Neriton, 2018.

Czarnecki, A., *Urbanizacja kraju i jej etapy*, [in:] *Ciągłość i zmiana. Sto lat rozwoju polskiej wsi* [Continuity and change. A hundred years of development in the Polish countryside], vol. 1, eds. M. Halamska, M. Stanny, J. Wilkin, Warsaw: PAN – Scholar, 2019.

Duda, M., *Patchwork. Architektura Jadwigi Grabowskiej-Hawrylak* [Patchwork. Architecture by Jadwiga Grabowska-Hawrylak], Wrocław: Museum of Architecture, 2010.

Frampton, K., *Towards a Critical Regionalism: Six Points for an Architecture of Resistance*, [in:] *The Anti-Aesthetic: Essays on Postmodern Culture*, ed. H. Foster, Port Townsend: Bay Press, 1983.

Frampton, K., *W stronę krytycznego regionalizmu. Sześć punktów architektury oporu* [Towards a Critical Regionalism: Six Points for an Architecture of Resistance], "Autoportret" 2017, no. 2(57).

Gabiś, A., *Całe morze budowania. Wrocławska architektura 1956–1970* [A whole sea of construction. Architecture in Wrocław 1956–1970], Wrocław: Museum of Architecture, 2019.

Gądek, Z., *Rekreacja a środowisko naturalne*, "Architektura" 1970, no. 12.

Górska, A., *Przegląd dorobku architektonicznego Zakopanego i okolic*, "Architektura" 1963, no. 5.

Hryniewiecki, J., Koniński przykład architektury sportowej, "Architektura" 1972, no. 5–6, s. 170.

Janković-Beguš, J. *"Between East and West": Socialist Modernism as the Official Paradigm of Serbian Art Music in the Socialist Federal Republic of Yugoslavia*, "International Journal of Music Studies" 2017, vol. 1, s. 149.

Jarosz, D., *Mieszkanie się należy . . . Studium z peerelowskich praktyk społecznych* [The flat is due . . . A study from the communist social practices], Warsaw: ASPRA, 2010.

Kardaszewski, B., *Dzielnica Wyższych Uczelni: Instytut Fizyki Uniwersytetu Łódzkiego* [Higher Education District: University of Łódź Phisics Institute], "Architektura" 1986, no. 429.

Karpińska, M., *Scenografie polityki historycznej. Realizacje pomnikowe Witolda Cęckiewicza z epoki rządków Władysława Gomułki* [Scenographies of historical policy. Monumental realizations of Witold Cęckiewicz from the era of Władysław Gomułka's rule], [in:] *Witold Cęckiewicz. Socrealizm, socmodernizm, postmodernizm. Eseje* [Witold Cęckiewicz. Socrealizm, socmodernizm, postmodernizm. Esseys], vol. 2, eds. M. Karpińska, D. Leśniak-Rychlak, M. Wiśniewski, Cracow: Instytut Architektury, 2015.

Kępiński, K., *Produkt osiedle* [Product Housing Estate], "Autoportret" 2019, no. 1(64).

Kulik, A., *Józef Niewiadomski. Wywiad rzeka z prezydentem Łodzi w latach 1978–1985* [Józef Niewiadomski. An extended interview with the president of Łódź from 1978 to 1985], Łódź: Księży Młyn, 2015.

Leszczyński, A., *Skok w nowoczesność. Polityka wzrostu w krajach peryferyjnych 1943–1980* [A leap into modernity. Growth policy in peripheral countries 1943–1980], Warsaw: Krytyka Polityczna, 2013.

Majmurek, J., *PRL jako projekt modernizacji peryferyjnej*, [in:] *PRL bez uprzedzeń* [PRL bez uprzedzeń], eds. J. Majmurek, P. Szumlewicz, Warsaw: Książka i Prasa, 2010.

Marciniak, P., *Architektura i urbanistyka Poznania w latach 1945–1989*Poznań, [in:], *Architektura i urbanistyka Poznania w XX wieku*, ed. T. Jakimowicz, Poznań: Posnania, 2005.

Marciniak, P., *Doświadczenia modernizmu. Architektura i urbanistyka Poznania w czasach PRL,* Poznań: Posnania, 2010.

Marcinkowski, H., *Projekt – miasto. Wspomnienia poznańskich architektów 1925–2005* [Project – city. Memories of Poznań architects], Poznań: Posnania, 2013.

152 *Architecture and Architects in Socialist Poland*

Miłobędzki, A., *Architektura ziem Polski* [Architecture of Poland], Cracow: Międzynarodowe Centrum Kultury, 2014.

Mycek, T., *Spotkania z mistrzami. Portrety 63 architektów polskich* [Encounters with the Masters. Portraits of 63 Polish architects], Warsaw: Nask-Service, 1998.

Nawratek, K., *Ideologie w przestrzeni – próby demistyfikacji* [Ideologies in space – attempts at demystification], Cracow: TAiWPN Universitas, 2005.

Pańkow, L., *Bloki w słońcu. Mała historia Ursynowa Północnego*, Wołowiec: Czarne, 2017.

Piątek, G., *Jadwiga Grabowska-Hawrylak. Rzeźba w prefabrykacie. Rozmawiał Grzegorz Piątek*, "Architektura-Murator" 2006a, no. 11.

Piątek, G., *Witold Milewski, Zygmunt Skupniewicz, Lech Sternal. Za mało kresek* [Witold Milewski, Zygmunt Skupniewicz, Lech Sternal. Too few lines], "Architektura" 2006b, no. 12.

Piechotka, M. & Piechotka, K., *Maria i Kazimierz Piechotkowie – wspomnienia architektów* [Maria and Kazimierz Piechotka – memories of architects], Warsaw: Dom Spotkań z Historią, 2021.

Popławski, B., *Projektowanie szkół wyższych* [University planning], Warsaw: Arkady, 1982.

Problem przebudowy Śródmiejskiej Dzielnicy Mieszkaniowej w Łodzi, Materiały z konkursu TUP nr 11/68, Łódź: TUP, 1969.

Przegalińska-Kruger, H., *Konkurs na centrum Łodzi* [Competition for the center of Łódź], "Architektura" 1965, no. 6.

Rączka, J.W., *Kroniki 50-lecia Wydziału Architektury Politechniki Cracowskiej*, Cracow: Cracow University of Technology, 1996.

Rogala, J., *Prefabrykowane cacka* [Prefabricated gems], "Tygodnik Polski": After: Ł. Wojciechowski, *Jadwiga Grabowska-Hawrylak*, *Architektki* [Female architects], ed. E.T. Kunz, Cracow: EMG, 2016.

Rogowski, L., *Centrum Warszawy. Konkurs zamknięty SARP nr 456* [Center of Warsaw. Closed competition SARP No. 456], "Architektura" 1971, no. 9.

Romanowicz, A., *Zostaliśmy w cieniu* [We were left in the shade], "Architektura" 2006, no. 6.

Roszewski, W., *Zbiorowisko rodzin* [Family community], "Stolica" 1983, no. 51.

Różański, M., *Uniwersytet Mikołaja Kopernika w Toruniu* [Nikolai Copernicus University in Toruń], "Architektura" 1971, no. 6.

Samujłło, J., *Realizacje i projektu budynków szkolnictwa wyższego w Łodzi* [Realizations and projects of higher education buildings in Łódź], "Architektura" 1970, no. 8.

Sigalin, J., *Warszawa 1944–1980. Z archiwum architekta* [Warsaw 1944–1980. From the architect's archive], vol. 3, Warsaw: PIW, 1986.

Skibniewska, H., *Problemy z Witruwiusza* [Problems from Vitruvius], "Architektura" 1977, no. 3–4.

Skoczek, A. & Radziewanowski, Z., *Architektura rekreacji na obszarach Polski południowej* [Leisure architecture in southern Poland], Cracow: Cracow University of Technology, 1987.

Skolimowska, A., *Modulor Polski. Historia osiedla Za Żelazną Bramą* [Polish Modulor. History of the housing estate Za Żelazną Bramą], [in:] *Mister Warszawy. Architektura mieszkaniowa lat 60. XX wieku* [Mister Warsaw. Residential architecture of the 1960s], eds. Ł. Gorczyca, M. Czapelski, Warsaw: Raster, 2012.

Stefański, K. & Ciarkowski, B., *Modernizm w architekturze Łodzi XX wieku* [Modernism in the architecture of 20th-century Łódź], Łódź: Księży Młyn, 2018.

Stępiński, Z., *Wejchertowie. Wokół miasta, wywiad Z. Stępińskiego z H. Adamczewską-Wejchert i K. Wejchertem* [The Wejcherts. Around the city, interview with H. Adamczewska-Wejchert and K. Wejchert by Z. Stępiński], "Architektura" 1977, no. 3–4.

Szafer, T.P., *Łódź odmieniona* [Łódź transformed], "Fundamenty" 1965, no. 8.

Szafer, T.P., *Nowa architektura polska: diariusz lat 1965–1970* [New Polish Architecture: A Diary of the Years 1965–1970], Warsaw: Arkady, 1972.

Szafer, T.P., *Nowa architektura polska: diariusz lat 1971–1975* [New Polish Architecture: A Diary of the Years 1971–1975], Warsaw: Arkady, 1979.

Szafer, T.P., *Współczesna architektura polska* [Contemporary Polish architecture], Warsaw: Arkady 1988.

Transcript of the 3rd meeting of the first session of the Sejm, Warsaw, 22.05.1980.

Transcript of the 6th meeting of the second session of the Sejm, Warsaw, 19.10.1972.

Transcript of the 8th meeting of the second session of the Sejm, Warsaw, 16.12.1972.

Transcript of the meeting of the Parliament committee on construction and building materials, BPS 34/VII term, Warsaw, 25.05.1976.

Trębacz, W., *Obraz Panoramy Racławickiej w obiektywie "bezpieki"* [Image of the Racławice Panorama through the lens of the 'security services'], "Biuletyn IPN" 2007, no. 3(74).

Uchwała nr 126 Rady Ministrów z dnia 13 maja 1966 r. w sprawie dalszego rozwoju typizacji w budownictwa [Resolution No. 126 of the Council of Ministers of May 13, 1966, on the further development of standardization in construction].

Urbańska, M., *Halina Skibniewska. Architektura, społeczeństwo, władza?* [Halina Skibniewska. Architecture, society, power?], [in:] *Architektki* [Female architects], ed. E.T. Kunz, Cracow: EMG, 2016.

Wojciechowski, Ł., *Pierwsze w Polsce: muzeum w krajobrazie* [A first in Poland: A museum in the landscape], "Architektura-Murator" 2014, no. 1.

Wojtkun, G., *Wielorodzinne budownictwo mieszkaniowe w Polsce. W cieniu wielkiej płyty* [Multi-family housing in Poland. In the shadow of large slab], "Przestrzeń i Forma" 2008, no. 10.

Wrońska, J., *Requiem dla nieboszczki* [Requiem for the deceased], "Odgłosy" 1986, no. 8.

Wujek, J., *Mity i utopie architektury XX wieku* [Myths and utopias of 20th-century architecture], Warsaw: Arkady, 1986.

Zabłocki, W., *Architektura* [Architecture], Olszanica: Bosz, 2007.

Zachwatowicz, J., *Budownictwo i architektura w Polsce 1945–1956* [Construction and architecture in Poland 1945–1966], Warsaw: Interpress, 1968.

Zarecor, K.E., *Manufacturing a Socialist Modernity: Housing in Czechoslovakia, 1945–1960*, Pittsburgh: University of Pittsburgh Press, 2011.

Z pracowni architektów Bolesława Kardaszewskiego i Włodzimierza Nowakowskiego [From the studio of architects Bolesław Kardaszewski and Włodzimierz Nowakowski], "Architektura" 1973, no. 6–7.

6 Post-soc-modernism

6.1 Post-socmodernism or soc-postmodernism?

How to overtake the Athens Charter? – wondered in 1980 by the editors of the monthly magazine "Architektura" (Bruszewski, 1982). The criticism of modernism, both in the sphere of practice and ideas, coincided in Poland with the political and economic crisis. When the 14th World Congress of the UIA (International Union of Architects) was held in Warsaw in 1981, some of its participants paid more attention to the ongoing so-called Solidarity carnival than to the papers and accompanying panel discussions (Crowley, 2018). Besides, the line between architecture and politics was very blurred at the time. A congratulatory letter to the designers was addressed by Pope John Paul II, and attendees were able to see a preview of Andrzej Wajda's film "Man of Iron." In turn, the deliberations themselves, and above all the visit of Charles Jencks, preceded by a series of publications on the essence of postmodernism, guided the transformations in domestic architecture of the next decade. It is worth noting that they anticipated changes in the political or economic sphere (Kurnicki, 2018).

Postmodernism, which in the realities of the West was a trend oscillating between populism (Sławińska, 1995) and the free-market turn of the times of Ronald Reagan and Margaret Thatcher, in communist-ruled Poland became a current of resistance to power. It was "a symbol of the renewal of architectural life during the 'Solidarity carnival'" (Sepioł, 2015, p. 28). Not coincidentally, the postmodern turn, which restored continuity, manifested itself forcefully in sacred architecture (Cichońska & Popera & Snopek, 2016) (Urban, 2021). Architects and Catholic Church representatives openly criticized "modernist forms" that are "derivative of the whole ideology born together with the house factories" (Budzyński & Wicha, 1982) and "imagination raped by Le Corbusier" (Pasierb, 1983, p. 67).

At this point, it is necessary to ask the question – what was postmodernism in Polish architecture and can we talk about its local distinctiveness and specificity (Węcławowicz-Gyurkovich, 1998)? What role did architectural theory and criticism play in its development? Architecture researcher Lidia Klein noted that "postmodernism in Poland lacked the theoretical background that accompanied American or Western European realizations" (Klein, 2013, p. 7). This is confirmed

DOI: 10.4324/9781003603153-7

by the voices of designers who implemented the new tendencies in the architecture of the declining communist Poland (Gzowska & Klein, 2013).

At the same time, in the 1980s, architects stressed that Polish postmodernism should remain "post" in relation to domestic modernism (Kardaszewski, 1996, p. 8). Although this thought was not developed at the time, it is worthwhile to dwell on it and consider the semantics. After all, if we use the term "socmodernism" (despite its limitations) to refer to modern architecture in the countries of the so-called Eastern Bloc, then perhaps we should speak of "post-socmodernism" as its logical successor. This seems justified for historical reasons. Postmodern (or post-socmodern) architecture was not only an expression of opposition to authority but also an attempt to "humanize" the system, as discussed by Cracow architect Romuald Loegler, who stressed that in the 1980s " 'consent' to postmodernism was a matter of the policy of the then authorities" (Gzowska & Karpińska & Leśniak-Rychlak, 2018, p. 13).

Regardless of the assessment of Polish postmodernism – whether as a phenomenon secondary to Western trends or bearing the mark of originality, it brought a significant revival to the domestic architectural discourse. The generation born in the 1940s and 1950s came to the fore. The generational rebellion was directed against the teacher-modernists. The young angry ones absorbed Western innovations. They read Jane Jacobs, Charles Jencks, and Christopher Alexander. They became enthralled with the deconstructivism of Peter Eisenmann and the work of James Stirling. The result of their reflections and the resulting design and implementation activities was postmodernism, which was as much "post to Polish modernism" as it was a reflection of currently fashionable trends in Western architecture. Trends with which they were able to familiarize themselves not through imported literature or articles in "Architektura," but personally, while working abroad. It is not a coincidence that native pioneers worked in Western Europe – in France (Czesław Bielecki), Austria (Romuald Loegler), Denmark (Marek Budzyński), or Finland (Jakub Wujek), or in the Middle East (Wojciech Jarząbek, Krzysztof Wiśniowski), where they could also come into contact with representatives of new trends in architecture.

Describing his experience during his time working in Kuwait, Wojciech Jarząbek recalled that, initially, the challenge was to reflect the "spirit of Islam" in the designed objects. "I began to apply the postmodern convention, in my understanding of the word, based on the books of Charles Jencks, the works of (Robert) Graves or (James) Stirling." Nevertheless, he stressed that he did not feel he was a postmodern architect. "I read that one of the markers of postmodernism was quotes from history. I think Graves said that, and Jencks adopted it as the canon of postmodern architecture," he said. – recounted the author of Wrocław's Solpol department store, an architectural icon of the times of political transformation and Polish postmodernism, which Jarząbek himself said he thought was "more deconstructivist."[1]

Associations with deconstructivism may be evoked by the early work of Romuald Loegler (Figure 6.1). When asked about the relationship between his

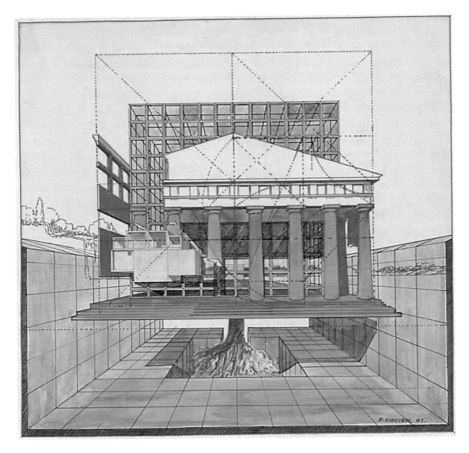

Figure 6.1 The form released out of order – drawing by architect Romuald Loegler.
Source: Museum of Architecture.

own achievements and the work of one of the leading representatives of the trend, American architect Peter Eisenmann, however, he remained reserved.

> Eisenmann placed great emphasis on the architectural-geometric dimension of the structure of the buildings he designed, and he believed that this rigor he imposed on himself was some kind of discipline of thought. And this largely coincides with my thoughts, but . . . I'll admit that this is the first time I've heard such a comparison. I think you could actually find a common denominator.[2]

Loegler pointed to experiences from studying classical architecture and its impact on modern times.

> I came to the conclusion that the value of classical architecture lies primarily in a great discipline of thought, which did not deprive it of artistic qualities,

but gave credibility to the proportions by a certain rule, which everyone, relating the modules to the human scale, began to understand as beauty, even if they did not feel it emotionally. A certain degree of objectification of the aesthetic qualities of architecture was created.

Indeed, an analysis of the diagrams created, both by Eisenman and Loegler, to justify certain design decisions reveals the overriding role of modules that organize architectural space. If we look at the diagrams of Case Study House III, published in the pages of "L'Architecture d'Aujourd'hui" in 1972, and concepts a few years younger by the Cracow architect, we can easily see some similarities. Loegler described the design work as building a form, based on a "spatial aesthetic module," by subtracting or adding submodules. This is how a house in Cracow's Ehrenberg Street was created in 1977, representing "an example of first attempts."[3] "It is not only the spatial structure that is the result of the adopted order. Its proportions are determined by the arrangement and mutual relation of the three cubes" – the author wrote years later (Loegler, 2001, p. 40). The "Florek" house in Cracow, completed a decade later, was based on a composition full of tensions and contrasts, using an "Eisenmanesque" rectangular skeleton, which Loegler derived from abstract art. "To the simple geometric solid of a recumbent prism with modular divisions is "added" at an acute angle a curved trellis, creating abstract raster divisions, transferred as if from op-art objects" (Loegler, 2001, p. 58).

Was Polish postmodern architecture really just a reflection of Western trends? Or, on the contrary, was it the result of individual creative explorations, whose similarity to what others were designing resulted from the intellectual climate of the era? It seems impossible to find unequivocal answers to these questions. However, their significance for the consideration of the history of Polish architecture is, in the author's opinion, marginal. It seems much more important that in the second decade of the 21st-century postmodernism in Polish architecture has become an "orphan." "There is no such thing in my practice that I would call postmodernism," said Łódź-based architect and urban planner Jakub Wujek (Gzowska & Klein, 2013, p. 152). Although for a dozen years or so it was a substitute for the West, a capitalist "forbidden fruit" in the coarse reality of declining socialism, after the first decade of freedom, when it informally played the role of "official style," postmodernism shared the fate of socialist realism. Architects were reluctant to admit participation in this trend, and when characterizing their achievements, they sought other terms (deconstructivism and eclecticism).

Many architects directly objected to being labelled a "postmodernist." "The moment postmodernism appeared in my thinking, I was simply an anti-modernist. Ideologically, philosophically, professionally," declared Warsaw architect-dissident Czesław Bielecki, in a conversation with architecture historians Alicja Gzowska and Lidia Klein (Gzowska & Klein, 2013, p. 70). Other architects spoke in a similar vein. Wojciech Jarząbek strongly dissociated himself from being included in the ranks of postmodernists (Gzowska & Klein, 2013, p. 202). Marek Budzyński spoke of "humanizing buildings, spaces" mutilated by modernism Gzowska & Klein, 2013, p. 8–13), and Jakub Wujek added that "postmodernism in Poland was not postmodernism as such" (Gzowska & Klein, 2013, p. 116). Perhaps one

158 *Architecture and Architects in Socialist Poland*

should wonder whether Polish postmodernism (soc-postmodernism) was not primarily anti-modernism (anti-socmodernism), which was constituted in the process of negation of the status quo.

6.2 Churches in the socialist state – architecture of resistance

Sacred architecture in People's Poland is a subject surrounded by a nimbus of legends and insinuations. For many, the very fact of building churches in a state with a socialist and programmatically anti-church system seems incomprehensible, while others point out that never in the history of Poland have so many temples been erected as "during communism." Some will draw attention to the formal imperfection of many realizations, while others will point to the liveliness that individually shaped blocks bring to the monotonous tissue of housing estates. Formal dissimilarity was described in a beautiful, metaphorical way by the authors of the book "Architecture of the Seventh Day." Looking from the height of the thirteenth floor at Katowice's Millennial Housing Estate, they pondered the genesis of the differences between the simple modernist blocks of flats designed by Henryk Buszka, Aleksander Franta, Tadeusz Szewczyk, and Marian Dziewoński and the organic, almost baroque shapes of the Church of the Elevation of the Holy Cross. Elevation of the Holy Cross and Our Lady of the Healing of the Sick were designed by the same artists. "There were two parallel architectures in People's Poland," ruled. Modernist "architecture of the six working days" and "architecture of the seventh day – churches . . . complementing and spiritually individualizing the thoroughly rationally planned space of the People's Republic" (Cichońska & Popera & Snopek, 2016, p. 30–32).

Architecture of the Seventh Day by Izabela Cichońska, Karolina Popera, and Kuba Snopek is a broad and in-depth analysis of the phenomenon that was Polish sacred architecture in the years 1945–1989. An attempt at its comprehensive characterization would therefore lead to inevitable repetitions and, given the cross-sectional nature of this book, simplifications. In view of this, the leading problem to which the reader's attention will be drawn is the attitude of the Church as a patron of architecture, seen from the perspective of those directly affected by it – architects.

For the first three decades of the Polish People's Republic, the communist authorities effectively hindered the construction of new temples (Opaliński, 2018). Permission to build a church could be obtained for the reconstruction or expansion of an existing building (Basista, 2001, p. 146). However, the realization of a new building was a much bigger problem, and "new temples were built in an atmosphere of constant struggle with the state" (Cichońska & Popera & Snopek, 2016, p. 167). Party decision-makers made attempts to block religious investments, although the chaotic, haphazard nature of such actions may indicate the lack of a specified policy of the authorities in this matter. On more than one occasion, however, the Church and architects acted on the basis of "accomplished facts, without the appropriate permits from administrative and political authorities" (Basista, 2001, p. 146).

When Gdańsk architect Szczepan Baum set about designing a temple in a small seaside town of Władysławów in the late 1950s, the striking modernist structure

Post-soc-modernism   159

was an extension of a small neo-Gothic church from 1930. The pre-war building was skillfully integrated into the modern body and was to play the role of a presbytery. A similar ploy was used a quarter century later in Ciechocinek by architect and preservationist Jan Tajchman. In the context of growing pastoral needs and the expectations of the faithful, it became necessary to build a new church, or, in the face of opposition from the authorities, to expand the existing one. Tajchman, initially sceptical, yielded to the bishop's persuasions, but the needs of the people proved decisive. So instead of a new church, a spacious transept and chancel were added to the existing 19th-century building.

The situation changed in the mid-1970s. Restrictive policies of the authorities were significantly relaxed, resulting in a real explosion of church construction. The days of building fortes were over. Construction was being done a lot and on a grand scale. Unfortunately, as architect and lecturer Konrad Kucza-Kuczynski stated, the new churches "from the point of view of architectural craftsmanship presented a level that did not qualify for any stylistic evaluation at all" (Kucza-Kuczyński & Mroczek, 1991, p. 15). Who is to be blamed for such a state of affairs? In most cases, it was the parish priest, who arbitrarily decided not only on the choice of architect but also on the final shape of the building. The positions of the bishops' committees for construction and project evaluation were often disregarded. "On the construction site remained the one who paid, that is, the parish priest, absolutely unprepared, without a construction program . . . undereducated even in basic matters of art history" (Szczypińska, 1984, p. 16).

Another problem was the location of temples within new housing estates and residential neighbourhoods. The history of the church in Nowa Huta is known even to those who are not normally interested in the history of domestic architecture in the past century. Residents of the exemplary socialist housing estate back in 1956, just before the Gomułka's thaw, petitioned the authorities to build a temple. To no avail. The situation changed with the assumption of the post of First Secretary of the PZPR Central Committee by Władysław Gomułka. However, Gomułka, who initially agreed to the erection of the church, just as quickly withdrew from the decision, resulting in riots. In the end, construction of the first Nowa Huta church did not begin until 1965, while it was put into operation in 1977. Architect Wojciech Pietrzyk wanted to build an open church, whose monolithic walls of cast concrete would, as it were, embrace the faithful gathered in the oval nave. Great attention to detail was noticeable – the outer edge of the oval roof was covered with wooden shingles, while the walls were covered with small river pebbles. It was not insignificant that both of the aforementioned materials were traditional local building materials. In this way, Pietrzyk combined the local with the international, as the mass of the Church of Our Lady Queen of Poland (commonly known as the Ark of the Lord) resembled the chapel of Notre Dame du Haut in Ronchamp by Le Corbusier, the inspiration of which the architect himself did not deny (Cymer, 2018, p. 426).

The problem of the presence of religious buildings in the space of socialist housing estates affected practically the entire country. Despite the unfavourable attitude of the authorities, architects and urban planners, in a way, anticipated the expectations of residents by providing space for churches in their designs. The exception was the J. Słowacki housing estate in Lublin, where Oskar and Zofia Hansen, as declared atheists, did not consider the possibility of building a church at all (Springer, 2013, p. 132). Sometimes, the authorities, fearing the development of vacant space for religious purposes, tried to "pre-empt" the designers. When designing the Piastowskie Housing Estate in Rzeszów, Józef Zbigniew Polak set aside a zone for the construction of a district service centre. Then a rumour rumbled through the city that residents wanted to build a church there. The Rzeszów authorities, with the approval of the city's architect, without a second thought "inserted" two typical residential blocks in the vacant space – not designed by Polak and located against all urban planning rules. Years have passed, times have changed, and with them, the "wisdom of the stage" has changed. Faced with the crisis, the Communist authorities sought an agreement with the Church and were ready to make numerous concessions. So, permission was given to build new temples (Kucza-Kuczyński & Mroczek, 1991, p. 12). "There was no place for a church in Ursynów in the original plan," recounted the estate's chief designer Marek Budzyński.[4] The search for a suitable location began. It was a stroke of luck (the parish priest saw it as divine intervention) that a reserve of land was left in the heart of the neighbourhood, near the main square intended for the market, for serving functions. Construction began. Surprisingly, the priest did not interfere with the shape of the body of the new church. He accepted the vision of Budzyński and the collaborating architect Piotr Wicha, who wanted to create "a bridge of the past with the present, i.e., to patch up the hole of the socialist period" (Kucza-Kuczyński & Mroczek, 1991, p. 12). Thus, between the blocks of Ursynów stood a church with a brick façade in a form reminiscent in part of the Baroque temples of the First Polish Republic and in part of Romanesque collegiate churches (Figure 6.2). The

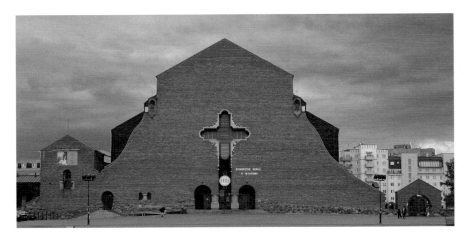

Figure 6.2 Postmodernist church of the Ascension between large panel housing blocks of North Ursynów in Warsaw. Architects Marek Budzyński and Piotr Wicha.

Source: Wikimedia Commons, author: Przemek Więch CC BY 2.0.

parish priest accepted all unconventional solutions, such as the lack of pillars in the interior or the entrance through the cross. Problems only began when it came to designing the interior. "The parish priest threw our design in the trash and did his own thing," complained Budzyński, who tried for a long time to fix what the clergyman had spoiled. He was not alone with his problems. In 1982, Łódź architect Witold Millo won first prize in a competition to design the St. Maximilian Kolbe Church at the Dąbrowa housing estate in Łódź. During the course of the project, which began a year later, and lasted a total of seventeen years (it took even longer, 27 years, to get permission to build the temple), the architect introduced a number of changes, the most important of which involved replacing the broken reinforced concrete roof with a steel structure. Difficult economic realities forced modifications, and on top of this, the developer himself tried to adapt the project to his own ability to procure building materials. Similar experiences were shared by many architects who were faced with the not-easy subject of creating a church. Stefan Müller recalled the construction of a temple in Wrocław, which was a dream come true for a parish priest who allocated every penny to its realization. "At some point I point out that he is going against the project. And he – give way to me, you will design yourself a few more churches, and this is my first and last," he recounted. "And all in all, he did the designing. I was just a draftsman."[5]

Wojciech Jarząbek, together with Wacław Hryniewicz and Jan Matkowski, designed the Church of the Blessed Virgin Mary Queen of Peace in Wrocław's Popowice housing estate in the 1980s (Figure 6.3). "Popowice are big soulless

Figure 6.3 The Church of the Blessed Virgin Mary Queen of Peace in Wrocław's Popowice housing estate. Designed by architects Wojciech Jarząbek, Wacław Hryniewicz, and Jan Matkowski.

Source: Wikimedia Commons, author: Masur, CC BY 4.0.

162   *Architecture and Architects in Socialist Poland*

blocks of flats and this church is as if in total opposition to them," he said. – he recalled the circumstances of the concept, which is close to the idea of "architecture of the seventh day" described by Cichońska, Popera, and Snopek. Bold architecture with postmodern forms aroused extreme opinions and emotions (Stanek, 2012, p. 33). Despite this, the concept first won first place in the competition and was later approved by the authorities and the architectural administration.

> The main supporter of the project, the man who supported it, was Father Alfons Kupka. He was an architect by profession and served as the head of the Oblate order for investments. He even had a church designed in Africa as an architect,"

– recounted the circumstances of Jarząbek's winning the competition. The completed project was also to the liking of Cardinal Henryk Gulbinowicz, who was said to have said during the cornerstone consecration ceremony that "there are monuments that are a hundred years old and monuments that have just been built." Indeed, the atmosphere of antiquity was an extremely important part of the concept, which Jarząbek characterized as follows:

> Our idea was to show a thousand years of history of the church. The entrance is Romanesque, the body is Gothic, the interior is Baroque, and the tower is futuristic, for the 21st century. At the same time, all the time we were striving to get this impression without being too literal, without using any literal quotes from history.[6]

Equally interesting was the Higher Seminary of the Congregation of the Resurrectionist Fathers erected in Cracow in 1985–1993, according to a design by architects Dariusz Kozłowski and Wacław Stefański. It was a postmodernism devoid of direct references to history, but affecting viewers and users with the unique atmosphere, the designers managed to create. The Wrocław architectural historian, author of the book "Antinomies of Modern Sacred Architecture," Cezary Wąs, described it as a rationally dispersed set of functions (residential buildings, refectory, church, teaching rooms), on which "an incredibly rich layer of scenography and decoration was superimposed" (C. Wąs, 2006, p. 77). He compared it to an enclosed world with the character of "a specific religious surrealism." Stanisław Niemczyk, architect of the Holy Spirit Church in Tychy (1978–1983), also presented his authorial vision of sacred architecture. Niemczyk's work, undeniably firmly rooted in the local context and history, eluded easy explanations, and he readily employed symbolism conducive to individual interpretations. In Tychy, he hid the interior under a huge hipped roof with a truncated gable, which for some was the Old Testament tent of the ark of the covenant, for others a barrow or heap. In essence, however, the most important thing was the isolation of the sacred from the urban profane, as Niemczyk's work was in line with the idea of domus dei – a temple that stands out from its secular surroundings. The architect used modern structural solutions, but the form itself, the materials (brick), and finally the method of construction

Post-soc-modernism 163

were thoroughly traditional, and Niemczyk saw the construction of the church as an almost mystical experience uniting the local community of believers involved (financially and physically) in the process of its creation.

In this context, it was interesting to see the influence of politics on the sacred architecture of the period of the decline of socialism in Poland. It is most often perceived (quite rightly) as a conflict between the Church and the state authorities, and the difficulties created by the latter in undertaking further investments. However, this is only part of the issue, as the Polish Church also pursued its own policy. It involved, among other things, questioning certain assumptions of the Second Vatican Council and, in the vast majority of cases, advocating the domus dei, the church distinguished from its surroundings, being a dominant and a sign in space. Indeed, the Polish Episcopate expressed the view that the temple was to be a visible sign of God's presence among the people and distinguished from secular architecture. Postmodern aesthetics, being the opposite of "state" modernism, became an expression of rebellion and growing conflict.

Sacred buildings were built in Poland, so to speak, on the margins of state reality, subject to less regulation than investments subject to central planning. Thanks to this, and the availability of extensive material resources, they were often spaces for architectural and aesthetic experimentation. They were financed by the weekly offerings of the faithful and formal and informal social donations (including foreign ones). They were built with materials, much of which was donated to the church, and with the help of volunteer labour. During the construction of the aforementioned Pentecostal church in Ursynów, the parish legally employed 40–50 labourers, and they operated almost like a private enterprise in a communist state. Architectural researcher Florian Urban saw a correlation between the Baroque-influenced form of the church designed by Marek Budzyński and Piotr Wicha, and the fact that, in the 1980s, the church, just like in the days of the Counter-Reformation, was gaining more and more power in the leaning socialist system (Urban, 2021).

6.3 Against the Athens Charter – postmodern urban planning

One of the most iconic images, which encapsulates virtually the entire philosophy of modernism, is a black-and-white photograph depicting Corbusier's concept for the redevelopment of Paris (Wujek, 1986; Leśniakowska, 2012). The architect's right hand hovers above a mock-up showing modern skyscrapers that were to replace 19th-century buildings. The fingers repeat a gesture familiar from the fresco depicting the creation of Adam on the vault of the Sistine Chapel. Le Corbusier takes on the role of God and, like him, with a single gesture brings a new existence into existence. The utopian vision of reality created from scratch by the designer demiurge became one of the main axes of criticism of the modern movement years later. "We already know that it is impossible to build the world on the model of a designer mock-up. If it is to be something alive and authentic, we are doomed to a combination of known and proven standards with the unknown," wrote Czesław Bielecki (Bielecki, 2016, p. 169). Bielecki's article entitled Continuity in

164 *Architecture and Architects in Socialist Poland*

Architecture, published in "Architektura" in 1978, was the first such clear and loud criticism of the prevailing doctrine on Polish soil. However, the author himself admitted that opposition to modernist ideas was born much earlier and was the result of many observations and reflections.

He began to notice the discrepancies between the history and theory of architecture and the daily practice around him as early as his studies at the Faculty of Architecture at the Warsaw University of Technology.

> I walked out of the room where I was taught about the history of architecture, about beauty, about its criteria, about geometry, about proportions, about their study, about utility and beauty and goodness. After a while, all of this was negated in a place where one of the lecturers would break the chalk and say that if you lay it flat, there are fives – five-story blocks, and if you lay it vertically, there are elevens, or tower blocks.

– recalled Bielecki's education.

> When I went abroad for the first time, I saw Vienna, Salzburg, Paris, Tel Aviv, Jerusalem. I saw cities where the whole history of architecture and modernity formed some other amalgam, but I also saw that in Paris, Angers, Tel Aviv, Jerusalem one builds against the climate, against tradition, according to the same modernist model.[7]

The diagnosis of modernism's flaws went hand in hand with calls for change. "In our time we keep building more technocratic urban visions," Bielecki wrote, stressing the need to return to the basics of urban planning. "Just as discussions about moral norms cannot abstract from the Decalogue, discussions about urban space cannot arbitrarily operate with terms such as square or street, which are elements of the spatial Decalogue" (Bielecki, 1978). Instead of a modernist anti-urbanism, he advocated a return to the broken continuity of urban evolution and market principles that, on a par with planning regulations, shaped the image of urban complexes for centuries. Bielecki recognized numerous absurdities resulting from the unreflective application of pseudo-modern design rules, and he saw their genesis not so much in the workshop or intellectual deficiencies of designers, but primarily in the very essence of modernism itself.

> I saw in Tel Aviv or Jerusalem the traditional narrow streets created during the British Mandate in Palestine. And all of a sudden I saw settlements like ours, with some horrific trampled spaces in between, which are sunbaked, on which no greenery can be maintained. It was again propaganda of a certain type of thinking about city space. Completely unsuited to Vitruvian criteria. For Vitruvius said that streets should be related to winds, sun and climatic conditions. I've seen glazed facades in the country, where you have to escape the sun.

Despite different socio-political realities, the prevailing doctrines in architecture seemed unchangeable, and the classical (or traditional) view of design issues "in a system of freedom, democracy, [free] market, was violated by this evil of modernist thinking, which is de facto totalitarian thinking."[8]

A natural outgrowth of Bielecki's views and his speeches and publications from the 1970s was the DiM Charter, a duplicator-printed manifesto handed out to participants in the Warsaw UIA Congress. The authors were the Home and City (DiM – Dom i Miasto) group, an informal organization of about 20 people intended as an alternative to the rigid, official structures of the Association of Polish Architects (*Karta DiM . . .*). Centred around Bielecki, the milieu consisted mainly of architects (including Andrzej Zielonka, Wojciech Szymborski, Tomasz Turczynowicz, and Maria Sołtys) clearly contested the communist reality of the early 1980s. The very form of the brochure, reminiscent of illegal underground prints, the fact that it was printed on a duplicator belonging to the Solidarity Mazovia Region, and the opposition activity of Bielecki himself, meant that the material could be read as a voice of opposition – both to the prevailing views in architecture and the political system. The author stressed that both the text and the exhibition had an "absolutely dissident" character. "This exhibition was in opposition to this official exhibition that SARP was doing."[9] "The greatest mistake of architecture born of the spirit of the Athens Charter was the rupture of the continuity of architecture," proclaimed the creators of the Charter, criticizing "the uncritical belief in progress, the mythologizing of science and technology" and succumbing to "the magic of large numbers." They restored the traditional meaning of the architectural profession, which "is neither an omnipotent creator nor a slave to universal or local spatial and cultural patterns." As the architecture researcher Dorota Jędruch pointed out, the word "modernism" was not mentioned even once in the manifesto, but its anti-modernist pronunciation seemed all too clear. The "Memento" that ended the text, on the other hand, carried a message of meaning that went beyond architecture and urban planning: "We are proclaiming this Charter in Warsaw, a city destroyed not only by the war, but also later by the meeting of the modern urban planning doctrine with the total socio-political doctrine" (*Karta DiM . . .*).

The retreat from modernist urbanist doctrines could be seen even in the case of such realizations, which from the very beginning were an attempt to revise the idea of CIAM. Among such was the Ursynów Północny project in Warsaw, which can be seen as an attempt to reform modernism – the changes in the disposition of space were clear but still took place within a single paradigm. However, when, in the mid-1980s, Marek Budzyński, in cooperation with architect Zbigniew Badowski, designed a quarter of the so-called Ursynów Passage, the change in approach was all too clear. The development was shaped in the form of a frontage with services in the ground floor (rather than in independent pavilions). The interiors of the "quarters" were filled with greenery (Budzyński clearly emphasized the need to combine culture and nature). Similar ideas, but on the scale of the entire neighbourhood, were embodied by Łódź architects Jakub Wujek, Zdzisław Lipski, and Andrzej Owczarek, authors of the Radogoszcz East neighbourhood project

166 *Architecture and Architects in Socialist Poland*

in Łódź (1979–1985). Aware of the changes taking place in Western architecture, they decided to create a housing estate with a character different from the previous experience while realizing that the chances of catching up with the world are illusory due to material and technological deficiencies. They tried to make up for the shortcomings with the quality of the project itself. Instead of a typical block of flats, the concept envisioned a housing development shaped like a traditional urban complex. The architects created quarters, squares, and pedestrian passages. They also introduced a clear division into public, semi-private, and private spaces. The architecture itself was designed in a prefabricated system, but Lipski, Owczarek, and Wujek made efforts to introduce details of traditional provenance and diversify the character of the buildings wherever possible. Around Słoneczny Square, which is the centre of the estate, buildings of larger dimensions and richer form appeared. In the frontages appeared arcades hiding commercial and service establishments, and the elevations were crowned with gables of individual shapes. In this way, with very limited resources at their disposal, Wujek, Lipski, and Owczarek tried to break the monotony so common in socialist housing estates.

There were many similar examples throughout Poland: Różany Potok in Poznań (architects Marian Fikus, Jerzy Gurawski, 1978–2010s) or Na Skarpie Estate in Cracow-Nowa Huta (architects Romuald Loegler, Wojciech Dobrzański, Ewa Fitzke, and Michał Szymanowski, 1987–1995). In 1978, an extremely interesting residential complex designed by Stanisław Niemczyk was built in the H-7 estate in Tychy. Multi-family buildings surrounded by terraced housing with a fragmented form. A square was created between them, which was the estate's public space. Niemczyk, like the aforementioned architects, wanted to break the settlement's monotony and anonymity. There was nothing surprising in this, since the general designers of Tychy, Kazimierz Wejchert and Hanna Adamczewska-Wejchert, had already promoted diversity in the forms and scale of buildings much earlier. Stanisław Niemczyk himself took a step further by designing the Nad Jamną housing development in Mikołów, Silesia (1983–1986) (Figure 6.4). As in the case of the Tychy development, here too the material was a large slab. However, the architect introduced varied building heights, sloping roofs, brick facing on the facades, and original details. Added to this was the undulating terrain and the curvilinear course of traffic routes. In the Nad Jamną estate, one could easily find references to 19th-century Silesian factory estates and districts such as Nikiszowiec in Katowice (Niemczyk himself grew up in Silesia and did not deny the influence the context had on him) (Cymer, 2013).

An important area of activity for architects and urban planners in a context strongly marked by local specifics was the reconstruction of old towns in cities and towns in the so-called Recovered Territories that were destroyed during World War II. Among the outstanding examples was the aforementioned Elbląg, which from 1983 was the arena (and at the same time the testing ground) for what the local conservator of historical monuments, Maria Lubocka-Hoffmann, termed retroversion. Gdańsk-based architects Szczepan Baum and Stefan Phillip were responsible for the project. Their goal was to preserve the original street layout and building lines, and, insofar as possible, to recreate a subdivision of townhouses that was

Post-soc-modernism 167

Figure 6.4 Nad Jamną housing development in Mikołów designed by architect Stanisław Niemczyk.
Source: Wikimedia Commons, author: Wjchmzn, CC BY 4.0.

consistent with the preserved foundations. The forms of the new tenements themselves, however, were postmodern interpretations of history, leaving no doubt as to their contemporary origins. Indeed, Baum, Phillip, and Lubocka-Hoffmann's goal was not a faithful reconstruction, but to restore the atmosphere of the Hanseatic port city that Elbląg once was (Figure 6.5).

Changes in the area of housing construction in People's Poland concerned not only the form of buildings and housing estates. In 1982, the "Program Assumptions of Housing Construction until 1990 with Changes in Certain Principles of Housing Policy" were created, which assumed an increased role for housing cooperatives, allowing private investment, breaking up the prefabrication monopoly, and expanding the offer of credit (which had a positive effect on the development of single-family housing). "Assumptions . . ." were supposed to be a response to the

Figure 6.5 Results of the retroversion of Elbląg's old town by architects Szczepan Baum and Stefan Phillip, and preservationist Maria Lubocka-Hoffman.

Source: Photograph by the author.

crisis and stagnation in construction. Although no reforms were able to halt the gradual decay of the system, the development of small-scale social cooperatives carrying out investments that were small compared to those of the state and often consisted of a few dozen single-family or row houses was evident in the 1980s.

Post-soc-modernism 169

Alongside them, cooperatives also functioned much larger, and their number in the last decade of the Polish People's Republic increased from about a thousand to more than three thousand (Śliwa, 2004, p. 30).

Notes

1 Wojciech Jarząbek, conversation with the author, Wrocław, 24.04.2019.
2 Romuald Loegler, conversation with the author, Cracow, 30.04.2019.
3 Romuald Loegler, conversation with the author, Cracow, 30.04.2019.
4 Marek Budzyński, conversation with the author, Warsaw, 16.09.2014.
5 Stefan Müller, conversation with the author, Wrocław, 04.07.2013.
6 Wojciech Jarząbek, conversation with the author, Wrocław, 24.04.2019.
7 Czesław Bielecki, conversation with the author, Bartoszówka, 27.04.2019.
8 Czesław Bielecki, conversation with the author, Bartoszówka, 27.04.2019.
9 Czesław Bielecki, conversation with the author, Bartoszówka, 27.04.2019.

References

Basista, A., *Betonowe dziedzictwo. Architektura w Polsce czasów komunizmu* [Concrete heritage. Architecture in communist Poland], Warsaw-Cracow: PWN Scientific Publishing House, 2001.
Bielecki, C., Ciągłość w architekturze [Continuity in Architecture], "Architektura" 1978, no. 3–4.
Bielecki, C., *Głowa. Instrukcja użytkowania* [Head. User manual], Warsaw: Zwierciadło, 2016.
Bruszewski, A., *Czym przebić Ateńską Kartę?* [How to overtake the Athens Charter?], "Architektura" 1982, no. 1.
Budzyński, M. & Wicha, P., *Kościół na Ursynowie Północnym w Warszawie* [Church in Ursynów Północny in Warsaw], Warsaw, "Architektura" 1982, no. 1.
Cichońska, I., Popera, K. & Snopek, K., *Architektura VII dnia* [Architecture of the 7th Day], Cracow: Międzynarodowe Centrum Kultury, 2016.
Crowley, D., *Modernizm realny około 1981 roku* [Real Modernism circa 1981], [in:] *Teksty modernizmu. Antologia polskiej teorii i krytyki architektury 1918–1981* [Texts of modernism. Anthology of Polish architectural theory and criticism 1918–1981], vol. 2: Essays, eds. D. Jędruch, M. Karpińska, D. Leśniak-Rychlak, Cracow: Instytut Architektury, 2018.
Cymer, A., *Architektura w Polsce 1945–1989* [Architecture in Poland 1945–1989], Warsaw: Centrum Architektury, 2018.
Cymer, A., *Stanisław Niemczyk – postmodernista średniowieczny* [Stanisław Niemczyk – a medieval postmodernist], [in:] *Polish Postmodernism. Architecture and urbanism. An anthology of texts*, ed. L. Klein, Warsaw: Stowarzyszenie 40 000 Malarzy, 2013.
Gzowska, A., Karpińska, M. & Leśniak-Rychlak, D., *Wszyscy wtedy czytali Derridę i wszystko wydawało się możliwe. Z architektami Krzysztofem Ingardenem, Dariuszem Kozłowskim oraz Romualdem Loeglerem rozmawiają historyczki architektury Alicja Gzowska, Marta Karpińska i Dorota Leśniak-Rychlak* [Everyone was reading Derrida at the time and everything seemed possible. Architectural historians Alicja Gzowska, Marta Karpińska and Dorota Leśniak-Rychlak talk with architects Krzysztof Ingarden, Dariusz Kozłowski and Romuald Loegler], "Autoportret" 2018, no. 4(63).
Gzowska, A. & Klein, L., *Postmodernizm polski: architektura i urbanistyka/z architektami rozmawiają Alicja Gzowska i Lidia Klein* [Polish Postmodernism. Architecture and urbanism. Architects are interviewed by Alicja Gzowska and Lidia Klein], Warsaw: Stowarzyszenie 40 000 Malarzy, 2013.
Kardaszewski, B., *Rozważania o teoretycznych i praktycznych uwarunkowaniach nauczania projektowania architektonicznego* [Reflections on theoretical and practical considerations

170 Architecture and Architects in Socialist Poland

for teaching architectural design], [in:] *Politechnika Łódzka. Zeszyty Naukowe – Budownictwo* vol. 47, Łódź: Łódź University of Technology, 1996.

Karta DiM [DiM Charter], compiled by. D. Jedruch, [in:] *Teksty modernizmu. Antologia polskiej teorii i krytyki architektury 1918–1981* [Texts of modernism. Anthology of Polish architectural theory and criticism 1918–1981], vol. 2: Essays, eds. D. Jędruch, M. Karpińska, D. Leśniak-Rychlak, Cracow: Instytut Architektury, 2018.

Klein, L., *Postmodernizm polski: od wielkiej płyty do architektury wczesnej transformacji* [Polish postmodernism. From the great plate to the architecture of early transformation], [in:] *Postmodernizm polski: architektura i urbanistyka: antologia tekstów* [Polish Postmodernism. Architecture and urbanism. An anthology of texts], ed. L. Klein, Warsaw: Stowarzyszenie 40 000 Malarzy, 2013.

Kucza-Kuczyński, K. & Mroczek, A., *Nowe kościoły w Polsce* [New churches in Poland], Warsaw: Instytut Wydawniczy PAX, 1991.

Kurnicki, K. *Postmodernizm albo logika kulturowa polskiej przestrzeni* [Postmodernism or the cultural logic of Polish space], "Autoportret" 2018, no. 4(63).

Leśniakowska, M., *Oczy Le Corbusiera* [Le Corbusier's Eyes], [in:] *W stronę architektury* [Towards Architecture], ed. Le Corbusier, Warsaw: Centrum Architektury, 2012.

Loegler, R., *Z porządku uwolniona forma* [Out of order released form], Cracow: RAM, 2001.

Opaliński, M., *"Zgody nie wyrażono": problem budownictwa sakralnego w diecezji łódzkiej 1945–1989* ["Consent was not expressed." The Problem of Sacral Construction in the Diocese of Łódź 1945–1989], Łódź: Księży Młyn, 2018.

Pasierb, J., *Współczesne wnętrze kościelne – style, potrzeby, gusty [Contemporary church interior - styles, needs, tastes], [in:] Seminarium SARP nt. architektury obiektów sakralnych. Kazimierz Dolny, 20–21 listopada 1982 rok. Wydawnictwo poseminaryjne* [SARP seminar on the architecture of sacred buildings. Kazimierz Dolny, 20–21 November 1982. Post-seminar publication], eds. R. Girtler, K. Kucza-Kuczyński, J. Miazek, J. Pełka, Warsaw: SARP, 1983.

Sepioł, J., *Architektura polskiej demokracji* [Architecture of Polish democracy], [in:] *Form follows freedom. Architektura dla kultury w Polsce 2000+* [Form follows freedom. Architecture for culture in Poland 2000+], eds. J. Purchla, J. Sepiol, Cracow: Międzynarodowe Centrum Kultury, 2015.

Sławińska, J., *Ruchy protestu w architekturze współczesnej* [Protest movements in contemporary architecture], Wrocław: Wrocław University of Technology, 1995.

Śliwa, Z., *Spółdzielczość mieszkaniowa w Polsce* [Housing cooperatives in Poland], Bydgoszcz: Qax manufaktura artystyczna, 2004.

Springer, F., *Zaczyn. O Zofii i Oskarze Hansenach* [Leaven. On Sophia and Oskar Hansen], Warsaw–Cracow: Karakter, 2013.

Stanek, Ł., *Postmodernizm jest prawie w porządku. Polska architektury po socjalistycznej globalizacji* [Postmodernism is almost right. Polish architecture after socialist globalization], Warsaw: Bęc Zmiana, 2012.

Szczypińska, H., *Jakie będą nasze świątynie?* [What will our temples be like?], "Przegląd Powszechny" 1984, no. 7–8.

Urban, F., *Postmodern architecture in socialist Poland. Transformation, symbolic form and national identity*, London: Routledge Taylor & Francis Group, 2021.

Wąs, C., *Bunt kwiatu przeciw korzeniom. Polska architektura sakralna lat 1980–2005 wobec modernizmu* [Revolt of the flower against the roots. Polish sacred architecture of 1980–2005 against modernism], "Quart" 2006, no. 1.

Węcławowicz-Gyurkovich, E., *Postmodernizm w polskiej architekturze* [Postmodernism in Polish architecture], Cracow: Cracow University of Technology, 1998.

Wujek, J., *Mity i utopie architektury XX wieku* [Myths and utopias of 20th-century architecture], Warsaw: Arkady, 1986.

Epilogue

Epilogue

The introduction to this book echoes the questions posed by Professor Andrzej Basista in 2001 – "why did it happen the way it did" and "who was to blame" (Basista, 2001). My goal, unlike that of the author of Concrete Heritage, was not to find fault but to paint a more empathetic picture of the past. After all, as Enzo Traverso wrote, one way of looking at history is to try to identify with the portrait of a "defeated ancestor" (Traverso, 2014). These "defeated ancestors" are the architects, who functioned in certain realities and whose achievements should be analysed only in their context. This does not absolve them of responsibility, as the architects themselves were aware. In the documentary "Blocks" (Bloki), directed by Konrad Królikowski (2017), the author of the wave houses in the Przymorze housing estate in Gdańsk, Danuta Olędzka, summed it up quite accurately. She did not try to apologize and did not express any forced remorse. All she said was: "One should not look away from what one once did."

The "Blocks" film itself was another manifestation of the growing interest in the heritage of communist architecture since around 2010. That was when, despite protests, one of the icons of socialist modernism in Poland – the train station in Katowice – was demolished. Before that, in 2006, Warsaw's Supersam was wiped off the face of the earth. The discussion about the legacy of socialist architecture began in earnest in 2012 with the publication of the book "Ill Born" by Filip Springer (2011). The merit of the book was not only to bring socialist architecture "under thathed roofs"[1] and change the language used to talk about it but also to introduce the term "ill born" into use. This term was used to refer to buildings built under socialism, which were therefore stigmatized in the Third Republic. Its synonym is the much more widely used term dissonant heritage, which is defined as the material representation of values with which most of modern society does not want to identify, although it is aware that they are an inseparable part of its history. Objects can have different meanings for different social groups, and the overlap of different narratives creates the very dissonance mentioned. Close, though not the same as "troubled heritage," are "ambivalent heritage" and "unwanted heritage." Despite the differences, all of these concepts are based on a common set of values and criteria.

DOI: 10.4324/9781003603153-8

172 *Architecture and Architects in Socialist Poland*

The discussion about preserving the "troublesome heritage" of post-war modernism has brought to light a number of problems that historic preservation has not had to face before. While the question of preserving the layout of a city, neighbourhood, or district is not entirely new (although modernism has given it a whole new dimension), the question of preserving typical and repetitive buildings is an entirely new one.

Kuba Snopek, in the pages of his book "Bielayevo. A Monument of the Future," points out that, in the case of objects without any individual uniqueness (such as prefabricated blocks of flats), "the understanding of uniqueness and authenticity should be considered in the context of the immaterial heritage connected with the existing architecture" (Snopek, 2014). In short, in addition to the protection of matter, attention should be paid to the protection of ideas.

The attitude towards the architectural heritage of socialism in Poland has evolved over decades. A clear example of this evolution is the aforementioned "Supersam" department store in Warsaw, designed by Jerzy Hryniewiecki and Maciej Krasiński, which received critical acclaim for its innovative suspended roof construction system. This was confirmed by the honourable mention at the São Paulo Biennial in 1965. The story of Supersam shows the turning points in the history of post-war Polish modernism, from the universal affirmation of the 1960s to the rejection of the 1990s. Michał Wiśniewski called this rejection "the anti-communist iconoclasm," which, for economic reasons, did not take place immediately after the fall of communism, but about a dozen years later (Wiśniewski, 2012). The final phase of this story was the vindication that began in the early 21st century, but the building itself did not survive to witness the rehabilitation.

The "anti-communist iconoclasm" itself took many different forms. It ranged from the capitalist recapture of economically attractive areas in large cities, which led to the demolition of many valuable post-war buildings, to the destruction of monuments to fallen soldiers of the Polish People's Army and the Soviet Red Army, inspired by the government and the IPN. The process of decommunization was, in fact, the war of collective memory declared by right-wing politicians against hundreds of sculptures, buildings, and street names. Analysing the post-communist transformation in Poland, and decommunization as an integral part of it, reveals the complexity of the phenomenon. It involves the privatization and commercialization of public goods, the revision of recent history, and the rejection of late modernist aesthetics. Obviously, the process of removing the remnants of socialism from the public space is based on much deeper premises than the evaluation of certain historical events or architectural trends. The common ground is anti-socialism.

The lack of broad public debate and dialogue has led to an oversimplified view of the world based on the Cold War identification of "good" and "red" ("red is bad" – this slogan became the name of a popular Polish clothing brand!) There are no case studies like the Buzludzha monument in Bulgaria, where the complex, multi-layered narrative is the crucial element of the preservation strategy. On the contrary, according to Emil Chartier, the prevailing opinion is that any description, any explanation "that boasts of being neutral is in fact an advocacy speech in favor of the status quo." Perhaps those who see the "anticommunist iconoclasm"

Epilogue 173

as a war of values are right to a certain extent. The real struggle is not between the dark forces of communism (or neo-Marxism) and the noble anti-communists. It is between those who want to heal the public space by removing the dissonant legacy and those who want to secure people's right to their own judgment and prefer to preserve history as it was – with all the good and bad memories.

Note

1 Reference to Adam Mickiewicz's "Pan Tadeusz," where in the Epilogue poet wrote: *O that I win to this pleasure some day/That these books under thatched roofs find their way.* Mickiewicz, A., Pan Tadeusz, czyli ostatni zajazd na Litwie. Historia szlachecka z roku 1811 i 1812 we dwunastu księgach wierszem [Pan Tadeusz or The Last Foray in Lithuania: A Tale of the Gentry During 1811–1812] translated by Marcel Weyland, 2004.

References

Basista, A., *Betonowe dziedzictwo: architektura w Polsce czasów komunizmu* [Concrete heritage: Architecture in communist Poland], Warsaw-Cracow: PWN Scientific Publishing House, 2001.
Królikowski, K., *Bloki* [Blocks], documentary, 57 min., Poland, 2017.
Snopek, K., *Bielajewo. Zabytek przyszłości* [Bielayevo. A monument of the future], Warsaw: Bęc-Zmiana, 2014.
Springer, F., *Źle urodzone. Reportaże o architekturze PRL-u* [Ill born. Reportages about architecture of Polish People's Republic], Cracow: Karakter, 2011.
Traverso, E., *Historia jako pole bitwy – interpretacja przemocy w XX wieku* [The history as a battlefield–interpretations of the violence in 20th century], Warsaw: "Książka i Prasa" Publishing Institute, 2014.
Wiśniewski, M., *Spóźnione ułaskawienie. Kilka uwag o nostalgii za niechcianym dziedzictwem PRL* [A belated pardon. Some remarks on the Nostalgia for the unwanted heritage of communist Poland], "Herito" 2012, no. 7.

Appendix 1
Biographies of selected architects mentioned in the book

Hanna ADAMCZEWSKA-WEJCHERT (1920–1996) graduated from the Faculty of Architecture at the Warsaw University of Technology (1946). Lecturer for many years and professor at the Warsaw University of Technology.

Kazimierz WEJCHERT (1912–1993) graduated from the Faculty of Architecture at the Warsaw University of Technology (1935). Lecturer and professor at the Warsaw University of Technology. Prominent architect and town planner, author of numerous publications, including Miasteczko polskie [Polish Town] (1947), Elementy kompozycji yrbanistycznej [Elements of Urban Composition] (1974), Kształtowanie zespołów mieszkaniowych [Shaping Residential Complexes] (1985, with H. Adamczewska-Wejchert), and Małe miasta [Small Cities] (1986, with H. Adamczewska-Wejchert).

The most important projects and realizations: Starachowice Town Development Plan (1947–49), Garwolin Town Development Plan (1947–1949), and New Tychy Town Development Plan (1951 – State Prize of the First Degree in 1964).

Tadeusz BARUCKI (1922–2022) studied mathematics at the UMCS in Lublin from 1944 to 1949, art history at the Catholic University in Lublin and the Jagiellonian University, and architecture at the Warsaw University of Technology and the AGH University of Science and Technology (Polytechnic Faculties) in Cracow. From 1949, he worked in design offices in Cracow, later at the Institute of Urban Planning and Architecture, and at the same time at the Office of Studies and Projects of the Ministry of Transport in Warsaw. Since 1949, he has been active in SARP, where he served as Secretary General (1956–1961) and Vice-President for Foreign Affairs (1972–1975).

Architect, independent architectural researcher, and publicist. Lecturer at the Schools of Architecture at North Carolina State University in Raleigh NC (1964), Iowa State University in Ames, Iowa (1967), and Department of Architecture at the Gdańsk University of Technology (1973), and guest lecturer at many universities around the world, including MIT, Harvard, and Columbia. Author of numerous publications, including: *Maciej Nowicki* (1980), Architecture of Poland (1985), Wacław Kłyszewski, Jerzy Mokrzyński, Eugeniusz Wierzbicki (1987), Stephan du Chateau (1995), Polish Architects on Architecture (2009), and Green Horses-Henryk Buszko, Aleksander Franta, Jerzy Gottfried (2015).

Appendix 1: Biographies of selected architects mentioned in the book 175

Important projects and realizations: Aviation School in Tęgoborze, Motor Transport Institute in Warsaw, PTTK House in Sandomierz (co-author: K. Muszyński), shelter in Morskie Oko (co-author: Tadeusz P. Szafer), and war cemeteries in Katyń, Kharkiv, and Mednoye.

Andrzej BASISTA (1932–2017) graduated from the Faculty of Architecture at the Cracow University of Technology (1956). Professor at the Academy of Fine Arts in Cracow. Lecturer in Cracow, Poznań and Białystok. Collaborator of the Miastoprojekt in Cracow. He taught at the University of Baghdad (1968–72) and created the General Housing Program for Iraq (1972–78).

Author of numerous publications, including *Opowieści budynków – Architektura czterech kultur* [Tales of Buildings – Architecture of Four Cultures] (1995), *Betonowe dziedzictwo – Architektura w Polsce czasów komunizmu* [Concrete Heritage – Architecture in Poland under Communism] (2001), *Kompozycja dzieła architektury* [Composition of a Work of Architecture] (2006), *Architektura i wartości* [Architecture and Values] (2009), and *Jak czytać architekturę* [How to Read Architecture] (2012, with Andrzej Nowakowski).

Szczepan BAUM (1931–2014) graduated from the Faculty of Architecture at the Silesian University of Technology in Gliwice (1954) and the Gdańsk University of Technology (1956). Professor at the Gdańsk University of Technology and long-time lecturer at the University. Worked at the Urban Planning Studio and Miastoprojekt in Gdańsk. Co-founder and long-term member and President of the Supervisory Board of ZAPA – ARCHITEKCI (since 1982).

The most important projects and realizations: the Church of the Assumption of the Blessed Virgin Mary Queen of Polish Emigrants in Władysławowo, the Delfin Resort in Jastrzębia Góra (co-authors: Jerzy Piaseczny, Stefan Philipp), the Miastoprojekt office building in Gdańsk, the Dom Technika in Gdańsk (co-author: Danuta Olędzka), the Orbis-Hevelius Hotel in Gdańsk (co-author: A. Matoń), Reconstruction of the Old Town in Elbląg, and Reconstruction of the Old Town in Malbork and Hotel Hanza in Gdańsk (co-author: A. Kwieciński).

Czesław BIELECKI (1948) graduated from the Warsaw University of Technology (1973). He worked in architectural offices in Warsaw, France, Israel, and West Germany. In 1984, he founded and directed the architectural office "Home and City." Opposition activist. Arrested in 1968 in connection with the March events. Member of the Solidarity trade union since 1980. During the Third Republic, he was a member of the Parliament in its third term.

Author of numerous publications, including *Gra w miasto* [Playing the City] (1996), *Plan akcji* [Action Plan] (1997), *Więcej niż architektura. Pochwała eklektyzmu* [More than Architecture. Praise of Eclecticism] (2005), *Scenarzysta* [Screenwriter] (2009), and *Wolność zrób to sam* [DIY Freedom] (2010).

The most important projects and realizations: own house in Bartoszówka, PSE headquarters in Konstancin, monument – Radegast Station in Łódź and TVP building in Warsaw.

Marek BUDZYŃSKI (1939) graduated from the Faculty of Architecture at the Warsaw University of Technology (1963). Architect and town planner. Lecturer at

176 *Appendix 1: Biographies of selected architects mentioned in the book*

the Faculty of Architecture at the Warsaw University of Technology and in the past also at the Łódź University of Technology and the Ärhus branch of the Copenhagen Academy of Fine Arts. From 1961 to 1988, he worked as a designer and general designer in state design offices. Since 1992, Badowski, Budzyński, Kowalewski Studio – currently Marek Budzyński Architect Ltd.

Major projects and realizations: competition design of the Victory Monument on Playa Giron (Cuba), North Ursynów housing estate (co-authors: Jerzy Szczepanik-Dzikowski, Andrzej Szkop), the Church of the Assumption in Warsaw (co-author: Piotr Wicha), the building of the University Library in Warsaw, the building of the Supreme Court in Warsaw, the competition design of the Church of Divine Providence in Warsaw, the Opera and Philharmonic House in Podlasie: European Art Center in Białystok, and the campus of the University of Białystok.

Henryk BUSZKO (1924–2015) graduated from the AGH University of Science and Technology in Cracow (1949). From 1949 to 1958, he worked at Miastoprojekt Katowice (together with Aleksander Franta), and then, together with A. Franta, managed the State Studio of General Building Design in Katowice. Lecturer at the Silesian University of Technology in 1970–1978.

Alexander FRANTA (1925–2019) graduated from the AGH University of Science and Technology in Cracow (1949). Creative activity connected with Silesia and the person of his long-time collaborator Henryk Buszko.

The most important projects and realizations by Buszko and Franta: the building of the District Council of Trade Unions in Katowice (co-author: Jerzy Gottfried), the Rybnik Land Theater in Rybnik (co-author: Jerzy Gottfried), the Rybnik Land Theater in Rybnik (co-author: Jerzy Gottfried): Jerzy Gottfried), the Millenium Housing Estate in Katowice, the Treatment and Rehabilitation District on Zawodzie in Ustroń, the Gwiazdy Housing Estate in Katowice, the Registry Office – Wedding Pavilion in Chorzów, the Górnik Sanatorium in Szczawnica, and the Church of the Elevation of the Holy Cross and the Healing of the Sick in Katowice.

Witold CĘKIEWICZ (1924–2023) graduated from the Faculty of Architecture at the Cracow University of Technology (1950). Architect of the City of Cracow in 1955–1960. Professor, long-time lecturer at the Faculty of Architecture. In 1970–1994, director of the Institute of Urban Design and head of the Department of Urban Composition. He also gave lectures in the USA and Germany. Soldier of the Home Army in the rank of Second Lieutenant, alias "Kropidło."

The most important projects and realizations: the Cathedral of Rome-.cat. in Rzeszów, the Divine Mercy Sanctuary in Cracow, the Cracovia Hotel, the Kyiv Cinema, the Grunwald Victory Monument (co-author: Jerzy Bandura), the Monument to the Revolutionary Deed in Sosnowiec (co-author: Helena and Roman Husarscy), the KL Płaszów Monument in Cracow (cooperation: Ryszard Szczypczyński), the Mistrzejowice Housing Estate in Cracow, the Polish Embassy in New Delhi (co-author: Stanisław Deńko), and the main designer of the Mistrzejowice Housing Estate and the Podwawelski (Dębniki) Housing Estate in Cracow.

Edmund GOLDZAMT (1921–1990). A graduate of architecture in Moscow. From 1952 to 1970, he was a lecturer at the Faculty of Architecture at the Warsaw

Appendix 1: Biographies of selected architects mentioned in the book 177

University of Technology. Since 1975, he has been a lecturer at the Faculty of Architecture in Moscow. One of the most important representatives of socialist realism in Polish architecture.

Selected publications: *Architektura zespołów śródmiejskich i problemy dziedzictwa* [Architecture of Inner-City Complexes and Problems of Heritage] (1956), *W miastach włoskich* [In Italian Cities] (1959), *Urbanistyka krajów socjalistycznych: problemy społeczne* [Urban Planning in Socialist Countries: Social Problems] (1968), Urban Planning in Socialist Countries (1974), and *Kultura urbanistyczna krajów socjalistycznych* [Urban Planning Culture of Socialist Countries] (1987, co-author with Oleg Shvidkovsky).

Among others, he is the author of a project for a sanatorium in Kołobrzeg (together with his wife Helena Gurjanova).

Jadwiga GRABOWSKA-HAWRYLAK (1920–2018) graduated from the Faculty of Architecture at the Wrocław University of Technology (1950). Associated with Wrocław throughout her professional life. She began her professional career during the reconstruction of the war-ravaged Old Town and later ran her own studio in the Wrocław Miastoprojekt. The first woman to receive the SARP Honorary Award (1974).

The most important projects and realizations: a residential building on Kollątaja Street (the so-called "Masoinette"), school buildings on Janiszewskiego and Grochowa Streets, a house of scientists on Grunwaldzki Square, a residential and commercial complex on Grunwaldzki Square, a private house on Kochanowskiego Street, and the Church of Christ the Redeemer of the World.

Wieslaw GRUSZKOWSKI (1920–2018) graduated from the Faculty of Architecture at the Gdańsk University of Technology (he began his studies at the Lviv Polytechnic before World War II). As an architect and town planner since 1945, he actively participated in the reconstruction of the capital. In 1952–1955, he was the chief architect of the province and then the head of the provincial urban planning laboratory. Lecturer at the Gdańsk University of Technology for many years.

Author of numerous publications, including *Planowanie przestrzenne miast portowych* [Spatial Planning of Port Cities] (1964, co-authors: Bohdan Szermerm and Stanisław Tomaszek), *Wspomnienia z odbudowy Głównego Miasta* [Memories of the Reconstruction of the Main City] (1978, co-author: Izabella Trojanowska), *Zarys historii urbanistyki* [Outline of the History of Urbanism] (1989), and *Ruiny. Fotografie Wiesława Gruszkowskiego*[Ruins. Photographs by Wiesław Gruszkowski] (2012).

Jerzy GURAWSKI (1935–2022) graduated from the Faculty of Architecture at the Cracow University of Technology (1960). Lecturer at the Faculty of Architecture at the Poznań University of Technology. Stage designer, from 1960 worked with Jerzy Grotowski's Laboratory Theater. From 1961 to 1974, he worked in Opole and then in Poznań Miastoprojekt (together with Marian Fikus). Since 1989, he has been working independently as "Jerzy Gurawski's Architectural Authorship Studio."

The most important projects and realizations: Spa and Holiday District in Kołobrzeg (co-author: M. Fikus), Residential District in Kędzierzyn (co-author: M.

178 *Appendix 1: Biographies of selected architects mentioned in the book*

Fikus), Campus of Adam Mickiewicz University in Poznań (co-author: M. Fikus), Buildings of Adam Mickiewicz University in Morasko, Extension of the Academy of Music in Poznań, and Residential Building "Wstęga Warty" in Poznań.

Romuald GUTT (1888–1974). Graduate of the Higher Technical School in Winterthur, Switzerland (1908). Lecturer and professor at the Warsaw University of Technology and the Academy of Fine Arts in Warsaw. Dean of the Faculty of Architecture at the Warsaw University of Technology (1947).

Important projects and realizations: The School of Political Science in Warsaw, numerous villas and residential buildings, the Central Statistical Office building, the Warsaw Nursing School, the project of the Polish Army House Theater (cooperation with Halina Skibniewska), the brine-thermal swimming pool in Ciechocinek (cooperation with Alexander Szniolis), the post office in Ciechocinek, and the post office in Kazimierz Dolny.

Zofia GARLIŃSKA-HANSEN (1924–2013). Graduate of Architecture at the Warsaw University of Technology (1952). Designer at the Warsaw Housing Association.

Oskar HANSEN (1922–2005) graduated from the Mechanical Department of the Vilnius Higher Technical School (1942) and the Faculty of Architecture at the Warsaw University of Technology (1951). He studied painting in the studio of Fernand Leger in Paris and practiced with Pierre Jeanneret. Lecturer at the Warsaw Academy of Fine Arts (1950–1983). Chief designer of the Warsaw Housing Cooperative.

Creator of the Open Form Theory and the Linear Continuous System. The most important projects and realizations: the Słowacki Housing Estate in Lublin (co-author: Z. Garlińska-Hansen), the "Przyczółek Grochowski" Housing Estate in Warsaw (co-author: Z. Garlińska-Hansen), the Rakowiec Housing Estate in Warsaw (co-author: Z. Garlińska-Hansen), the design of the "Słowacki" Housing Estate in Warsaw (co-author: Z. Garlińska-Hansen), the design of the City Hall in Warsaw, the roofs of the Polish pavilion in Izmir (co-author: Lech Tomaszewski), the design of the extension of the Zachęta Gallery (co-authors: L. Tomaszewski and Stanisław Zamecznik), the monument to the Auschwitz concentration camp, and the design of the Museum of Modern Art in Skopje and his own house in Shumin.

Władysław HENNIG (1930–2014) graduated from the Faculty of Architecture at the Cracow University of Technology (1956). Architect and town planner. From 1956 to 1990, he worked in urban planning studios and offices in Rzeszów. For many years, president of the Rzeszów branch of SARP.

The most important projects and realizations: general development plans for Strzyżów, Jarosław, Przemyśl, Rzeszów, and Sandomierz, Drabianka Housing Estate in Rzeszów, and Solidarność City Garden in Rzeszów.

Author of numerous publications on the practice and theory of urban planning, history of urban development, and Rzeszów and its surroundings. He has produced a series of programs "Rzeszów Lessons of Architecture."

Jerzy HRYNIEWIECKI (1908–1989) graduated from the Warsaw University of Technology (1936). From 1937, he worked in the Capital City Planning Office. After World War II, he headed the studio of the Office for the Reconstruction of the

Appendix 1: Biographies of selected architects mentioned in the book 179

Capital. He also worked for the Warsaw Bureau of Industrial Construction Design. Lecturer at the Faculty of Architecture at the Warsaw University of Technology. Non-party member of the Sejm of the People's Republic of Poland for the second and third terms.

Important projects and realizations: Exhibition of Recovered Territories in Wrocław – designer and client of the exhibition, Tenth Anniversary Stadium (co-author: Marek Leykam, Czesław Rajewski), "Supersam" in Warsaw (co-author: Maciej Krasiński), and Sports and Entertainment Hall "Spodek" in Katowice (co-author: M. Krasiński, Maciej Gintowt).

Stanisław JANKOWSKI (1911–2002) graduated from the Faculty of Architecture at the Warsaw University of Technology (1938) and from the Faculty of Urban Planning at the Polish School of Architecture at the University of Liverpool (1946). Assistant at the Faculty of Architecture at the Warsaw University of Technology (1938–39). After the war, he worked at the BOS Capital and then at the Warsaw Urban Planning Studio (Warsaw Development Planning Bureau). A soldier of the Home Army, a silent-covert, alias "Agaton," participant in the Warsaw Uprising.

Important projects and realizations: W-Z Route in Warsaw (co-authors: Jan Knothe, Józef Sigalin, and Zygmunt Stępiński), Marszałkowska Housing District in Warsaw (co-authors: J. Knothe, J. Sigalin, and Z. Stępiński), Ministry of Agriculture and Agrarian Reform in Warsaw (co-authors: Jerzy Czepkowski, Jan Grabowski, Jerzy Jezierski, J. Knothe, and Zofia Krzewińska), the design of the Okęcie Airport Station, and the design of the Museum of Revolutionary and Liberation Struggles in Warsaw.

Stanisław JUCHNOWICZ (1923–2020) graduated from the Faculty of Architecture at the Gdańsk University of Technology (1948). Assistant at the Faculty of Architecture in PG, lecturer at the Cracow University of Technology for many years, in 1984 elected Dean of the Faculty of Architecture in PK. Scholarship in the United States (1959–1960). From 1973 to 1981, he worked in West Africa.

The most important projects and realizations: the project for the reconstruction of the Main Town in Gdańsk, the concept of the spatial layout of Nowa Huta (under the direction of Tadeusz Ptaszycki), the residential district of Nowa Huta – Bieńczyce, the main building of the Catholic University in Lublin, projects for the centres of Polish cities of Cracow, Lublin, Chorzów and others, and projects for the expansion of cities in Southern Nigeria.

Bolesław KARDASZEWSKI (1931–2000) graduated from the Faculty of Architecture at the Warsaw University of Technology (1962). Lecturer at the Łódź University of Technology for many years, and in 1995, appointed Director of the Institute of Architecture and Urban Planning Didactics. Collaborator of the Łódź Miastoprojekt. Member of the Sejm of the People's Republic of Poland in the seventh term.

The most important projects and realizations: the project of the University District in Łódź (co-authors: Włodzimierz Nowakowski, Anna Wiśniowska), the building of the Institute of Physics of the University of Łódź, the Pavilion of Civil Engineering of the University of Łódź (co-author: Ludwik Mackiewicz), the State

180   *Appendix 1: Biographies of selected architects mentioned in the book*

University of Fine Arts in Łódź (co-author: W. Nowakowski), and residential buildings in the centre of Łódź.

Witold MILEWSKI (1930–2021) graduated from the Poznań School of Engineering (1953) and the Wrocław University of Technology (1963). He worked in the Old Town Workshop for the reconstruction of the Old Town of Poznań (under the direction of Zbigniew Zieliński). From 1952, he worked in the Poznań Miastoprojekt, where from 1963 to 1980, he created the Higher Education Studio (with Lech Sternal and Zygmunt Skupniewicz).

The most important projects and realizations: Jowita student dormitory of the Adam Mickiewicz University in Poznań (co-author: Z. Skupniewicz), Eskulap Student House (co-authors: L. Sternal, Z. Skupniewicz), buildings of the Faculty of Mechanical Engineering and the Faculty of Electrical Engineering of the Poznań University of Technology (co-authors: L. Sternal, Z. Skupniewicz). Sternal, Z. Skupniewicz), The Main Library and the Teaching Building of the Academy of Economics – Collegium Altum (co-authors: L. Sternal, Z. Skupniewicz), The Veterans' House (co-authors: L. Sternal, Z. Skupniewicz), and The Restoration of the Royal Castle in Poznań.

Witold MILLO (1932–2019) graduated from the Faculty of Architecture at the Gdańsk University of Technology (1954) and postgraduate studies in Spatial Planning at the University of Łódź (1971). Employee of the Łódź Miastoprojekt and the Studio of the Presidium of the National Council in Łódź.

Important projects and realizations: Jaracz Theatre in Łódź, New Theatre Project, Łódź Liberty Square Redevelopment, Łódź Cultural Complex Project, Łódź Philharmonic Orchestra Project, Łódź Medical Academy Library, and Dębrowa Estate Church in Łódź.

Stefan MÜLLER (1934–2018). Graduated from the Faculty of Architecture at the Wrocław University of Technology (1956). Lecturer at the Wrocław University of Technology for many years (since 1964). Since 1956, he has been associated with the studio of the Wrocław Miastoprojekt. At the same time, together with his wife Maria, he ran an author's architectural studio. He held the post of Architect of the City of Wrocław and Director of the Department of Architecture and Geodesy of the City Council in Wrocław (1990–1992). Organizer of the international architecture exhibitions TERRA 1 and TERRA 2. Major projects and realizations: reconstruction of the market in Jawor (co-author: Maria Müller), "Granit" Resort in Szklarska Poręba, project of the "Kamienny Szaniec" Resort in Kołobrzeg, residential buildings on Grabiszyńska Street in Wrocław, the Church of the Blessed Virgin Mary Queen of Poland in Domaszowice, and the Church of St. Stanisław Kostka in Wrocław.

Tadeusz MYCEK (1929–2019) graduated from the Faculty of Architecture at the Warsaw University of Technology (1951). Lecturer at the Faculty of Architecture at the Warsaw University of Technology (1970–1976). Designer of numerous industrial and public buildings. Draftsman whose works have been presented at many exhibitions.

The most important projects and realizations: the Central Gardening Cooperative, the extension of the Geographical Institute building, the reconstruction of

Appendix 1: Biographies of selected architects mentioned in the book 181

the Contemporary Theatre in Warsaw, the Medical Academy in Cracow, and the American Częstochowa in Doylestown (United States).

Maria PIECHOTKA (1920–2020) graduated from the Warsaw University of Technology (1948). She worked in the State Historic Preservation Office and later in the Miastoprojekt of the capital. Non-partisan deputy of the Sejm of the People's Republic of Poland in the third term.

Together with her husband, she conducted research on synagogues, which resulted in a number of publications: *Bramy nieba. Bożnice drewniane na ziemiach dawnej Rzeczypospolitej* [Gates of Heaven. Wooden Synagogues on the Lands of the Former Republic of Poland] (1957), *Bramy nieba. Bożnice murowane* [Gates of Heaven. Brick Synagogues] (1999), and *Krajobraz z menorą* [Landscape with a Menorah] (2008).

Kazimierz Maciej PIECHOTKA (1919–2010) graduated from the Warsaw University of Technology (1946). Until 1952, he worked at the Department of Polish Architecture at the Faculty of Architecture at the Warsaw University of Technology. He worked for BOS and Miastoprojekt in the capital.

The most important projects and realizations: development of the W-70 and Wk-70 large panel building systems, the Bielany I-IV housing estate, a complex of buildings including a hotel for the Institute of Medical Improvement, and a complex of detached houses in Ursynów.

Roman PIOTROWSKI (1895–1988). A graduate of architecture at the Warsaw University of Technology (1924). Member of the Praesens Group. Architect in the studio of ZUS (1930–34) and the Society of Workers' Housing (1934–44). Head of the BOS (1945–49). Commissioner for the Reconstruction of the Capital and Vice-President of Warsaw (1945–47). In 1949–51, he held the post of Head of the Ministry of Construction, and from 1951 to 1956 – Minister of Construction. Member of PPR and PZPR. Member of the Legislative Parliament and the Parliament of the Polish People's Republic of the first term.

Important projects and realizations: WSM Rakowiec Housing Estate (co-authors: Szymon Syrkus, Helena Syrkus, Zygmunt Skibniewski, Aleksander Szniolis), ZUS Building in Gdynia, and ZUS Colony in Warsaw (co-authors: Bohdan Lachert, Romuald Miller, Józef Szanajca).

Bohdan PNIEWSKI (1897–1965) graduated from the Faculty of Architecture at the Warsaw University of Technology (1923). Lecturer at the Faculty of Architecture at the Warsaw University of Technology and at the Academy of Fine Arts.

His most important projects include the Patria Guest House in Krynica, the Magistrate's Court building in Warsaw, the Ministry of Communications building, the Peasant House in Warsaw (in collaboration with Małgorzata Handzelewicz-Wacławek), the reconstruction and extension of the Grand Theatre, the National Bank of Poland building, the extension of the Parliament building, and the design of the Temple of Divine Providence.

Józef Zbigniew POLAK (1923–2021) graduated from the Warsaw University of Technology (1949). He worked at the Faculty of Architecture at the Warsaw University of Technology, as well as at ZOR and the Central Research and Design

182 Appendix 1: Biographies of selected architects mentioned in the book

Center for General Construction in Warsaw and abroad, including Afghanistan, the United States, Libya, and Saudi Arabia.

Major projects and realizations: Cultural Center in Rzeszów, Cultural Center in Léopoldville, Kabul Downtown Project, Tel Aviv Downtown Project, Chicago Downtown Redevelopment Project – Central Plaza XX, and Crystal Cathedral of the Divine Mercy Project in Osny near Paris.

Arseniusz ROMANOWICZ (1910–2008) graduated from the Warsaw University of Technology (1936). Before World War II, he worked in the Central Office for Railway Construction in Warsaw. In 1951, he joined the Central Office for Railway Design and Projects (together with Piotr Szymaniak).

Piotr SZYMANIAK (1911–1967) graduated from the Faculty of Architecture at the Warsaw University of Technology (1938). Since 1951, designer at the Central Office for Railway Design and Projects.

The most important projects and realizations: YMCA Rowing Harbor at Wał Miedzeszyński in Warsaw, stations of the Cross-City Line in Warsaw – Powiśle, Ochota, Warsaw-Stadium, Śródmieście, Warsaw Śródmieście Railway Station, Warsaw Wschodnia Railway Station, and Warsaw Central Railway Station.

Józef SIGALIN (1909–1983). Graduated from the Faculty of Architecture at the Warsaw University of Technology (1946). Co-founder of the Planning and Reconstruction Office of the PKWN. Deputy head of the BOS. Chief Architect of Warsaw in 1951–56 and co-author of the General Plan of Warsaw.

The most important projects and realizations: W-Z line in Warsaw (co-author: S. Jankowski, J. Knothe, Z. Stępiński), Marszałkowska Housing Estate (co-author: S. Jankowski, J. Knothe, Z. Stępiński).

Halina SKIBNIEWSKA (1921–2011) graduated from the Warsaw University of Technology (1948). From 1948 to 1949, she worked at the Office for the Reconstruction of the Capital, and from 1957 at the Warsaw Housing Association. Lecturer at the Faculty of Architecture at the Warsaw University of Technology. Member of the Parliament of the Polish People's Republic in the fourth, fifth, sixth, seventh, and eighth terms. From 1971 to 1985, she was the first woman in the history of the Polish Parliament to serve as Deputy Speaker of the House of Parliament.

The most important projects and realizations are the Sady Żoliborskie housing estate in Warsaw, the Sadyba estate in Warsaw, the Community School in Sadyba, the Szwoleżerów estate in Warsaw, and the Białołęka Dworska estate project.

Jerzy SOŁTAN (1913–2005) graduated from the Warsaw University of Technology (1935). After World War II, he worked in the studio of Le Corbusier. From 1954 to 1967, he worked at the Academy of Fine Arts in Warsaw. 1959–1961 visiting professor at Harvard University (USA), then full professor. 1967–74 Dean of the Faculty of Architecture there.

The most important projects and realizations: the project of the building of the Air Defense League, the sports complex SKS "Warszawianka" in Warsaw (cooperation: Zbigniew Ihnatowicz, Lech Tomaszewski, Włodzimierz Wittek, Wiktor Gessler), the "Venice" Bar in Warsaw (co-authors: Z. Ihnatowicz, Adolf Jan Szczepiński), and the "Dukat" PDT in Olsztyn (co-author: Z. Ihnatowicz).

Appendix 1: Biographies of selected architects mentioned in the book 183

Zygmunt STĘPIŃSKI (1908–1982) graduated from the Faculty of Architecture at the Warsaw University of Technology (1933). Designer at the Warsaw Development Planning Office. Author of publications on the history of architecture and urbanism: Gawędy warszawskiego architekta [Stories from a Warsaw architect] (1984) and Siedem placów Warszawy [Seven squares of Warsaw] (1988).

The most important projects and realizations: W-Z route in Warsaw (co-authors: S. Jankowski, J. Knothe, J. Sigalin), Reconstruction of the Palace of the Government Commission for Internal and Religious Affairs in Warsaw (co-author: Mieczyslaw Kuzma), Reconstruction of tenement houses in the Old Town of Warsaw, Reconstruction of the Krasiński Palace (co-author: M. Kuzma), MDM (co-authors: S. Jankowski, J. Knothe, J. Sigalin), and International Press Club in Warsaw (co-author: M. Kuzma).

Helena SYRKUS (1900–1982) graduated from the Faculty of Architecture at the Warsaw University of Technology (1925) and from the Faculty of Philosophy at the University of Warsaw (1923). Lecturer at the Faculty of Architecture at the Warsaw University of Technology for many years. From 1948 to 1955, she was one of the vice-presidents of CIAM. Author of many important publications, including Ku idei osiedla społecznego [Towards the Idea of Social Settlement] (1976) and Społeczne cele urbanizacji [Social Goals of Urbanization] (1984).

Szymon SYRKUS (1893–1964) He studied architecture in Vienna, Graz, Riga, Moscow, and Warsaw from 1911 to 1922. In 1920–1921, he studied sculpture and painting at the Academy of Fine Arts in Cracow. Associated with the "Blok" group. Lecturer at the Faculty of Architecture at the Warsaw University of Technology. Member of CIAM. Founder of the "Praesens" group (1925).

The most important projects and realizations: the District Health Insurance Fund in Kutno, the Fertilizer Factory Pavilion at the General National Exhibition in Poznań, the WSM Rakowiec Housing Estate in Warsaw, the WSM Kolo-East Housing Estate in Warsaw, and the ZOR Housing Estate in Praga.

Jakub WUJEK (1937–2014). Graduated from the Faculty of Architecture at the Gdańsk University of Technology (1961). Lecturer at the Łódź University of Technology for many years. From 1963 to 1964, he worked in an architectural office in Helsinki. In 1967, he formed a design team with Zdzisław Lipski and Andrzej Owczarek, which was transformed into the "Lipski and Wujek" design office in 1990.

Major projects: Church of the Blessed Sacrament in Łódź (co-author: Zdzisław Lipski), Church of the Assumption in Łódź (co-author: Z. Lipski), housing estates in Łódź (including Radogoszcz-East), zoning plans for selected areas of Wloclawek, Katowice and Łódź, Drama Theatre in Płock, and reconstruction of the Jaracz Theatre in Łódź.

Jan ZACHWATOWICZ (1900–1983) graduated from the Institute of Civil Engineering in St. Petersburg and the Faculty of Architecture at the Warsaw University of Technology (1930). For many years, he worked as a lecturer at the Department of Polish Architecture at the Warsaw University of Technology. During World War II, he was active in the government delegation for Poland. After the war, he directed the reconstruction of Warsaw. Author of numerous publications,

184 *Appendix 1: Biographies of selected architects mentioned in the book*

including Monument Protection in Poland (1965), Polish Architecture (1967), and Royal Castle in Warsaw (1972).

Major projects and realizations: Reconstruction of the Basilica of St. John the Baptist in Warsaw (cooperation: Maria Piechotka and Kazimierz Piechotka) and Reconstruction of the Potocki Palace in Warsaw.

Konrad KUCZA-KUCZYŃSKI (1941) graduated from the Faculty of Architecture at the Warsaw University of Technology (1964). Lecturer at Białystok University of Technology (1980–85) and Warsaw University of Technology. Former member of the Presidium and Chairman of the Architecture Section of the Architecture and Urban Planning Committee of the Polish Academy of Sciences. Since 1991, he has led the Atelier 2 studio (together with Andrzej Miklaszewski).

Important projects and realizations: Main Library of Nicolaus Copernicus University in Toruń (co-author: Witold Benedek), Radio Astronomy Observatory in Piwnice near Toruń (co-author: Jacek Nalewajski), Church of the Conversion of St. Paul the Apostle in Warsaw (co-author: A. Miklaszewski), Church of the Good Shepherd in Warsaw, and Assembly Hall in Jasna Góra.

Janusz WYŻNIKIEWICZ (1931–2019) graduated from the Faculty of Architecture at the Gdańsk University of Technology (1956) and completed postgraduate studies at the Faculty of Architecture at the Warsaw University of Technology (1968). Employee of Łódź Miastoprojekt and the Municipal Design Office in Łódź. Since 2000, he has been working at the author's studio, "Janusz Wyżnikiewicz Pracownia Projektowa."

Major projects and realizations: MOSiR Sports Hall in Łódź, Copernicus Hospital in Łódź, Polish Mother's Health Center Institute, and CKD Clinical Hospital in Łódź.

Zbigniew GĄDEK (1925–1998) graduated from the Faculty of Architecture at the AGH University of Science and Technology in Cracow (1951). Lecturer at the Faculty of Architecture at the Cracow University of Technology, at the Faculty of Architecture at the Silesian University of Technology in Gliwice, at the Hull School of Architecture, and at the Faculty of Architecture at the University of Sheffield.

In his work, he searches for a native expression of architecture and tries to humanize large buildings. He presented his works at exhibitions in Poland (including Terra-1 and Terra-2 in Wrocław) and abroad (XIV Art Biennial in São Paulo in 1977). Winner of competitions (e.g., for a tourist centre in Bukowina Tatrzańska and for the development of the centre of Łódź).

Ewa DZIEKOŃSKA (1929) graduated from the Faculty of Architecture at the Wroc³aw University of Technology (1955). Worked in the Office of Rural Construction Projects in Wrocław, and from 1959 in Miastoprojekt – Tychy. Pioneer of participatory planning (F6 housing estate in Tychy). From 1986 to 1989, she cooperated with the Polish Academy of Sciences, working on the issue of designing energy-efficient houses. Involved in ecological activities, founder and long-term president of the Polish Ecological Club in Tychy.

Marek DZIEKOŃSKI (1930–2002). A graduate of the Faculty of Architecture at the Wrocław University of Technology. Lecturer at the Wrocław University of Technology and the Silesian University of Technology.

Appendix 1: Biographies of selected architects mentioned in the book 185

Major projects: Rotunda of the Racławicka Panorama in Wrocław (co-author: Ewa Dziekońska), Railway Station in Tychy, Fast Food Bar in the M Housing Estate in Tychy (co-author: Ewa Dziekońska), and Building of the NOT Mining Club in Tychy.

Włodzimierz GRUSZCZYŃSKI (1906–1973). Graduate of the School of Construction in Cracow (1925). Graduate of the Faculty of Architecture at the Academy of Fine Arts in Cracow (1930). Graduate of the Faculty of Architecture at the Warsaw University of Technology (1936). Professor at the Cracow University of Technology. Co-organizer of the Faculty of Architecture in Cracow after World War II, where he was head of the Department of Architectural Composition, then head of the Department of Landscape Design.

Jan BOGUSŁAWSKI (1910–1982) graduated from the Faculty of Architecture at the Warsaw University of Technology (1933). Professor at the Faculty of Architecture at the Warsaw University of Technology and at the Higher School of Fine Arts in Poznań. Winner of 28 awards in national and international competitions, including first prizes for theater and opera designs in Madrid and Budapest and first prize for the design of the Embassy of the Polish People's Republic in Moscow.

The most important projects and realizations: Praha Cinema, Zodiak Pavilion, Chemia Pavilion (all in Warsaw), and reconstruction of the Royal Castle in Warsaw.

Przemysław GAWOR (1927) – graduate of the Cracow University of Technology (1952). He started his professional career in 1949 in Miastoprojekt – Cracow.

Major projects and realizations: competition for the design of a shelter in Morskie Oko in the Tatra Mountains (co-authors: L. Filar, Z. Perchal, and J. Pilitowski), House of Culture in Chrzanów (co-authors: L. Filar, Z. Perchal, and J. Pilitowski), and holiday house Harnaś in Bukowina Tatrzańska (co-authors: L. Filar, Z. Perchal, and J. Pilitowski).

Stanisław SPYT (1924). Graduate of the Faculty of Architecture at the Cracow University of Technology (1950). Designer at Miastoprojekt Cracow.

Major projects and realizations: the building of the Chemical Institute of the Jagiellonian University in Cracow, the Tourist House in Cracow (co-author: Z. Mikołajewski), the Silesia Rest House in Krynica (co-author: Z. Mikołajewski), and the Mineral Water Drinking Hall in Krynica (co-author: Z. Mikołajewski).

Marek LEYKAM (1898–1983), a graduate of the Faculty of Architecture at the Warsaw University of Technology (1933). Soldier in the September campaign of 1939 and the 1940 campaign in France. Interned in Switzerland. Lecturer at the Faculty of Architecture at the Warsaw University of Technology and at the Engineering School in Szczecin. Designer at the Office of Industrial Construction Projects in Warsaw.

The most important projects and realizations: the building of the Supreme Chamber of Control and the District Court for the capital city of Warsaw (co-author Jerzy Hryniewiecki), the department store "Okrąglak" in Poznań; the Ministry of National Defense in Warsaw (co-author J. Hryniewiecki), the Office Building of the Presidium of the Government in Warsaw, the Tenth Anniversary Stadium in Warsaw (co-authors: J. Hryniewiecki, Czesław Rajewski), and the Tourist House in Płock.

186 *Appendix 1: Biographies of selected architects mentioned in the book*

Wacław KŁYSZEWSKI (1910–2000). Graduated from the Faculty of Architecture at the Warsaw University of Technology (1936). Participant in the War of Independence in 1939. Prisoner of war in camps: in Spittal on the Drau and in the IIC camp in Woldenberg.

Jerzy MOKRZYŇSKI (1909–1997). Student of the Faculty of Architecture at the Lviv Polytechnic. Graduated from the Faculty of Architecture at the Warsaw University of Technology (1935). Fought in the September Campaign and then in the Home Army. In the 1970s, a member of the Minister of Culture and Art's Commission for Architectural Creativity.

Eugeniusz WIERZBICKI (1909–1991) Graduated from the Faculty of Architecture at the Warsaw Technical University (1936). Participant in the September Campaign of 1939. Prisoner of war camp: II B Arnswalde and II D Gross Born.

Kłyszewski, Mokrzyński, and Wierzbicki worked together and their team became known as the "Tigers."

Important projects and realizations: Party House in Warsaw, apartment building at 8 Kredytowa St. in Warsaw, train station in Katowice, Museum of Modern Art in Skopje, and Philharmonic Hall in Rzeszów.

Barbara BRUKALSKA (1899–1980) graduated from the Faculty of Architecture at the Warsaw University of Technology (1934). Professor at the Warsaw University of Technology. Co-founder, with Stanisław Brukalski, Bohdan Lachert, Józef Szanajca, Helena Syrkus, and Szymon Syrkus, of the creative group Praesens, which became the Polish section of CIAM.

Stanisław BRUKALSKI (1894–1967). Student at the Polytechnic University of Milan. Graduate of the Faculty of Architecture at the Warsaw University of Technology (1925). Professor at the Warsaw University of Technology.

The most important projects and realizations: own house, 8 Niegolewskiego Street, Warsaw (co-author B. Brukalska), ZUS and WSM buildings in Warsaw (S. Brukalski + B. Brukalska), and Komedia Theater and Social House of Culture in Warsaw.

Aleksander ZWIERKO (1924–2003) graduated from the Faculty of Architecture at the Wrocław University of Technology (1951). Then he worked as a designer in the Office of Industrial Construction Projects in Wrocław, the Miastoprojekt Office in Wrocław, and the Miastoprojekt Office in Łódź.

Major projects and realizations: skyscrapers in the area of Main Street in Łódź, office buildings "Cetebe" and "Confexim" in Łódź, and downtown residential district in Łódź.

Wojciech ZABŁOCKI (1930–2020) graduated from the Faculty of Architecture at the AGH University of Science and Technology in Cracow (1954). Lecturer at the Institute of Architecture of the Łódź University of Technology and at the Faculty of Architecture of the University of Ecology and Management in Warsaw. Designer at the Office of Studies and Typical Projects of Industrial Construction. Four-time Olympian in fencing (three-time medalist). Multiple participant and ten-time medalist in World Fencing Championships.

Major projects and realizations: Sports Hall of the Academy of Physical Education in Warsaw, Olympic Preparation Center in Warsaw, Sports Complex in Konin,

Appendix 1: Biographies of selected architects mentioned in the book 187

Sports Center in Puławy, Sports Center in Aleppo (Syria), Olympic Center in Latakia (Syria), and Monument to Silesian Insurgents in Katowice (co-author Gustaw Zemla).

Author of publications, including "With Feather and Saber," "Architecture for active recreation in urban agglomerations," and "Architecture."

Tadeusz PTASZYCKI (1908–1980). Graduate of the Faculty of Architecture at the Warsaw University of Technology (1936). Researcher at the Faculty of Architecture at the Warsaw University of Technology. General Director of the Wrocław Reconstruction Directorate, Director of the Wrocław Planning Office, Director of the Central Design Office of the ZOR in Warsaw, and General Designer of the City of Nowa Huta. Participant in the September Campaign of 1939. Prisoner of war in the officers' POW camps of Brunswick, Oflag IIC – Woldenberg, Murnau.

Member of the Committee for Town Planning and Architecture, the Committee for Construction, Town Planning and Architecture, and the Committee for Science and Technology.

Juliusz ŻÓRAWSKI (1898–1967). Graduate of the Faculty of Architecture at the Warsaw University of Technology (1927). Researcher at the Faculty of Architecture at the Warsaw University of Technology. During World War II, he received his PhD at the secret Faculty of Architecture of the Warsaw University of Technology. He spent 1943–1945 in Zakopane.

The most important projects and realizations: the Wedel House in Warsaw, the Postal Savings Bank in Vilnius, the tenement house of the State Mutual Insurance Company of Intellectual Workers in Warsaw, and the apartment house on Przyjaciół Street in Warsaw.

Author of "On the Construction of Architectural Form."

Bohdan LISOWSKI (1924–1992) graduated from the Faculty of Architecture at the AGH University of Science and Technology in Cracow (1948). Professor at the Cracow University of Technology. Pioneer in ergonomics research and designer in the field of industrial design.

Major projects and realizations: "House of Hundred Balconies in Cracow, TAMEL Electric Motors Factory in Tarnow, STOMIL Factory in Debica."

Author of, among others, publications: Genealogy of Extreme Avant-Garde Architecture of the 20th Century 1800–1900," "Extreme Avant-Garde Architecture of the 20th Century 1900–1944," and "Systematic of Architecture of the 20th Century – World and Poland (1981–84)."

Wojciech PIETRZYK (1930–2017) graduated from the Faculty of Architecture at the AGH University of Science and Technology in Cracow (1956).

Important projects and realizations: Willa Książków in Tarnów, Church of Our Lady Queen of Poland (Ark of the Lord) in Nowa Huta, and Church of the Lord Jesus the Good Shepherd in Cracow.

Stanisław NIEMCZYK (1943–2019) graduated from the Faculty of Architecture at the Cracow University of Technology (1968). Designer at Miastoprojekt Nowe Tychy.

Major projects and realizations: complex of suburban recreational buildings, Tychy-Paprocany, Glinka housing complex – H7 housing estate in Tychy, Nad

188 *Appendix 1: Biographies of selected architects mentioned in the book*

Jamną housing complex in Mikołów, Church of the Holy Spirit in Tychy, Divine Mercy Church in Cracow, and Church and Monastery of the Franciscan Order of Friars Minor in Tychy.

Dariusz KOZŁOWSKI (1942) graduated from the Faculty of Architecture at the Cracow University of Technology. Professor at the Cracow University of Technology. Dean of the Faculty of Architecture at the Cracow University of Technology from 2005 to 2012.

Important projects and realizations: The Alchemist's House in Cracow, the Higher Seminary of the Congregation of the Resurrection Fathers (co-authors: Maria Misiągiewicz and Wacław Stefański).

Anna GÓRSKA (1914–2002) student at the Faculty of Architecture, Lviv Polytechnic. Graduate of the Faculty of Architecture at the Warsaw University of Technology (1939). Designer: at the London County Council, Urban Development Department (Great Britain), at the Construction Design and Research Office "Miastoprojekt" Cracow Branch in Zakopane, at the Industrial Construction Design Office "Pracownia" in Zakopane. Head of the Construction, Urban Planning, and Architecture Department in the Presidium of the Municipal National Council in Zakopane.

Major projects and realizations: Mountain Lodge on Hala pod Ornakiem, – Mountain Lodge in the Valley of Five Ponds (co-authors: Jan Chmielewski, Jerzy Mokrzyński, Gerard Ciołek, and Jędrzej Czerniak), ORBIS Hotel in Zakopane (co-authors: Stefan Żychoń and others), and "Granit" Co-operative Trading House in Zakopane.

Adolf CIBOROWSKI (1919–1987) graduated from the Faculty of Architecture at the Warsaw University of Technology (1946). Associate professor at the Warsaw University of Technology. Worked in the Office for the Reconstruction of the Capital, Head of the Urban Planning Office in Szczecin, Head of the Urban Planning Department of the Department of Workers' Estates in Warsaw, Chief Urban Planner in the Committee for Urban Planning and Architecture. Chief Architect of Warsaw, Chief Director of the UN Reconstruction Program in Skopje (Macedonia), and Advisor to the UN Secretariat on Urban Planning. Member of the Parliament of the Polish People's Republic. Member of the Council of State.

Consultant to United Nations Educational, Scientific and Cultural Organization (UNESCO), United Nations Disaster Relief Office (UNDRO), and United Nations Centre for Human Settlements (UNCHS) on the reconstruction of cities destroyed by earthquakes. Author of many scientific publications.

Zbigniew KARPIŃSKI (1906–1983). Graduate of the Faculty of Architecture at the Warsaw University of Technology (1937). Associate professor at the Warsaw University of Technology. Designer at the Office for Reconstruction of the Capital. Dean of the Faculty of Architecture at the Warsaw University of Technology (1971–73).

Important projects and realizations: Courthouse in Gdynia (co-authors: Tadeusz Sieczkowski and Roman Sołtyński), Metalexport Office Building in Warsaw, Embassy of the People's Republic of Poland in Beijing, and "Eastern Wall" development at Marszałkowska Street in Warsaw.

Appendix 1: Biographies of selected architects mentioned in the book 189

Danuta OLĘDZKA (1927–1925) graduated from the Faculty of Architecture at the Gdańsk University of Technology (1952). Assistant at the Department of Utility and Industrial Construction at the Faculty of Architecture at the Gdańsk University of Technology and designer at the Gdańsk Office of General Construction Projects Miastoprojekt in Gdańsk.

Major projects and realizations: Dom Technika NOT in Gdańsk (co-author: S. Baum), multi-family buildings "falowce" on the Przymorze estate in Gdańsk (co-authors: Tadeusz Różański and Janusz Morek), and Neptun Holiday Resort, Jurata (co-author: Daniel Olędzki)

Daniel OLĘDZKI (1925–1991) graduated from the Faculty of Architecture at the Gdańsk University of Technology (1952). Designer in the Gdańsk Office of General Construction Projects Miastoprojekt in Gdańsk. Co-founder and designer in the ZAPA team of Authorial Architectural Laboratories.

His most important projects include the Stare Przedmieście Housing Estate in Gdańsk, the urban design of the Grunwald Housing Estate in Gdańsk (co-authors: R. Hordyński and others), the Wybrzeże Theatre in Gdańsk (co-author: Lech Kadłubowski), the Musical Theatre in Gdynia (co-author: Józef Chmiel), and the extension of the Baltic Opera in Gdańsk (co-author: Józef Chmiel).

Zygmunt SKIBNIEWSKI (1905–1994) graduated from the Faculty of Architecture at the Warsaw University of Technology (1933). Studied in Paris under Le Corbusier. Associate professor at the Warsaw University of Technology. Had an architectural studio in Warsaw until 1939. After the war, co-founder of the Bureau for Reconstruction of the Capital (BOS), director of the Warsaw City Planning Office, and chairman of the Committee for City Planning and Architecture. Member of the Parliament of the Polish People's Republic (1952–1956).

Volunteer in the defence of Lviv and in the Polish-Bolshevik war (1918–1920). Soldier in the Home Army. During the occupation, as part of the Urban Planning and Architectural Workshop (PAU), he worked with other Warsaw architects on a secret plan for the reconstruction of Warsaw.

Jerzy BUSZKIEWICZ (1930–2000) graduated from the Faculty of Architecture at the Poznań University of Technology (1953) and from the Faculty of Architecture at the Cracow University of Technology (1956). Assistant at Miastoprojekt Poznań and designer at the Provincial Office of Architecture and Construction in Poznań and the Office of Industrial Construction Projects in Poznań. Scholarship holder at the Office of the Chief Architect of London (London County Council). Head of the Urban Planning and Architecture Department of the City of Poznań and Chief Architect of the City and Director of the Spatial Management and Environmental Protection Department of the Poznań City Hall. Director of the Provincial Office for Urban and Rural Development and Chief Architect of the Province. Second Vice-President of the UIA (1978–81) and First Vice-President of the UIA (1981–85). Honorary member of the American Institute of Architecture and Honorary member of the Bund Deutscher Architekten.

The most important projects and realizations: the building of the Provincial Office in Poznań, the Hotel "Poznań" in Poznań, 32 Wielkopolska Inns – roadside

190   *Appendix 1: Biographies of selected architects mentioned in the book*

inns, the Monument to the Victims of the Nazi Extermination Camp Kulmhof on the Nehr.

Bohdan LACHERT (1900–1987) graduated from the Faculty of Architecture at the Warsaw University of Technology (1926). Professor at the Warsaw University of Technology. Dean of the Faculty of Architecture at the Warsaw University of Technology (1950–54). Co-founder of the creative group Praesens, which was transformed into the Polish section of CIAM.

Major projects and realizations: the Lachert family's three-family house on Katowicka Street in Warsaw (co-author: Józef Szanajca), the tenement house for officials of the State Mutual Insurance Company of Mind Employees in Warsaw (co-author: J. Szanajca), the PKO office building in Warsaw, the Muranów housing estate in Warsaw, the cemetery of Soviet Army soldiers in Warsaw, and the National Library in Tehran.

Ryszard KARŁOWICZ (1919–2007) graduated from the Faculty of Architecture at the Warsaw University of Technology. Professor at the Warsaw University of Technology. Lecturer at the Faculty of Architecture at the Warsaw University of Technology. Employed at the Office for Reconstruction of the Capital.UN expert (1964–66).

Major projects and realizations: Nicolaus Copernicus University Complex in Toruń (chief architect), Staromiejskie Housing Estate in Łódź (chief architect).

Author of publications, including "The Development of Large Agglomerations in Poland."

Marian FIKUS (1938). Graduate of the Faculty of Architecture at the Wrocław University of Technology (1963). Lecturer and professor at the Poznań University of Technology for many years. Worked in Opole: in the Municipal Studio of Urban Planning, then in the Opole Office of Miastoprojekt. Since 1974 – in Miastoprojekt Poznań. In 1988, together with his wife Elzbieta Kosinska-Fikus, he founded the "Studio Fikus" architectural office.

Winner of numerous awards and prizes in national and international competitions. Major projects and realizations: Campus of Adam Mickiewicz University in Poznań (co-author: J. Gurawski), Spa and Holiday District in Kołobrzeg (co-author: J. Gurawski), and Residential District in Kędzierzyn (co-author: J. Gurawski).

Bogdan WYPOREK (1928). Graduate of the Faculty of Architecture at the Warsaw University of Technology. President of the Polish Association of Town Planners and Vice-President of the European Council of Town Planners. UN expert on urban planning.

Major projects: Reconstruction Plan for Skopje, Reconstruction of Chimbote (Peru), National Spatial Development Plan of Libya, and Warsaw Center Development Project.

Romuald LOEGLER (1940) graduated from the Faculty of Architecture at the Cracow University of Technology (1964). Worked at the Office of Projects and Technical Services in Cracow and then as part of a team of authors with Jacek Czekaj and Marek Piotrowski. In 1987, he opened his own architectural office "Atelier Loegler and Partners." In 1985, he was a co-founder of the Architecture Biennial

Appendix 1: Biographies of selected architects mentioned in the book   191

in Cracow; from 1985 to 1991, he was editor-in-chief of the magazine "Architekt" and later published the monthly magazine "Architektura & Biznes."

Major projects and realizations: Church of St. Jadwiga the Queen in Cracow (co-author J. Czekaj), Church of Our Lady of the Rosary in Rzeszów (co-author J. Czekaj), apartment building in Berlin on Dessauer Strasse, E Center in Nowa Huta, extension of the Jagiellonian Library in Cracow, new building of the Łódź Philharmonic, and building of the Cracow Opera.

Wojciech JARZĄBEK (1950) graduated from the Faculty of Architecture at the Wrocław University of Technology (1973). Worked in the Inwestprojekt office. In the late 1970s and early 1980s, he worked in design offices in Kuwait. In 1991, co-founder of the private studio "Studio Ar-5" and member of the NSZZ "Solidarity."

Major projects and realizations: housing estate Nowy Dwór in Wrocław, Church of the Blessed Virgin Mary Queen of Peace in Wrocław, tenement house on Wybrzeze Wyspiańskiego, department stores Solpol I and Solpol II (all in Wrocław), and building Central Agency for Information Tech in Kuwait (co-author Edward Lach)

Krzysztof WIŚNIOWSKI (1944) graduated from the Faculty of Architecture at the Wrocław University of Technology. Worked in the Inwestprojekt office. In the late 1970s and early 1980s, he worked for Shiber Consult in Kuwait and then for INCO.

Major projects and realizations: Łódź City Centre Housing Estate (co-authors: Mieczysław Sowa, Ryszard Żabiński et al.), Kozanów Housing Estate in Wrocław (co-authors Andrzej Bohdanowicz, Ryszard Daczkowski and Edward Lach), Library in Damascus (Syria), Sabah al Salem Housing Estate, Port Authority Headquarters in Kuwait, Al-Baloush Bus Station in Kuwait, and Ministry of Interior (MOI) Headquarters commissioned by the Ministry of Public Works in Kuwait.

Index

20th Congress of the Communist Party of the Soviet Union 8

Aalto, Alvar 51
Abu-Dhabi 72
Accra 68, 69
Adamczewska-Wejchert, Hanna 94, 95, 109, 166, 174
Adegbite, Vic 68, 69
al-Assad, Hafez 70
Aleppo 70, 71, 187
Alexander, Christopher 53, 54, 155
Algiers 68
Amanowicz, Wojciech 63
Architectural and Urban Planning Studio (Pracownia Architektoniczno-Urbanistyczna–PAU) 15, 189
Architecture d'Aujourd'hui (journal) 52
Architekt (journal) 53, 191
Architektura (journal) 22, 38, 49–51, 53–55, 64, 68, 83, 95, 127, 154, 155, 164
Architektura i Budownictwo (journal) 11
Ärhus 176
as-Asad, Basil 72
Association of Polish Architects (SARP) 26, 28–30, 36, 38, 43, 48, 49, 52, 55, 60, 63, 82, 83, 93, 98, 114, 140, 148, 165, 174, 177, 178
Aswan 68
Athens Charter 84, 145, 154, 163, 165
Auschwitz 15, 50, 178

Baghdad 67–69, 175
Bald, Wacław 136
Ballenstedt, Janusz 63, 90, 91
Baloush 73, 191
Balzac, Honore 84
Banaszewski, Bogdan 61

Bandura, Jerzy 123, 176
Banham, Reyner 52
Barucki, Tadeusz 25, 26, 29, 39, 55, 60, 61, 89, 114, 174
Basista, Andrzej xv, 1, 3, 22, 24, 32, 34, 43, 45, 52, 55, 69, 121, 150, 171, 175
Batlle y Ordonez, Jose 61, 62
Bauen un Wohnen (journal) 52
Baum, Szczepan 29, 107, 108, 136, 158, 166–168, 175, 189
Baumeister (journal) 52
Baumiller, Jerzy 68, 69
Behrens, Peter 11
Benedek, Witold 117, 184
Berlage, H. P. 11
Berlin 56, 57, 191
Białystok 86, 175, 176, 184
Biegański, Piotr 2, 96, 174
Bielany (Warsaw) 93, 143, 144, 181
Bielecki, Czesław 52, 54, 155, 157, 163–165, 175
Bień, Krzysztof 129
Bieńkuński, Stanisław 79, 86
Bierut, Bolesław 36, 51, 81, 83, 96–98, 122
Bierut Decree 96
Bigus, Antoni 37
Blok (group) 11, 183
Bogusławski, Jan 31, 63, 80, 185
Bohdanowicz, Andrzej 72, 191
Borawski, Ludwik 146, 147
Brabander, Jerzy 94
Brasilia 59
Brezhnev, Leonid 125, 126
Brukalska, Barbara 11, 12, 81, 87, 186
Brukalski, Stanisław 11, 12, 81, 87, 100, 186
Bruszewski, Andrzej 54

Index 193

Budapest 50, 63, 185
Budzyński, Marek 55, 56, 146–148,
155, 157, 160, 161, 163, 165,
175, 176
Bukowina Tatrzańska 130, 131, 184, 185
Bulganin, Nikolai 88
Buszkiewicz, Jerzy 35, 37, 40, 63–66, 119,
125, 189
Buszko, Henryk 26, 86, 132, 145,
174, 176
Bzie Zameckie 139

Catherine II 125
Cęckiewicz, Witold 19, 20, 31, 35, 37, 40,
65, 123, 124, 127, 176
Chartres Cathedral 19
Chełmno nad Nerem (Kulmhof am Nehr)
125, 190
Chicago 58, 182
Chmiel, Józef 29, 189
Chmielewski, Jan 12, 64, 65, 188
Chomątowska, Beata 90
Chorzów 176, 179
Chronowski, Jerzy 33
Chyrosz, Jacek 68, 69
Ciborowski, Adolf 40, 43, 50, 67, 188
Cichońska, Izabela 158, 162
Ciechocinek 14, 159, 178
Committee for Construction, Urban
Planning and Architecture (KBUA) 36
Committee for Urban Planning and
Architecture (KUA) 35, 36
The Company for Workers' Housing Estate
(Zakład Osiedli Robotniczych-ZOR) 26,
81, 181, 183, 187
Congrés Internationaux d'Architecture
Moderne (CIAM) 11, 14, 58, 77, 145,
165, 183, 186, 190
Copernicus, Nicolaus 86, 117
Courbet, Gustave 84
Cracow 7, 10, 15, 19, 23, 27, 28, 31–34,
37, 38, 40, 50, 53, 59, 60, 63, 64, 67,
69, 70, 84, 85, 89, 90, 92, 97, 107,
117, 120, 127, 129, 131, 135, 157,
162, 166, 174–179, 181, 183–185,
187–191
critical regionalism 3, 129, 130, 131
Curzon Line 5
Cymer, Anna 1, 91, 93
Cyrankiewicz, Józef 6, 114, 115, 122
Czarnecki, Maciej 17
Czekaj, Jacek 60, 190, 191
Czeladź 116
Czepkowski, Jerzy 179

Czyżewska, Maria 117
Czyżewski, Andrzej 117

Damascus 70–72, 191
Democratic Party (SD) 6
Deńko, Stanisław 65, 176
Dobrzański, Wojciech 166
Domus (journal) 52
Doylestown 181
Drozd, Piotr 60
Drzewiecki, Henryk 53
Dubai 72
du Chateau, Stephan 174
Duda, Michał 103, 137, 138
Dummar 70
Dunikowski, Marek 70
Duszeńko, Franciszek 125
Dziekońska, Ewa 27, 124, 125, 147,
184, 185
Dziekoński, Marek 124, 125, 184, 185
Dziewoński, Marian 145, 158

Edmund, Osmańczyk 103
Eisenmann, Peter 155–157
Elbląg 108, 166–168, 175
Espoo 56, 64, 65

Fangor, Wojciech 59
Fikus, Marian 40, 63, 65, 118, 166, 177,
178, 190
Filar, Leszek 129–131, 185
Fitzke, Ewa 166
Foster, Norman 72
Frampton, Kenneth 130, 131
Franta, Aleksander xiv, 23, 26, 86, 132,
133, 145, 158, 174, 176
Freud, Sigmund 23
Froebel's blocks 19
Frydecki, Andrzej 65
Functional Warsaw 12, 15

Gabiś, Agata 139
Gaddafi, Muammar 72
Gądek, Zbigniew 65, 130, 184
Gadomska, Barbara 54
Galica, Józef 131
Garwolin 174
Gawor, Przemysław 23, 33, 130,
131, 185
Gdańsk 5, 7–9, 29, 33, 36–38, 40, 52, 56,
87, 93, 100, 102–104, 117, 120, 127,
133, 135, 136, 144, 145, 171, 174, 175,
177, 179, 180, 183, 184, 189
Gessler, Wiktor 182

194   Index

Ghirardo, Diane 52
Giedion, Siegfried 51, 96
Gierek, Edward 9, 10, 42, 126, 137, 139, 140, 147
Gintowt, Maciej 127, 179
Gistedt, Elna 12
Gliszczyński, Mieczysław 27, 63
Gliwice 95, 175, 184
Global South 3, 55, 67, 70
Główczewski, Jerzy 68
Gniewiewski, Bohdan 63
Godlewski, Jan 118
Gołąb, Józef 117
Goldzamt, Edmund 83, 88, 89, 98, 114, 177
Gomułka, Władysław 9, 60, 102, 108, 116, 123–125, 159
Görres, Guido 50
Górska, Anna 130, 188
Gottfried, Jerzy 86, 174, 176
Grabowska-Hawrylak, Jadwiga 102, 103, 116, 137–139, 142, 177
Grabowski, Jan 86, 179
Graves, Robert 155
Graz 183
Grębecka, Jadwiga 61, 63
Gropius Walter 51, 65
Grunwald 122–125
Gruszkowski, Wiesław 35–37, 40, 100, 103, 104, 177
Gulbinowicz, Henryk 162
Gurjanova, Helena 178
Gutman Ignacy (Izaak) 14
Gutt, Romuald 14, 21, 25, 32, 49, 60, 78, 88, 89, 141, 178
Gzowska, Alicja 157

Hadid, Zaha 72
Hałas, Henryk 44
Handzelewicz-Wacławek, Małgorzata 181
Hansen (Garlińska-Hansen) Zofia 145, 160, 178
Hansen, Oskar 58, 59, 145, 160, 178
Haupt, Adam 125
Hennig, Władysław 27, 35, 37, 38, 40, 41, 128, 178
Herbst, Krzysztof 30
Herburt, Tadeusz 116
Högsbro Sven 55
Holzbauer, Wilhelm 64
Home Army 41, 57, 176, 179, 186, 189
Homs 70
Hordyński, Roman 93, 189
Howard, Ebenezer 145
Hryniewicz, Wacław 161

Hryniewiecka, Katarzyna 49
Hryniewiecki, Jerzy 15–17, 31, 32, 34, 37, 43, 79, 88, 122, 124, 127, 138, 172, 178, 185
Humięcki, Wiktor 71
Husarska, Helena 124, 176
Husarski, Roman 124, 176

Ihnatowicz, Zbigniew 79, 182
Ingarden, Janusz 90, 91
Ingarden, Marta 90, 91
Institute of National Remembrance (IPN) 56, 57, 172
International Committee for the Resolution of Problems in Contemporary Architecture (CIRPAC) 12
International Meeting Architects and Local Government Activists 49
International Union of Architects (UIA) 154, 165, 189
Iron Curtain 2, 3, 48, 48, 49, 52–54, 64, 126, 139, 141

Jacobs, Jane 54, 155
Janković-Beguš, Jelena 115
Jankowski, Karol 11
Jankowski, Stanisław 59, 86, 88, 91, 92, 100, 179, 182, 183
Janowski, Tadeusz 90
Jarosław 38, 178
Jarząbek, Wojciech 73, 74, 148, 155, 157, 161, 162, 191
Jastrzębia, Góra 175
Jawor 107, 108, 180
Jeanneret, Pierre 11, 178
Jencks, Charles 52, 154, 155
Jerusalem 164
Jerzy, Grotowski 177
Jerzy, Gurawski 34, 65, 118, 119, 166, 177, 190
Jezierski, Jerzy 179
John Paul II (Pope) 154
Johnson, Philip 19, 65
Juchnowicz, Stanisław 90, 179
Juszczyk, Stanisław 28

Kabul 182
Kaczorowski, Michał 24
Kadłubowski, Lech 36, 52, 189
Kaganovich Lazar 88
Kalinin Mikhail 88
Kalkowski, Leszek 44
Kamieniec Pomorski 109
Kammel, Leo 57, 58

Index 195

Kardaszewska, Irena 28
Kardaszewski, Bolesław 23, 28, 33, 34, 39, 40, 43, 44, 120, 141, 149, 150, 179
Karłowicz, Ryszard 39, 40, 68, 94, 117, 120, 121, 190
Karpiel, Stanisław 130
Karpiński, Zbigniew 13, 32, 79, 134, 135, 188
Karpowicz, Andrzej 54
Katowice 9, 14, 26, 86, 117, 127, 134, 135, 144, 145, 158, 166, 171, 176, 179, 183, 186, 187
Katyń 175
Kazimierz, Dolny 85, 178
Kazubiński, Janusz 64, 65
Kędzierzyn 177, 190
Khalifa, Fauzi 71
Kharkiv 175
Khurshchev, Nikita 50, 88, 125
Kielce 15, 86
Kilarski, Jan 103
Kiltynowicz, Witold 12
Kirov, Sergei 88
Klein, Lidia 54, 154, 157
Klewin, Jan 134
Kłosiewicz, Lech 64
Kłyszewski, Wacław 79, 127, 174, 186
Knothe, Jan 86, 91, 92, 100, 179, 182, 183
Kobylański, Tadeusz 61
Kołacz, Leszek 88
Kołobrzeg 107, 177, 180, 190
Komunikat SARP (journal) 38, 48, 51
Konin 127, 128, 186
Konstancin 175
Korski, Witold 60
Kosciuszko, Tadeusz 39, 124
Kossak, Wojciech 124
Kotarbiński, Adam 51, 81, 84
Kotela, Czesław 40
Kozłowski, Dariusz 53, 162, 188
Kozłowski, Tadeusz 14
Kożuchów (Freystadt) 107
Krasińska, Ewa 127
Krasiński, Maciej 127, 172, 179, 183
Krier, Leon 53
Król, Mieczysław 144
Królikowski, Jeremi 53
Królikowski, Konrad 171
Krosno 38, 128
Krug, Jan 65, 79
Krzewińska, Zofia 179
Krzyszkowski, Adam 49
Kucza-Kuczyński, Konrad 159, 184
Kupka, Alfons 162

Kuraś, Krzysztof 64, 65
Kurmanowicz, Helena 58
Kurmanowicz, Jerzy 57, 58
Kuryłowicz, Ewa 142
Kuś, Stanisław 70, 127
Kuzma, Mieczysław 183
Kwaśniewicz, Stanisław 117
Kwieciński, A. 175

Lach, Edward 72, 191
Lachert, Bohdan 11, 12, 39, 94, 96, 181, 186, 190
Lalewicz, Marian 10
Lappo, Osmo 56
Larsson, Naomi 115
Latakia 71, 72, 187
Latour, Stanisław 17
Le Corbusier, Charles Jeanneret xiv, 11, 14, 51, 55, 60, 79, 129, 154, 159, 163, 182, 189
Leder, Andrzej 15
Ledkiewicz, Maria 124
Lenin, Vladimir 84, 122
Leopoldville 61, 62, 66, 182
Lettström, Gustaf 49
Leykam, Marek 79, 80, 88, 124, 179, 185
Libera, Adalberto 12
Lilpop, Franciszek 11
Linear Continuous System (LSC) 145, 178
Lipski, Zdzisław 65, 165, 166, 183
Liśniewicz, Jerzy 136
Lisowski, Bohdan 2, 17, 23, 34, 187
Łódź 14, 23, 24, 28, 29, 31, 33, 34, 40, 79, 94, 97, 116, 117, 120, 125, 136, 137, 141, 149, 150, 161, 165, 166, 175, 176, 179, 180, 183, 184, 186, 190, 191
Loegler, Romuald 53, 54, 59, 60, 155–157, 166, 190
London 12, 58, 59, 61, 64, 188, 189
Łowiński, Józef 25, 80
Lubicz-Nycz, Jan 64
Lublin 48, 94, 102, 120, 125, 145, 160, 174, 178, 179
Lubocka-Hoffmann, Maria 108, 166–168
Lviv 5, 10, 37, 39, 73, 95, 177, 186, 188, 189

Maciejewska, Beata 107
Mackiewicz, Ludwik 179
Mączeński, Zdzisław 13
Madejski, Andrzej 63
Madrid 63, 185
Malbork 107, 175
Mańkowski, Tomasz 32, 33
Marciniak, Piotr 118, 120, 136

196 *Index*

Marczewski, Kazimierz 80
Marshall Plan 6
Marszałkowska Residential District
  (Marszałkowska Dzielnica Mieszkaniowa–
  MDM) 84, 88, 92, 93, 179, 182
Matkowski, Jan 161
Matoń, A. 175
Mednoye 175
Meissner, Jan 33, 70
Mexico City 50
Mezga, Duane 98
Mickiewicz, Adam 86, 183
Miklaszewski, Andrzej 184
Mikołajewski, Zbigniew 185
Mikołów 166, 167, 188
Milewski, Witold 106, 107, 118, 119, 180
Miller, Romuald 14
Millo, Witold 161, 180
Miłobędzki, Adam jr. 53
Miłobędzki, Adam sr. 115
Minc, Hilary 8
Minorski, Jan 49, 51, 83, 88, 114
Mokrzyński, Jerzy 79, 127, 174, 186, 188
Molotov, Vyacheslav 88
Montecatini 63
Montevideo 61, 62
Morek, Janusz 189
Moscow 35, 50, 51, 63, 83, 85, 176, 177,
  183, 185
Moser, Karl 96
Mrówczyński, Tadeusz 148
Müller, Maria 107, 108, 180
Müller, Stefan 61, 64, 65, 107, 108,
  161, 180
Muranów 44, 94, 190
Murawski, Michał 98
Murczyński, Stanisław 28
Mussolini, Benito 12
Muszyński, K. 175
Mycek, Tadeusz 21, 31, 122, 180

Nalewajski, Jacek 184
National Meeting of Architects 21, 25, 88,
  89, 114
National Meeting of Party Architects 83
Nawratek, Krzysztof 36
Nędzi, Andrzej 137
Neutra, Richard 61, 62, 104
New Delhi 176
Nidzica 107
Niemczyk, Stanisław 162, 163, 166,
  167, 187
Niemeyer, Oscar 65
Niemojewski, Lech 11, 31, 32

Niewiadomski, Stanisław 70, 117
Niverød 55
Nkrumah, Kwame 68
North Ursynów 56, 141, 146–148, 160,
  163, 165, 176, 181
Nowa Huta 7, 8, 28, 50, 84, 89, 90, 91, 92,
  94, 95, 102, 117, 159, 166, 179, 187, 191
Nowakowska, Zofia 33
Nowakowski, Andrzej 175
Nowakowski, Włodzimierz 120, 179, 180
Nowe Tychy 50, 94, 95, 117, 147, 162, 166,
  174, 184, 185, 187, 188
Nowicki, Maciej 77–79, 96, 174
Nowy Dwór (Wrocław) 74, 148, 191
Nowy Sącz 109

Olędzka, Danuta 33, 136, 144, 171,
  175, 189
Olędzki, Daniel 29, 52, 93, 190
Olszewski, Andrzej K. 10, 11
Olsztyn 182
Opole 118, 177, 190
Orlik, Edmund Roman 31, 120
Osny 182
Ostrowski, Wacław 96
Owczarek, Andrzej 29, 165, 166, 183

Palace of Culture and Science 84–86, 89,
  91, 93, 114, 133, 134
Parandowski, Zbigniew 63
Paris 65, 163, 164, 182
Pelli, César 64
People's Party (SL) 6
Petelenz, Jerzy 65
Pevsner, Nikolaus 52
Philipp, Stefan 108, 166–168
Piacentini, Marcello 12
Piano, Renzo 65
Piaseczny, Jerzy 175
Piechotka, Kazimierz 63, 93, 140, 143, 144,
  181, 184
Piechotka, Maria 20, 41–44, 63, 68, 69, 93,
  100, 140, 143, 144, 181, 184
Pietrusiewicz, Stefan 44
Pietrzyk, Wojciech 159, 187
Pilitowski, Jerzy 129–131, 185
Piotrowski, Marek 60, 190
Piotrowski, Roman 20, 24, 25, 82, 96, 97, 181
Płaszów 176
Pławiński, Konrad 93
Playa Giron 176
Płock 9, 183, 185
Pniewski, Bohdan 11, 13–15, 26, 49, 77,
  78, 181

Index 197

Polak, Józef Zbigniew 57, 58, 61, 62, 64, 86, 87, 160, 181
Polish Committee of National Liberation (PKWN) 5, 182
Polish Socialist Party (PPS) 6, 40
Polish Workers' Party (PPR) 6, 181
Ponti, Gio 63
Popera, Karolina 158, 162
Popper, Karl 16
Poronin 122
Poznań 37, 63, 79, 80, 117–120, 136, 166, 175, 177, 178, 180, 183, 185, 189, 190
Praesens 11, 14, 181, 183, 186, 190
Pronaszko, Andrzej 12
Provisional Government of the Republic of Poland 5, 97
Pruska-Buszkiewicz, Ewa 64, 66
Przyczółek Grochowski 145, 178
Przymorze 127, 144, 145, 171, 189
Ptaszycki, Tadeusz 28, 63, 67, 69, 89, 90, 102, 179, 187
Puławy 127, 187
Purchla, Jacek 4
Putowski, Stefan 80

Radziewanowski, Zbigniew 129
Rajewski, Czesław 88, 124, 179, 185
Rakowski, Witold 87
Raleigh, North Carolina 77, 174
Raymond Camus and Company (construction enterprise) 51, 139
Reagan, Ronald 154
Recovered Territories (Northern Territories and Western Territories) 5, 101, 102, 103, 106, 107, 166, 179
Riga 183
Rio de Janeiro 50, 61
Rogers, Richard 65
Rolek, Ireneusz 63
Romanowicz, Arseniusz 126, 182
Romański, Jerzy 79
Różański, Tadeusz 144, 189
Rudnev, Lev 84, 85
Rusu, Dumitru 115
Rybnik 139, 176
Rychłowski, Stanisław 86
Rykwert, Joseph 54
Rymaszewski, Bohdan 107
Rymaszewski, Stanisław 68, 69
Ryszard Daczkowski 72, 191
Rzepecki, Zbigniew 86
Rzeszów 27, 37, 38, 40, 41, 86, 87, 160, 176, 178, 182, 186

Sabah al-Salem 72, 73, 191
Sady Żoliborskie 141–143, 182
Sandomierz 38, 90, 175, 178
Schmidt, Hans 49
Schulze-Rohr, Jakob 56
Schwanzer, Karl 59, 60
Second Vatican Council 163
Seruga, Wacław 65
Sidorov, Aleksey 49
Sieczkowski, Tadeusz 13, 188
Sigalin, Józef 35, 36, 83, 85, 88, 91, 92, 96, 100, 115, 179, 182, 183
Skalimowski, Andrzej 96
Skibniewska, Halina 41–43, 116, 141–143, 149, 178, 182
Skibniewski, Zygmunt 22, 36, 37, 41, 43–45, 50, 122, 143, 181, 189
Skoczek, Andrzej 129, 130
Skopje 178, 186, 188, 190
Skrzypczak, Jerzy 134
Skupniewicz, Zygmunt 118, 119, 180
Słupsk 107
Ślusarczyk, Jan 86
Snopek, Kuba 158, 162, 172
Sobiepan, Jerzy 67
Social Insurance Institution (ZUS) 82, 181, 186
Solidarity (NSZZ Solidarity) trade union 9, 10, 29, 159, 165, 175, 191
Sołtan, Jerzy 41, 182
Sołtyński, Roman 13, 188
Sołtys, Maria 96, 165
Soria y Mata, Arturo 145
Sowa, Mieczysław 137, 191
Springer, Filip 30, 171
Spyt, Stanisław 28, 185
St. Petersburg 10, 84, 85, 183
Stalin, Joseph xiv, 5, 15, 36, 85, 88, 97
Starachowice 174
State National Council 5
Stefański, Wacław 162, 188
Steiger, Rudolf 96
Stępiński, Zygmunt 88, 91, 92, 100, 101, 179, 182, 183
Sternal, Lech 118, 119, 180
Stirling, James 155
Strzałkowska, Jasna 136
Strzyżów 38, 178
Styka Jan 124
Sumorok, Aleksandra 84, 91
Świdnica 107
Świerczyński, Rudolf 13
Syrkus, Helena 11, 12, 14, 15, 24, 25, 39, 51, 81, 82, 181, 183, 186

198 Index

Syrkus, Szymon 11, 12, 14, 15, 24, 25, 81, 82, 100, 181, 183, 186
Szafer, Tadeusz P. 2, 16, 17, 128, 133, 136, 141, 144, 145, 175
Szanajca, Józef 11, 12, 181, 186, 190
Szczawnica 176
Szczecin 5, 7, 8, 102, 104–106, 133, 139, 185, 188
Szczepanik-Dzikowski, Jerzy 146, 147, 176
Szczepiński Adolf, Jan 182
Szczuka, Mieczysław 11
Szczypczyński, Ryszard 176
Szermerm, Bohdan 177
Szewczyk, Tadeusz 132, 145, 158
Szklarska Poręba 180
Szkop, Andrzej 146, 147, 176
Szmidt, Bolesław 21, 25
Szniolis, Aleksander 178, 181
Szymanowski, Michał 166
Szymański, Wojciech 63
Szymborski, Wojciech 165
Szymski, Adam M. 2, 17
Szyszko-Bohusz, Adolf 10, 14, 15, 20, 31

Tajchman, Jan 159
Tange, Kenzo 51
Tatarkiewicz, Bolesław 97, 120
Tatra Mountains 122, 129–131, 185
Tęgoborze 175
Tehran 190
Tel Aviv, Tel Aviv–Yafo 64, 164, 182
Teodorowicz-Talowski, Tadeusz 95
Thatcher, Margaret 154
thaw (post-stalinist thaw, Gomułka's thaw) 3, 8, 15, 32, 36, 42, 50, 54, 60, 107, 122, 124, 141, 159
Titkow, Walenty 41
Tobolczyk, Stanisław 136
Tołwiński, Stanisław 15
Tomaszek, Stanisław 177
Tomaszewski, Lech 178, 182
Toruń 85, 117, 120, 121, 184, 190
Treblinka 125
Trojanowska, Izabella 177
Tunikowski, Roman 93
Turczynowicz, Tomasz 165
Tychy, Nowe Tychy 50, 94, 95, 117, 147, 162, 166, 174, 184, 185, 187

Union of Armed Struggle (ZWZ) 41
United Nations Centre for Human Settlements (UNCHS) 188
United Nations Disaster Relief Office (UNDRO) 188

United Nations Educational, Scientific and Cultural Organization (UNESCO) 188
Urban, Florian 163
Urbańska, Marta 142
Ustroń, Ustroń–Zawodzie 132, 176
Utzon, Jørn 65

Vago, Pierre 63
Venturi, Robert 53, 54
Vienna 57–60, 64, 164, 183
Vilnius 5, 73, 178, 187
Vitruvius 164

Wacławek, Zbigniew 134
Wajda, Andrzej 154
Warsaw 7, 10–15, 19–21, 24, 26, 31, 32, 35, 38–42, 44, 50, 55, 56, 61, 67, 77–85, 87, 88, 91–94, 96, 96–101, 103, 106, 107, 115, 116, 124, 126, 127, 133–136, 141–143, 145, 146, 148, 154, 160, 165, 171, 172, 174–176, 178–190
Warsaw Housing Cooperative (WSM) 12, 87, 181, 183, 186
Warsaw Reconstruction Office (BOS) 24, 39, 94, 96–100, 179, 181, 182, 189
Wąs, Cezary 162
Wejchert, Kazimierz 94, 95, 166, 174
Wicha, Piotr 160, 163, 176
Wierzbicki, Eugeniusz 25, 79, 127, 174, 186
Wierzbicki, Jerzy 26, 114, 115
Wierzbicki, Konrad 65
Wiktor, Tołkin 125
Wilczek, Mieczysław 10
Wiśniewski, Michał 84, 172
Wiśniowska, Anna 73, 120, 179
Wiśniowski, Krzysztof 72, 73, 137, 155, 191
Wittek, Włodzimierz 182
Władysławowo 175
Włodzimierz, Gruszczyński 129–131, 185
Wright, Frank Lloyd 19, 65
Wright, Tom 72
Wrocław 5, 7, 28, 55, 74, 93, 102, 103, 107, 116, 120, 122–124, 135, 137–139, 148, 155, 161, 177, 179, 180, 184–187, 191
Wujek, Andrzej 55
Wujek, Jakub 52, 55, 56, 65, 155, 157, 165, 166, 183
Wyka, Kazimierz 97
Wyporek, Bogdan 40, 96, 97, 134, 190

Yalta Conference, Yalta Treaty 5, 101

Żabiński, Ryszard 137, 191
Zabłocki, Wojciech 56, 70–72, 127, 128, 186

Zachwatowicz, Jan 1, 15, 90, 96, 97, 100, 103, 106, 183
Zakopane 130, 187, 188
Zalewski, Wacław 127
Zamość 85, 90
ZAPA (Zespół Autorskich Pracowni Architektonicznych–Team of Author's Architectural Studios) 29, 175, 189
Zaremba, Piotr 104–106

Zaufal, Bogumił 130
Zieliński, Tadeusz 63, 180
Zielonka, Andrzej 165
Zielonka, Jacek 53
Ziętek, Jerzy 134
Ziołowski, Stefan 14
Zipser, Tadeusz 53
Żórawski, Andrzej 127
Żórawski, Juliusz 14, 23, 31–34, 187
Zwierko, Aleksander 136, 137, 186